Palgrave Advances in Sex Work Studies

This series takes a broad and interdisciplinary view of the sex industry, prioritizing transnational and intersectional work and marginalized sex workers. It seeks to center underrepresented groups such as Black, Indigenous, and other people of color; transfeminine, transmasculine, and non-binary people; LGBTQIA+ sex workers; people with disabilities; and workers outside of the US and UK. Books in the series cover a wide range of sex industries including camming, full-service sex work in a range of contexts e.g. street-based, brothel work, and escorts), hostessing, phone sex, pornography, pro-dommes, stripping, sugar relationship, and other forms of individual sexual entrepreneurship online. They are attentive to lateral whorephobia which points to the privileges of certain forms of sex work over others and how sex workers practicing privileged forms of erotic labor often look down upon workers in more stigmatized sectors. This series also discusses criminal justice approaches to sex work and seeks titles that explore the complexities and wide range of sex worker experiences in the whorearchy to reflect the multiple positions, experiences, and perspectives of those within the sex work community.

Teela Sanders · Jane Scoular ·
Barbara G. Brents · Susie Balderston ·
Gillian Abel
Editors

Voicing Consent

Sex Workers, Sexual Violation and Legal Consciousness in Cross-National Contexts

palgrave
macmillan

Editors
Teela Sanders
University of Leicester
Leicester, UK

Barbara G. Brents
University of Nevada
Las Vegas, Nevada, USA

Gillian Abel
University of Otago
Dunedin, New Zealand

Jane Scoular
Strathclyde Law School
University of Strathclyde
Glasgow, UK

Susie Balderston
Strathclyde Law School
University of Strathclyde
Glasgow, UK

ISSN 2731-376X ISSN 2731-3778 (electronic)
Palgrave Advances in Sex Work Studies
ISBN 978-3-031-77714-1 ISBN 978-3-031-77715-8 (eBook)
https://doi.org/10.1007/978-3-031-77715-8

Cover illustration: Justin Kase zsixz/Alamy Stock Photo

This Palgrave Macmillan imprint is published by the registered company Springer Nature Switzerland AG
The registered company address is: Gewerbestrasse 11, 6330 Cham, Switzerland

Acknowledgements

The book is the accumulation of a team project, which started back in 2019 and has gathered pace and people during the years. We are indebted to the researchers Alessandra Lanti, Samuel Thomson, Jessica Hyer Griffin, Cherida Fraser, and Caoimhe Ní Dhónaill, whose vision and critical engagement have enabled the project to be informed by expertise. We would also like to acknowledge the engagement of sex work organisations in each site, particularly The Cupcake Girls, SWOP Behind Bars, Savannah Sly, Las Vegas Red Umbrella Collective, Aotearoa New Zealand Sex Workers Collective—NZPC, UglyMugs Ireland, and Sex Workers Alliance Ireland, Manchester Action for Street Health and Basis Yorkshire. Each site had an active advisory board and we are thankful for their input throughout this long journey and equally thankful to all the organisations that supported this project. We will remember the late Dr Susie Balderston for her passion and commitment to rights and assisting with the project during the three years that she was involved. We are very grateful for others who assisted greatly with the project: Rachel Howard, Chris Wakefield, Harriet Smailes, and Fanni Gyurkó, for their expertise, insightful perspectives, and energy to get this over the line, and James Milton and Didi Herman for their attention to detail. We must also thank Josie Taylor at Palgrave and the team at Nifty Fox Productions for their patience and belief that we would deliver.

Contents

Notes on Contributors

Gillian Abel is a public health academic at the Department of Population Health, University of Otago, New Zealand with over 20 years' experience in the field of sex work research. She uses her public health lens to examine how government legislation and local bylaws affect sex workers and their practices. New Zealand decriminalised sex work with the passing of the Prostitution Reform Act 2003, and Gillian's research provided a major contribution to the review of the Act. Since then, she has continued to focus on how policy in New Zealand affects the health and safety of migrant sex workers, who are made vulnerable to exploitation through immigration policies, and how the diversity of sex workers experience work in a decriminalised environment. Gillian is regarded as an international expert in this area of research and has been consulted by policymakers in a number of other countries considering change to their sex work laws.

Susie Balderston is Research Fellow in the Law School at the University of Strathclyde. She has led and delivered £1.3m of user-led, participative, and survey research with disabled/Deaf people, victims of sexual and domestic violence, hate crime, and institutional abuse. Previously, Susie was at the UNESCO Centre for Violence and Society at Lancaster University, evaluating victim assistance projects for the European Commission, Lankelly Chase, and National Citizens Advice. For the University of Birmingham Trauma, Social Harm and Health Team, she was validating an international justice tool to minimise harm and improve third-sector support for women. Before academia, Susie was Policy Director for a social enterprise, where she designed service changes in 32 government, police, social care, and health bodies, to improve independent living and safety for disabled people. She also conducted Care and Treatment reviews for high and medium secure detention. Susie authored a Shadow Report about disabled women and criminal justice for the UN Inquiry into Human Rights Violations in the UK. Susie is proud to be a disabled woman and a Geordie. Rape makes Susie very angry, but ice cream, data analysis, and puppies make her very happy.

Barbara G. Brents a Sociology professor at the University of Nevada, Las Vegas, brings over 30 years of experience in teaching and researching politics, sex, and gender in market culture, specialising in sexual commerce. Among other peer-reviewed work she co-authored 'The State of Sex,' a study of Nevada's legal brothels (2010) and 'Paying for Sex in the Digital Age' (2020) and is a co-editor of 'Sex Work Today: Erotic Labor in the 21st Century' (2024). Brents actively engages in promoting evidence-based law reforms and advocating for sex-worker rights. Brents has helped make UNLV's Sociology Department a national frontrunner in cultivating leaders in sex work/sex worker research at the Ph.D. level over the last three decades.

Caoimhe Ní Dhónaill is a researcher with a particular interest in Identity. She gained her Ph.D. in 2012 from Queens University, with a focus on social isolation, ageing, and Comparative International Sociology. She has been involved in research around domestic violence, disability, ageing, isolation, and sex work throughout her career.

Cherida Fraser is a community liaison, advocate, and researcher at NZPC: Aotearoa New Zealand Sex Workers' Collective, a peer organisation established in 1987. With lived experience of sex work, she has a strong interest in the rights and well-being of communities who have historically experienced marginalisation or stigma, and has worked in the community sector since graduating with a Master's of Cross-cultural Psychology in 2014. Her research contributions include action research with a Māori community described as 'hard to reach' due to the impacts of colonisation, and exploring the lived experiences of sex workers in the contexts of the Canterbury earthquakes (NZ) and the impact of decriminalisation in relation to stigma and discrimination.

Fanni Gyurko is currently a postdoctoral researcher at the University of Oxford, Centre for Socio-Legal Studies, Faculty of Law. She has a strong interest in exploring the relationship between law and society, focusing on the social norms that drive people's interactions. Her Ph.D. explored how migrants experience 'law' (both legal norms and non-state norms) when they are moving into a new social context (University of Glasgow). Gyurko has a Master's degree in Sociology of Law from Lund University (Sweden). She is also interested in issues around access to justice, in particular migrants' access to their legal rights.

Rachel Howard attended the University of Nevada Las Vegas where she received her B.A. in Criminal Justice in 2018. She then attended the William S. Boyd School of Law in Las Vegas, Nevada where she received her J. D. in 2022. Currently, she is completing her M.A. in sociology at the University of Nevada Las Vegas. Her research focuses on sexual violence, intersectionality, and the law.

Jessica Hyer Griffin is the founder, CEO, and support lead at Support for Student Sex Workers—a confidential sex worker-led peer support organisation which provides support to anyone who identifies with the sex work community. As a public speaker and mental health professional specialising in sexual trauma, she has consistently used her experiences as disabled full service sex worker to support others in similar positions.

She campaigns for the decriminalisation and destigmatisation of the sex work industry and acts as an advocate on behalf of sex-working students who need support within their university structure. Alongside training university staff on disclosures around sex work, her work across universities has encouraged an open dialogue to promote safety within the sex work community and seen the implementation of sex work policies across universities nationally. She is currently involved in a multinational project which intends to improve justice for sex workers who have experienced crimes involving sexual violence across the UK, Ireland, Nevada, and New Zealand, is training to become an ISVA and is working towards an MS in Psychology focusing on destigmatising sex work to support individuals coping with shame.

Alessandra Lanti holds a Master of Arts degree in Clinical Psychology and a Ph.D. in Sociology from The University of Nevada, Las Vegas (UNLV). Her research interests lie in the areas of gender and sexuality, social psychology, commercial sex, and stigma. She decided to obtain a Ph.D. in sociology rather than psychology because of a concern for the many social and cultural factors that influence mental health. She is also a licensed clinical professional counsellor and has been doing therapy since August of 2010. She is more specifically trained in supporting sex and gender-diverse folks and sex workers. In Las Vegas, she has facilitated no-cost, non-judgmental, resilience-based, weekly support groups for the local sex workers' community beginning in 2017. Since the start of the COVIDS-19 pandemic, all support services have moved online. Alessandra now lives in Italy where she works as a counsellor, and researcher and is developing a book of therapists' guidelines for best practices to improve clinical services to sex workers.

Teela Sanders is Professor of Criminology and currently the Pro Vice Chancellor and Head of College of Social Sciences, Arts and Humanities at the University of Leicester. She is a leading international scholar in research on the intersections between gender, regulation, governance, and crime, specifically in the sex industry. Sanders has written 7 books, edited 10, and has over 60 peer-reviewed journal articles, based on research projects funded by major research councils. Teela was PI on the ESRC funded, Beyond the Gaze project, on internet sex work and outcomes have involved practitioners and police good practice, safety resources for sex workers, and police and practitioner training. She has long-standing research relationships in Nairobi with third-sector and academic networks in relation to gender-based violence. She has received a Leverhulme Research Fellowship for 2019–2021. She has recently completed a large four-year ESRC international project: '*Understanding sexual violence in sex working populations: Law, legal consciousness and practice in four countries*' and an AHRC grant on the prevention of modern slavery on adult service websites partnered with Unseen, the National Crime Agency and National Police Chiefs Council. Teela is a long-standing member of the NPCC Sex Work and Policing group which informs and shapes policy and practice in policing. Her work has influenced government policy and policing guidance, and has been published in major newspapers and outlets. She has sat on the ESRC Strategic Advisory Network for the past four years and is currently involved in the Strategic delivery plan developments.

Jane Scoular is Professor of Law University of Strathclyde and is an internationally recognised scholar whose work is a primary reference in the field of the legal regulation of commercial sex. Her scholarship includes original theoretical expositions in books (The Subject of Prostitution: Sex/work, Law and Social Theory) and internationally peer-refereed journals (What's law got to do with it? How and why law matters in the regulation of sex work) as well as ground-breaking national and international empirical studies, funded by the EU, government bodies, the ESRC and the Joseph Rowntree Foundation. With colleagues, she undertook the largest study of internet-based sex work and its regulation, in the ESRC-funded project 'Beyond the Gaze' [2015–2018]. Among the project's publications, which included a monograph and numerous articles, was the winner of the SLSA Best Article Prize in 2020. She has been a Visiting Scholar at New York University and at the University of Stockholm, researching the Swedish law relating to prostitution. She served on the Management Committee and co-chaired the scientific programme Comparing European Prostitution Policies: Understanding Scales and Cultures of Governance (2013–2017). She is the Principal Investigator on the ESRC-funded project 'Sex work and Sexual Violence' (2021–2023) the work of which informs this book.

Harriet Smailes is a researcher in the fields of sexual violence and domestic abuse. Her research has primarily focused on institutional responses to violence and abuse, with a special interest in Universities in the UK. Harriet has worked as a practitioner, supporting students subjected to sexual violence at university, and as a volunteer emotional support worker at a Rape Crisis service. Harriet also has experience developing and delivering training and consultancy services to other sexual violence support staff.

Samuel Thomson is an advocate for survivors of sexual violence from all walks of life. He has previously worked for several years in the charity sector specialising in supporting survivors from marginalised communities. Samuel has worked on the frontline providing individual and group support to those affected by sexual violence, many of whom felt silenced by society due to their identity. He continues to train organisations in various sectors on how to provide safe spaces for survivors of multiple forms of violence alongside creating and galvanising communities that wish to see the difficult landscape for survivors change for the better. Now, Samuel is part of an international project that is amplifying the voices of sex workers who have experienced forms of sexual violence and employing their bravery to improve the criminal justice system. He is also currently training as a clinical associate psychologist specialising in children and young people with mental health difficulties.

Chris Wakefield is Assistant Professor of Sociology at Whitman College. Chris received a Ph.D. in sociology from the University of Nevada, Las Vegas in 2023 after teaching a range of courses on crime, theory, statistics, and gender. Chris has co-authored *Paying for Sex in the Digital Age* alongside Teela Sanders and Barbara Brents as well as multiple publications related to clients of sex work. Chris's expertise is in mixed methods research and intersections of law and sexuality. Chris's dissertation research examined how sex offenders in the US adapted their lives to registration and notification schemes.

List of Figures

List of Tables

1

Introduction: Understanding Consent and Legal Consciousness in Sex Work

Jane Scoular, Fanni Gyurko, Barbara G. Brents, Teela Sanders, and Gillian Abel

Introduction

> Just because you think what I do is wrong, doesn't make my safety and life worth less. And that's really what it comes down to: just because you don't agree with it, doesn't mean I shouldn't have a safe place to work, the same as anybody else.
> (Abbey, USA, independent)

J. Scoular
Strathclyde Law School, University of Strathclyde, Glasgow, UK

F. Gyurko
University of Oxford, Oxford, UK

B. G. Brents
University of Nevada, Las Vegas, Nevada, USA

T. Sanders (✉)
University of Leicester, Leicester, UK
e-mail: teela.sanders@leicester.ac.uk

T. Sanders et al. (eds.), *Voicing Consent*, Palgrave Advances in Sex Work Studies,
https://doi.org/10.1007/978-3-031-77715-8_1

We began this project with three primary goals: first, to understand how sex workers experience sexual violence in their work, by exploring a nuanced, victim-led definition of consent and harm; second, to examine the dynamics between different legal contexts (criminalised, legalised, and decriminalised systems) and victims' responses to sexual violence and unwanted sexual contact, focusing on how laws, awareness of legal rights, and law enforcement actions help or hinder in managing these experiences; and third, to explore the extent to which the legal context affects sex workers' actions, perceptions, understandings and experiences of sexual violence and unwanted contact.

To achieve these goals, we conducted a multi-country research project, involving surveys and interviews with sex workers.[1] This study spanned four different legal environments: Nevada in the USA (where legal brothels exist), the rest of the USA (where all sex work is criminalised), Aotearoa New Zealand (where sex work is decriminalised), and the UK[2] (where partial criminalisation exists).

We focus on sex workers' legal consciousness. Legal consciousness research aims to understand how people experience, perceive, understand, and act in relation to the law in their everyday lives (Chua & Engel, 2019; Cowan, 2004). This approach allows us to examine the law 'from below' (Engel, 1998), providing a bottom-up perspective on how legal systems impact sex workers.

Our findings reveal significant differences in sex workers' experiences across different legal contexts. In decriminalised settings like Aotearoa New Zealand (ANZ), sex workers often feel more empowered to handle violations. In contrast, in criminalised settings, fear of legal repercussions frequently prevents them from seeking help. These insights highlight

G. Abel
University of Otago, Dunedin, New Zealand

[1] We also interviewed health and social service providers and professionals in the criminal-legal system at the same time as part of a larger project, but we do not include that data in this book.

[2] While we hoped to collect data to understand Northern Ireland's legal environment of criminalising clients, the numbers we collected there were too small, both to protect anonymity and to make meaningful conclusions. Consequently, we included our Northern Ireland data as part of the United Kingdom.

how the legal environment can either support or hinder sex workers in managing their safety.

While the legal context and formal regulations are significant, they are just one of many factors influencing sex workers' legal consciousness. Sex workers operate in various sectors and under diverse conditions, whether independently or in brothels, which influences their experiences. But also, both formal (state) laws and informal (non-state) rules and norms are essential to understanding our empirical findings (Hertogh, 2004). Informal norms and community support play a pivotal role in how individuals prevent, define, manage, and respond to unwanted sexual contact.

Additionally, we found that consent in sex work is dynamic, involving ongoing negotiations with clients and the ability of sex workers to set both clear and flexible boundaries as necessary. This complexity is often misunderstood or oversimplified by legal systems, leading to inadequate protections for sex workers.

Throughout the book, we explore sex workers' experiences of unwanted contact, ranging from bothersome to violent. Typically, sexual violence is associated with physical injury, but our findings reveal a broader range of incidents, including payment problems and 'stealthing'. These incidents are rarely covered by sexual violence laws. By examining these diverse experiences and how sex workers prevent and manage them, we highlight the need to acknowledge the full range of their encounters in their work.

These insights set the stage for a deeper exploration of sex workers' legal consciousness, providing a foundation for understanding how law, community support, and various legal contexts shape sex workers' perceptions and interactions with the legal system.

But before we introduce our findings in the coming chapters, we need to back up several steps. We will discuss the complexities in defining sexual violence and consent, lay out the concept of legal consciousness, discuss the differences between formal law and informal norms, and finally lay out the research project itself.

Defining Sexual Violence

What surprised us most during our research was how differently people define sexual violence, which made comparing the contexts difficult, but which is also a central theme in our findings.

Sexual violence can refer to any form of unwanted sexual activity or behaviour. We know, however, that this is not how it is defined in law. As we will see in Chapter 2, legal definitions of sexual violence vary widely across jurisdictions, but they generally encompass two components: (1) acts of a sexual nature; and (2) acts that are done without an individual's clear and voluntary consent. However, in real life, sexual violence can comprise a variety and wide range of acts. It can include what many people most clearly think of as violence, such as rape, sexual assault, abuse, and sexual actions that cause physical harm. It also includes, however, actions ranging from unwanted sexual comments, harassment (in person or online), and posting photos without consent, to stalking, 'stealthing' (removing a condom without consent), and unwanted touching.

Years of advocacy around women's and LGBTQ + rights have taught us that existing legal definitions of sexual violence are fraught. What an individual counts as a violation and what criminal legal institutions affirm can be two very different things. Definitions can vary widely across legal jurisdictions and from person to person. Questions arise: When does a consensual sex act become non-consensual? What actions indicate consent? Whose account matters more in cases of disputed sexual contact? And what is considered reasonable to endure? These issues challenge those who experience them first-hand, as well as the police, judges, and juries.

Once an individual defines an incident as a violation, what happens next? Fear of retaliation, exposure, disbelief, societal stigma, differing gender and sexual norms, lack of awareness about legal rights and resources, and emotional trauma all influence outcomes. Because of this, only about 40% of female rape survivors identify their experiences as rape (Wilson & Miller, 2016). The vast majority of those who experience unwanted sexual contact tell no one. And if they do, the legal system determines justice. However, its standards for evidence, definitions of consent, and ideas of justice may not match the perspectives or desires of those involved.

The way the legal system defines and deals with sexual assault and rape cases has sparked intense debates in politics, policy, and academia. While the criminal justice system has made great strides in handling rape cases, few cases see a resolution. In 2019, the UK witnessed the lowest prosecution rates in a decade (Barr et al., 2019). Regarding conviction rates, meanwhile, there has been, since 2016—when the conviction rate was recorded at 57.7%—a steady increase, with some fluctuation (see, for e.g. End Violence Against Women, 2023); but there is more work to be done, and rape case attrition, where there is not any kind of resolution, continues to be a problem. Case attrition is even worse for victims from stigmatised and marginalised groups.

When it comes to sex work, these issues are even more complex. Generations of prejudice, fuelled by contentious policy, media, and advocacy group debates, drive questions rooted in stigma, such as "Can a sex worker be raped?". Meanwhile, some radical feminist perspectives define sex work as inherently violent against women and girls (Barry, 1995), driving questions, such as "Does all sex work constitute rape?". The key to understanding these questions lies in the concept of clear and voluntary consent. Yet, there is significant disagreement on what constitutes consent and how freely it can be given in the context of sex work.

Our work seeks to bring empirical data to this often abstract debate by highlighting the importance of context in sex work. For sex workers, consent is not a vague notion of 'sex'. It involves negotiating a verbal contract, detailing specific acts and behaviours involved in the exchange. This job requires managing consent around various sexual pleasures and desires, ensuring that boundaries are respected. Many factors can lead to unwanted contact, making the structures that support a worker's ability to negotiate and prevent such occurrences crucial.

International organisations have urged nations to address violence against sex workers as both a public health (Alexander, 1998; Kinnell, 2008; Platt et al., 2018) and human rights priority (Amnesty International 2016a; WHO et al., 2012;). Despite widespread assertions on the relationship between prostitution and gendered violence, it remains a daunting challenge to systematically assess this in sex-worker populations (cf. Benoit et al., 2015). A 2014 meta-analysis of mostly qualitative or small sample studies indicates that sex workers face disproportionately high levels of violence, but data on the nature, range, and sources varies (Deering et al., 2014). Sex workers can be targeted due to their vulnerability, isolation, and marginalisation; some are easy targets because of their work location or conditions (Lowman, 2000; Sanders & Campbell, 2007), while others experience no violence at all.

The recent '#MeToo' movement makes clear that we need better solutions for preventing and stopping sexual victimisation and for increasing access to justice for sex workers, as well as for non-sex workers (West & Horn, Eds., 2021). We need better ways to understand why violence is seldom reported amongst sex worker groups and why achieving justice is so hard.

As social scientists, we understand that social norms, institutions, and structural power dynamics—such as race, class, gender, sexuality, citizenship, and ability—shape the occurrence and recognition of any sexual violations in the general population and in sex work. The control of sexual pleasure and desire is deeply intertwined with classism, racism, ableism, heterosexism, ageism, xenophobia, cisnormativity, sizeism, systems of white supremacy, patriarchy, immigration policies, and the legacies of colonialism. While our project did not measure these variables quantitatively, as we discuss in our methodology chapter (Chapter 9), their influence on our findings is unmistakable.

Despite extensive research on law and sexual violence in general, and vigorous debates on the most effective prostitution laws to combat sexual violations experienced by sex workers, little attention has been given to questions about defining sexual violence (Scoular, 2015). Although there is much attention given to preventing 'violence' in sex work, the concept itself often goes undefined and is not typically explored in a comparative fashion. If our goal is to stop acts that violate a person's sexual autonomy and dignity, and to seek justice when they do occur, we need to understand all the dynamics involved in defining and dealing with unwanted sexual contact. This requires evidence of the kind that we will present in this book.

Defining Legal Consciousness

'Legal consciousness' is a useful framework by which to study how sex workers understand, interact with, and use the law in their daily lives and work in different legal contexts. Legal consciousness is a broad concept that encompasses ordinary people's understanding of both official formal law and other legal norms that shape their world (Gill & Creutzfeldt, 2018, p. 372). For us, it is not just their knowledge and opinion of official formal laws, but it includes their broad experience of other less formal norms and rules, as well as their own constructions of what 'law' is.

Indeed, legal consciousness research does not just focus on people's knowledge of statutory law. Scholar Marc Hertogh has suggested that people connect their perceptions of and attitudes towards formal law to what they experience in their own social worlds as comprising law. An approach that combines both the social significance of statutory law and takes seriously people's own ideas of law and justice (2004, p. 480) is helpful in analysing sex workers' actions and understandings around sexual violence and unwanted contact.

In this book, we focus on the individual legal consciousness of sex workers while also considering how relational and structural factors affect this consciousness. We align with Chua and Engel's (2019, p. 335) conceptualisation that "legal consciousness research should be imagined on a continuum ranging from individual thought and action to interactive, co-constitutive relations with others". Young (2014, p. 500) has found that legal consciousness also involves people's perceptions of how others understand law: "a person's belief about and attitude towards a particular law or set of laws is influenced not only by his [sic.] own experience but by his understanding of others' experiences with and beliefs about the law". This concept is useful for exploring factors beyond statutory law that impact sex workers' understanding of consent, sexual assault, and their perceived chances of reporting and seeking justice.

Our investigation uses mixed-method research to study this legal meaning-making. We examine wider ideas of legality, as well as particular legal provisions. Given the marginalised and stigmatised position of our sex-worker research participants, we also explore the relevance (and irrelevance) of formal laws to people's behaviours, drawing here on the concept of legal alienation and questions around legal mobilisation (Aidinlis, 2019).

Legal alienation is defined as a cognitive state of psychological disconnection from official state law and the justice system (Hertogh, 2018, p. 55). Research finds that sex workers often disregard, resist, or even show hostility towards formal law (Klambauer, 2019). The concept of legal alienation helps us to understand the gap between what state law dictates and what people actually do, recognise as law, and whether they are aware of and identify with state law (Hertogh, 2018). Aidinlis (2019, p. 509) has argued that attention to legal alienation urges us to identify forces other than formal law that shape social action (or inaction), and to find non-legal resources to address these problems.

Ewick and Silbey (1998, p. 192) have suggested that powerless individuals are more likely to display an 'against the law' dimension of legal consciousness. In this orientation, "legality is characterised as something to be avoided. Because it is a product of arbitrary power, legality is seen as capricious and thus dangerous to invoke, rather than conditionally appropriate or useful" (Ewick & Silbey, 1998, p. 192).

Legal alienation also aligns with important questions around legal mobilisation, such as, "To what extent, if at all, do people use or invoke the law?" (See Aidinlis, 2019, p. 509). Research on sexual violence finds that individuals must work through stages of legal consciousness by identifying a behaviour as harmful (*naming*), holding an individual responsible through some action (*blaming*), and seeking remedial action from the individual responsible or through another remedy, such as the criminal justice system (*claiming*) (Felstiner et al., 1980).

We recognise that sex workers' interactions with and experiences of the law are dynamic and evolving. Ewick and Silbey (1998) describe legal consciousness as a dynamic process, where individuals experience events, interpret them, and respond accordingly. For the reasons we have just been discussing, this framework is particularly useful for examining sex workers' experiences with the law.

Defining 'Law'

As noted above, both formal law and informal norms are essential for understanding our empirical findings. Grasping these differences is critical in comparing the effect of different legal systems on sex workers' experience of sexual violations.

In this book, 'formal law' refers to rules, regulations, and procedures codified by federal, regional, or local governments and their administrative agencies. This includes laws passed by legislatures, case rulings from judicial institutions, and executive orders guiding agency enforcement. We examine formal laws that govern two distinct realms: laws regulating sex work, which can criminalise or decriminalise it in various ways, and laws addressing unwanted sexual contact.

When people think of laws related to both prostitution and sexual violence they often think about criminal law. Criminal law involves prosecuting and punishing individuals who engage in criminal activities, holding offenders accountable to the public, and requiring proof beyond a reasonable doubt. But civil law also operates in these areas, addressing disputes and remedies between individuals and/or organisations. Civil law holds defendants accountable to victims, not the public. In civil cases, the standard of evidence is less, and compensation is usually monetary. In different legal contexts, both criminal and civil law can matter for sex workers.

However, rules also exist outside governmental institutions. Workplaces have their own rules to maintain order and to manage and sanction employees and customers. These organisations can enforce rules in a variety of ways, from firing employees to withholding pay to blocking customers. The level of codification of rules varies. Sex workers usually work for smaller, more informal organisations or contract with larger companies. In both cases, the rules can be relatively informal.

Informal norms and rules relate to or are informed by formal law, but generally operate outside of it. These can be unwritten or verbal, involving shared expectations. They govern organisational culture, communicated as unofficial advice from management or between workers. Informal norms include the 'rules of the game', shared among sex workers or clients, or learned patterns for dealing with clients.

Informal norms can, therefore, also influence informal methods of resolution (discussed further in Chapter 5).

Table 1.1, below, summarises the range of 'law' we will be talking about in this book.

We adopt a broad view of law, encompassing formal law and informal norms. Our research explores how these dimensions interact, to understand sex workers' responses to sexual violence and unwanted contact.

We also consider the relation between law and the practice of that law based on Baier et al., 2019:

- Formal legal norms ('law in books': laws as formal order, e.g. legal theory, case rulings, and legal codes);
- Legal practices ('law in action': law's effect, e.g. what police, lawyers, and judges actually do);
- Social norms (socially constructed norms, e.g. informal norms of the brothel, the 'rules of the game' (how to negotiate consent)); and
- Social practice ('living law': laws of everyday life, e.g. social norms realised in practice).

Table 1.1 Definitions of formal and informal 'law' used in this book

Category	Description
1. Formal law	Rules, regulations, and procedures codified by federal, regional, or local governments and their administrative agencies
a. Criminal law	Aims to punish guilty parties, holding them accountable to the public. Requires proof beyond a reasonable doubt, with incarceration or fines as punishment
b. Civil law	Holds defendants accountable to victims, requiring evidence that is more likely than not correct. Compensation is usually monetary
2. Workplace rules	Regulations codified formally or informally by employers to manage and sanction employees and customers, and maintain order. Enforcement takes place in the workplace
3. Informal norms	Unwritten or verbal rules, often informed by formal law or broader notions of legality, that govern acceptable behaviour. These can range from management decisions, including an individual manager's ways of handling violations, to the workplace culture or norms established among sex workers themselves for independent or collective work

The Research

To examine the legal consciousness of sex workers, we conducted interviews and surveys as part of a comprehensive research project that took place between 2022 and 2023 and that encompassed four distinct legal environments: Nevada (USA), with its legal brothels; the rest of the USA, where all sex work is illegal; Aotearoa New Zealand, where sex work is decriminalised, and the UK, with partial criminalisation. Our aim was to explore how legal consciousness (sex workers' perceptions and understandings of the law, their boundaries of consent, and decisions on reporting), legal norms (legal theory, case rulings, legal codes), and legal practices (the actions of police, lawyers, and judges) interact to affect sexual violence against sex workers, varying by demographics, sex market, and legal regime.

We employed an innovative methodology involving sex-worker peers as 'expert advisors', as advocated by Deering et al. (2014). Collaborations between academic researchers and 'experts by experience' are recognised as best practice when researching marginalised populations such as sex workers (Connelly & Sanders, 2020; Huysamen & Sanders, 2021). This approach ensures that research benefits the communities involved and strengthens the scientific project, leading to more robust knowledge and positive change (Keighley et al., 2023; Lewis & Maticka-Tyndale, 2000; O'Neill, 1996).

These expert advisors were involved at all stages of our project— from designing research tools and analysing data from various perspectives, to delivering and sharing project results. We will continue to prioritise the voices and experiences of sex workers, using our findings to influence policy and practice. The expertise of sex workers has been crucial in shaping the research and will be pivotal in creating strategies to combat sexual violence and unwanted contact. For a detailed overview of our methodological process and learning experiences, please see Chapter 9.

Survey

We developed our survey to gather empirical data on sex workers' and ex-sex workers' experiences of unwanted sexual contact, as well as their interactions with health services, advocacy, and the criminal justice system, across each of our study sites.

Our recruitment process for the survey and interviews, detailed in Chapter 9, targeted participants who had experienced unwanted contact. Although this is not a representative sample of all sex workers, as we lack the data on the total sex-worker population necessary to construct such a sample, we followed researcher Ron Weitzer's guidance:

> ... the best that we can hope for are studies that do an exceptional job of sampling people in different geographical locations in different types of prostitution and doing both the sampling and the interviewing in a rigorous and impartial manner. (2005, p. 942)

This book, then, analyses data from 483 sex-worker survey respondents who reported experiencing unwanted contact. We analysed the survey data using SPSS, with text-based responses entered into Nvivo. By exploring the quantitative and qualitative data together, we identified trends and mapped emerging patterns.

Interviews

We also interviewed 40 sex workers from each of our study sites. We developed a semi-structured interviewing approach based on an interview schedule created by the peer experts. The schedule included open-ended questions to encourage participants to provide detailed accounts of their experiences. With participants' permission, all interviews were audio-recorded and then transcribed in anonymised form. Transcripts were coded according to key themes aligned with the research questions (e.g. investigations, legal consciousness, witness support, stigma, trauma).

This approach allowed us to develop theory while generating data and conducting analysis in a dialectical process that established connections between emergent themes (Attride-Stirling, 2001). The themes were collaboratively checked and rated by the team.

Chapter Outlines

Chapter Two reviews the different laws in each of the sites in our project that are relevant to sex workers' experiences. The chapter covers the formal laws and court cases governing sex work, sexual violence and consent, and relevant workplace laws in each country. (Detailed information on these formal laws is included in Appendix 1: Prostitution; Sexual Violence and Workers Rights Laws Across Sites.)

Chapter Three explores how sex workers set boundaries and negotiate their conditions of consent. The chapter examines how they establish their own working routines to prevent violations, which involves negotiating with clients to set and maintain boundaries. The chapter also discusses the role of formal and informal norms, including how sex workers learn to negotiate or improve their negotiation skills from others in the industry.

Chapter Four explores how sex workers define and interpret incidents of unwanted sexual contact within their work. Using the data from both the survey and the qualitative interviews, we explore the types of unwanted contact that sex workers encounter and how the law influences their understanding, interpretation, and definition of these incidents. It highlights the varied interpretations of consent and harm among sex workers, emphasising the influence of legal and social contexts on these definitions.

Chapter Five explores what sex workers do after incidents of unwanted contact. It covers a wide range of actions, including no action, informal actions, and formal legal actions. It illustrates how legal consciousness and the immediate workplace environment, shape these responses, with a focus on the practical barriers and strategies used by sex workers.

Chapter Six examines how sex workers interact with the criminal legal system. It focuses on the challenges they face in reporting violations and seeking justice. We look at data on reporting, police interactions during investigations, and, for the few that had progressed to criminal proceedings, the court processes involved. The chapter emphasises how important the legal context is in shaping sex workers' alienation from and mistrust of law enforcement.

Chapter Seven introduces recommendations generated from the research by the expert peer researchers. These recommendations are based on the analysis of interviews with sex workers, suggestions provided by sex workers themselves, and the personal experiences of the peer researchers who have worked in the field as sex workers or practitioners. The key recommendations focus on improving healthcare, criminal justice, and support organisations, to address the rights and equity of sex workers and enhance the quality of services they receive.

Chapter Eight concludes by underscoring the profound effect of different legal frameworks on how sex workers feel they can and cannot interact with the law. We summarise the findings of the book, focusing on the disparity between sex workers' real-life experiences and formal legal regulations. We discuss interactions between formal legal norms and informal practices, and how these shape sex workers' understandings of sexual violence. The chapter calls for adaptable and supportive legal frameworks that recognise the dynamic nature of consent and the diverse circumstances of sex workers' lives.

Chapter Nine details the research methods used in this project. We discuss the values and ethics that have guided the research and outline the demographics of research participants.

References

Aidinlis, S. (2019). Defining the 'legal': Two conceptions of legal consciousness and legal alienation in administrative justice research. *Journal of Social Welfare and Family Law, 41*(4), 495–513.

Alexander, P. (1998). Sex work and health: A question of safety in the workplace. *Journal of the American Medical Women's Association, 53*(2), 77–82. https://pubmed.ncbi.nlm.nih.gov/9595900/

Amnesty International. (2016a). *Sex workers at risk: A research summary on human rights abuses against sex workers*. Retrieved July 14, 2024, from https://www.amnesty.org/en/documents/pol40/4061/2016/en/

Attride-Stirling, J. (2001). Thematic networks: An analytic tool for qualitative research. *Qualitative Research, 1*(3), 385–405. https://doi.org/10.1177/146879410100100307

Barry, K. (1995). *The prostitution of sexuality*. NYU Press. http://www.jstor.org/stable/j.ctt9qg779

Barr, C., Topping, A., & Bowcott, O. (2019). Rape prosecutions in England and Wales at lowest level in a decade. *The Guardian*. Retrieved May 21, 2024, from https://www.theguardian.com/law/2019/sep/12/prosecutions-in-england-and-wales-at-lowest-level-in-a-decade

Baier, M., Svensson, M., & Nafstad, I. (2019). *Understanding sociology of law*. Studentlitteratur AB.

Benoit, C., McCarthy, B., & Jansson, M. (2015). Stigma, sex work, and substance use: A comparative analysis. *Sociology of Health & Illness, 37*(3), 437–451. https://doi.org/10.1111/1467-9566.12201

Connelly, L., & Sanders, T. (2020). Disrupting the boundaries of the academe: Co-creating knowledge and sex work 'academic-activism'. In S. Walklate, K. Fitz-Gibbon, J. Maher, & J. McCulloch (Eds.), *The Emerald handbook of criminology, feminism and social change* (pp. 203–218). Emerald Publishing. https://eprints.whiterose.ac.uk/181379/

Cowan, D. (2004). Legal consciousness: Some observations. *Modern Law Review, 67*(6), 928–958. https://doi.org/10.1111/j.1468-2230.2004.00518.x

Chua, L. J., & Engel, D. M. (2019). Legal consciousness reconsidered. *Annual Review of Law and Social Science, 15*(1), 335–353. https://doi.org/10.1146/annurev-lawsocsci-101518-042717

Deering, K. N., Amin, A., Shoveller, J., Nesbitt, A., Garcia-Moreno, C., Duff, P., Argento, E., & Shannon, K. (2014). A systematic review of the correlates of violence against sex workers. *American Journal of Public Health, 104*(5), 42–54.

Engel, D. (1998). How does law matter in the constitution of legal consciousness? In B. G. Garth & A. Sarat (Eds.), *How does law matter?* (pp. 109–144). Northwestern University Press.

End Violence Against Women. (2023). *Latest data shows the criminal justice system isn't working for women*. Retrieved July 25, 2024, from https://www.endviolenceagainstwomen.org.uk/latest-data-shows-the-criminal-justice-system-isnt-working-for-women/

Ewick, P., & Silbey, S. S. (1998). *The common place of law: Stories from everyday life*. University of Chicago Press.

Felstiner, W. L. F., Abel, R. L., & Sarat, A. (1980). The emergence and transformation of disputes: Naming, blaming, claiming… *Law & Society Review, 15*(3/4), 631–654. https://doi.org/10.2307/3053505

Gill, C., & Creutzfeldt, N. (2018). The 'ombuds watchers': Collective dissent and legal protest amongst users of public services ombuds. *Social and Legal Studies., 27*(3), 367–388. https://doi.org/10.1177/0964663917721313

Hertogh, M. (2004). A 'European' conception of legal consciousness: Rediscovering Eugen Ehrlich. *Journal of Law and Society, 31*(4), 457–481. https://doi.org/10.1111/j.1467-6478.2004.00299.x

Hertogh, M. (2018). *Nobody's law: Legal consciousness and legal alienation in everyday life*. Palgrave Pivot.

Huysamen, M., & Sanders, T. (2021). Institutional ethics challenges to sex work researchers: Committees, communities, and collaboration. *Sociological Research Online, 26*(4), 942–958. https://doi.org/10.1177/13607804211002847

Keighley, R., Sanders, T., Saunders, L., & Agg, H. (2023). Participatory action research: Developing a collaborative approach to modern slavery research with survivors of exploitation. *Methodological Innovations, 16*(3), 393–404. https://doi.org/10.1177/20597991231208441

Kinnell, H. (2008). *Violence and sex work in Britain* (1st ed.). Willan. https://doi.org/10.4324/9781843926887

Klambauer, E. (2019). On the edges of the law: Sex workers' legal consciousness in England. *International Journal of Law in Context, 15*(03), 327–343. https://doi.org/10.1017/s1744552319000041

Lewis, J., & Maticka-Tyndale, E. (2000). Licensing sex work: Public policy and women's lives. *Canadian Public Policy, 26*(4), 437–449. https://ideas.repec.org/a/cpp/issued/v26y2000i4p437-449.html

Lowman, J. (2000). Violence and the outlaw status of (street) prostitution in Canada. *Violence against Women, 6*(9), 987–1011. https://doi.org/10.1177/10778010022182245

O'Neill, M. (1996). Researching prostitution and violence: Towards a feminist praxis. In M. Hester, L. Kelly, & J. Radford (Eds.), *Women, violence and male power*. London: Open University Press.

Platt, L., Grenfell, P., Meiksin, R., Elmes, J., Sherman, S. G., Sanders, T., Mwangi, P., & Crago, A. L. (2018). Associations between sex work laws and sex workers' health: A systematic review and meta-analysis of quantitative and qualitative studies. *PLOS Medicine, 15*(12), e1002680.

Sanders, T., & Campbell, R. (2007). Designing out vulnerability, building in respect: Violence, safety and sex work policy. *The British Journal of Sociology, 58*(1), 1–19.

Scoular, J. (2015). *The subject of prostitution: Sex work, law and social theory*. Routledge.

Wilson, L. C., & Miller, K. E. (2016). Meta-analysis of the prevalence of unacknowledged rape. *Trauma, Violence, & Abuse, 17*(2), 149–159. https://doi.org/10.1177/1524838015576391%3c/RefSource%3e

West, N., & Horn, T. (Eds.) (2021). *We too: Essays on sex work and survival: Essays on sex work and survival*. Feminist Press at CUNY.

Weitzer, R. (2005). Flawed theory and method in studies of prostitution. *Violence against Women, 11*(7), 934–949. https://doi.org/10.1177/1077801205276986

WHO, UNFPA, UNAIDS, & NSWP. (2012). *Prevention and treatment of HIV and other sexually transmitted infections for sex workers in low- and middle-income countries*. Retrieved May 21, 2024, from https://www.unfpa.org/sites/default/files/pub-pdf/9789241504744_eng.pdf

Young, K. M. (2014). Everyone knows the game: Legal consciousness in the Hawaiian cockfight. *Law & Society Review, 48*(3), 499–530. https://doi.org/10.1111/lasr.12094

2

Sex Work and Sexual Violence Laws in Each Jurisdiction

Jane Scoular, Rachel Howard, Barbara G. Brents, Teela Sanders, and Gillian Abel

Introduction

This chapter begins our analysis by outlining the formal laws that operate[1] in each of our case-study jurisdictions in relation to sex work and sexual violence. Looking at the varied and distinct legal contexts of

[1] The authors wish to acknowledge and thank Bridie Sweetman for her legal expertise, which has informed the Aotearoa New Zealand sections of this chapter.

J. Scoular
Strathclyde Law School, University of Strathclyde, Glasgow, UK

R. Howard · B. G. Brents
University of Nevada, Las Vegas, Nevada, USA

T. Sanders (✉)
University of Leicester, Leicester, UK
e-mail: teela.sanders@leicester.ac.uk

G. Abel
University of Otago, Dunedin, New Zealand

T. Sanders et al. (eds.), *Voicing Consent*, Palgrave Advances in Sex Work Studies,
https://doi.org/10.1007/978-3-031-77715-8_2

the UK (England and Wales, Scotland, and Northern Ireland),[2] Aotearoa New Zealand, and the USA, we consider the formal laws, legal regulations and court cases that directly concern prostitution, sexual violence, and workers' rights in each of these sites.The chapter also looks in detail at the operation of consent and the growing recognition, in some jurisdictions, of conditional consent, before we go on to consider the real-life application and relevance of these legal norms. Taken together, these discussions provide necessary framing for our subsequent empirical chapters, in which we seek to understand whether and how legislative context affects sex workers' attitudes, perceptions of, and behaviours towards the formal law and their experience of the law.

Laws Concerning Prostitution and Workers' Rights

United Kingdom

England and Wales

In England and Wales, sex work is partially criminalised. This means that offering or providing sexual services for money is not illegal, but working in brothels, brothel keeping or paying for services from someone forced into sex work is against the law (Sexual Offences Act, 2003). Loitering and persistent public solicitation (trying to get clients) in a street or public place for the purpose of prostitution is an offence; meanwhile, 'kerb crawling' (driving to find a sex worker) is also now charged as soliciting (Policing & Crime Act, 2009). It is not illegal to advertise sexual services, although rules prohibit obscene publications (Obscene Publications Act, 1959, Section 2), indecent displays (Indecent Displays (Control) Act,1981, s.1) and 'carding' (Criminal Justice & Police Act, 2001, s.46).

[2] We use the word 'prostitution' in the context of legal regulations that deploy this term.

Scotland

Sex work is also partially criminalised in Scotland. Street prostitution is dealt with under the Civic Government (Scotland) Act 1982, Section 46(1). 'Kerb crawling', soliciting a prostitute for sex in a public place, and loitering for the same purpose are also criminal under the Prostitution (Public Places) (Scotland) Act 2007.

It is not illegal to advertise sexual services, though there have been attempts to make it so in the context of efforts to criminalise the purchase of sex. These have so far failed, but sex work has been increasingly defined across a number of Scots social policies as a form of commercial exploitation (Scottish Government, 2024).

A Prostitution Tolerance Zones Bill was introduced into the Scottish Parliament in 2003 but failed to become law.[3]

Northern Ireland[4]

Paying for sexual activity with a person became illegal in Northern Ireland in 2015, with the passing of the Human Trafficking and Exploitation (Criminal Justice and Support for Victims) Act. Offering or providing sexual services for money and public solicitation is not illegal, but paying for sexual services is a summary offence subject to a £1000 fine and/or a maximum sentence of one year in prison. Offences relating to forced or coercive prostitution and brothel keeping are not within the scope of the above legislation and are prosecuted separately, as is the case in the rest of the UK. Similarly, as in the rest of the UK, paying for sex with someone under the age of 18 is subject to a maximum penalty of imprisonment ranging from seven years to life. The Sex Workers Alliance Ireland (SWAI) is the main advocacy group for sex workers in Northern Ireland.

[3] The Bill was withdrawn in 2015: https://webarchive.nrscotland.gov.uk/20240327012607/https://archive2021.parliament.scot/parliamentarybusiness/Bills/24985.aspx

[4] As noted in the introductory chapter, due to small numbers and in order to protect anonymity we included Northern Ireland data as part of the UK in the analysis that follows. The distinction in legal systems should, however, be noted and could be the focus of future study.

Policing in the UK

Police enforcement of these laws is discretionary. National policy discourages enforcement against street workers and encourages protecting sex workers and focusing attention on exploiters (NPCC, 2024). Great Britain has 43 territorial police forces (39 in England, four in Wales), with Police Scotland constituting its own force. Within this, there is a diversity of approaches to sex work and differing practices in working with sex-worker-led organisations, including the largest, National Ugly Mugs (NUM). This has led to what Feis-Bryce describes as a 'patchwork' approach to policing (Feis-Bryce, 2017) and, while there are policy attempts to bring consistency across the forces through models such as the 'harm-reduction compass' (Sanders et al., 2020a), discretionary element in policing means a myriad of approaches still exists, from safeguarding to enforcement. Some areas provide special liaison officers to sex workers reporting rape and serious physical harm. These officers are trained to understand the stigma and structural barriers that sex workers face (see Brown et al., 2024). A few areas treat all crimes against sex workers as hate crimes, allocating additional police resources and procedures to facilitate access to justice (Sanders et al., 2022).

Workers' Rights Laws in the UK

Labour law currently offers some level of protection for the formally self-employed stripping sector (see *Nowak v Chandler Bars Group Ltd*, 2019 in Barbagallo & Cruz, 2022); in Scotland, *KR v Mick Costello and others* (2021); Cruz (2020), but these protections do not, as yet, extend to other forms of sex work—such as prostitution and pornography—currently considered 'illegal', despite the fact they resemble stripping's labour processes (Barbagallo & Cruz, 2022).

Aotearoa New Zealand

Sex work has been decriminalised in Aotearoa New Zealand since the Prostitution Reform Act (PRA) was passed in 2003. Offering and providing commercial sexual services for money is legal and sex workers have the same employment, health, and safety rights as any other employee. Up to four sex workers can work together without the need to obtain a brothel operator's certificate. If there are more than four sex workers in a business entity, these workers need to obtain operators' certificates and must follow the same rules as other businesses, although, additionally, local councils can regulate location. In addition, there are specific protections just for sex workers.

In this decriminalised context, the police consider their role as one of providing support and preventing violence (Armstrong, 2017). The law is focused on concerns for worker and client health, and the welfare of trafficked people (although their legal status remains precarious), rather than on prosecuting people for participating in this trade. Under the PRA, sex workers are guaranteed the right to refuse to provide or continue to provide sexual services to any client. Section 17 of the PRA applies even when there is a previous agreement in place—the 'right to say no' supersedes contract law and the Consumer Guarantees Act (1993).

This guarantee was confirmed in the High Court decision of NR v MR (2014), in which the judge ruled that a sex worker had the right to end a two-hour booking early when she discovered the client had been looking up personal information about her. The client, who had refused to accept a refund, tried to argue that the worker had breached Section 28 of the Consumer Guarantees Act (CGA) (1993). The judge ruled that the respondent had no obligation to continue to supply sexual services and that she had a right under the Prostitution Reform Act to refuse to do so.

Introduced in part to address public health concerns, Section 8 and 9 of the PRA require both clients and workers to use prophylactic devices for oral, vaginal, and anal sex. Operators must promote this, and there is a $2000 fine for not practising safe sex.

As for migrant sex workers, Section 19 (PRA) was introduced as an anti-trafficking measure, to "ensure that in decriminalising the laws on prostitution, we do not unwittingly allow people to be brought into the country for the purposes of prostitution" (Dalziel, 2003). However, research indicates that s.19 is inconsistent with decriminalisation, as it creates two tiers of workers: legal (Aotearoa New Zealand citizens; permanent residents) and illegal (migrant workers with temporary visas). Temporary visa holders tend, therefore, to be more vulnerable to exploitation: unprotected by the PRA and fearing deportation, they are unlikely to report breaches or acts of violence (Armstrong, 2021; Bennachie et al., 2021; Harris, 2021; also see recent decision in case *AQ Thailand* [2022]).

Workers' Rights in Aotearoa New Zealand

Before the PRA passed in 2003, sex work was illegal. Post-PRA, sex workers no longer fear prosecution and can, accordingly, use criminal law to bring complaints about violence, theft, and other acts (Abel et al., 2010). As sex workers are independent contractors and not employees, however, they can be subjected to fines and other exploitative practices in contravention of the PRA, and have to take disputes with clients or brothel operators (e.g. over non-payment) to a mediation service, rather than employing labour law to enforce their rights. They can also report exploitation or abuse through various early resolution mechanisms provided by the Ministry of Business, and disputes with employers can be heard by the Human Rights Review Tribunal. Further information and support on criminal and breach-of-contract matters is available via the Aotearoa New Zealand Sex Workers' Collective.

United States of America

In most USA jurisdictions, governed by individual state laws, paying for services from someone forced into sex work is illegal, as is offering or providing sexual services for money, including keeping brothels, advertising, solicitation (public or private), and managing or controlling sex workers. The penalties for sex workers include fines or small prison sentences; and, in many states, any third-party involvement is subject to long-term prison sentences and large fines. Third parties include anyone seen as facilitating prostitution—from managers to persons referred to as pimps, to taxi drivers, to accountants if they know or should have known about their client's involvement in prostitution. The laws are worded differently in each state, with different penalties, and local police departments also have much discretion. Police are encouraged to prioritise clients and exploiters, but frequently arrest sex workers to encourage them to turn in exploiters; they also pose as sex workers online, to lure unsuspecting clients (Fernandez, 2016, p. 26).

The Stop Enabling Sex Traffickers Act (SESTA) and The Fight Online Sex Trafficking Act (FOSTA) were passed in 2017, both intended to fight sex trafficking by making it illegal to assist, facilitate or support sex trafficking through advertising. These laws suspended Section 230 of the Communication Decency Act of 1996 that protected platforms from liability for actions by users. These laws, moreover, put pressure on platforms to censor users—or risk civil and criminal penalties. Researchers note, however, that, rather than preventing online exploitation of trafficked persons, the legislation has pushed sex workers and trafficking victims into more dangerous and exploitative situations, by hampering their access to communication (Blunt & Wolf, 2020; Decriminalise Sex Work, 2024).

Nevada

Prostitution is legal in only one state: Nevada. Its laws on prostitution are contained in the Nevada Revised Statutes ('NRS') Chapter 201—Crimes Against Public Decency and Good Morals. These define prostitution as "engaging in sexual conduct with another person in return for a fee, monetary consideration or other thing of value" (Nevada Revised Statutes, (NRS) 201.295). Throughout the state, it is illegal for any person to "engage in prostitution or solicitation therefor, *except in a licensed house of prostitution*" (NRS 201.354.1; original emphasis), and these "licensed houses", which are allowed only in counties with less than

700,000 people (NRS 244.345.8), currently exist in 10 of Nevada's 17 counties. Only brothel owners, brothel staff, and sex workers themselves can legally gain money from prostitution. Nevada health codes specify regular testing for HIV and sexually transmitted infections for legal sex workers, who must use condoms.

Legal brothels are highly regulated. State law requires that "houses of ill fame" cannot be within 400 yards of a school or place of worship (NRS 201.380.1) and brothels are not allowed to advertise in areas where prostitution is illegal (NRS 201.430.9). Additionally, brothels are not permitted to operate from a building that fronts, or has entrances/exits onto, a principal business street or thoroughfare anywhere in the state (NRS 201.390.1). Most of the regulations covering brothels are set and governed by each city or county government, and enforced by local police. Ordinances, which vary greatly, specify where brothels can be located, conditions for revoking licences, and restrictions on advertising and signage (Brents & Hausbeck, 2005). Applying for a licence is difficult, with detailed business and financial histories required, and licensing fees can be up to $200,000 annually. Sex workers must be at least 21 years old in some counties, and 18 in others, and all brothel employees must obtain work cards from the police department.

As in most USA jurisdictions, Nevada law criminalises the solicitation of prostitution; if offering or agreeing to commit prostitution, a person can be arrested for solicitation, even if the sexual act never actually happens. Penalties for solicitation and prostitution are the same: a client or provider arrested for solicitation will incur fines of up to $1,000 and/or up to six months imprisonment. 'Pandering' (NRS 201.300.1) and 'pimping' (NRS 201.320.1) are also considered offences in Nevada and other USA states. Pandering refers to inducing or encouraging another "***without*** physical force or immediate threat" (emphasis added) to engage, or continue to engage, in prostitution, whether legal or illegal. It has a penalty of one to five years in prison and a fine of up to $10,000. Pimping—living off the earnings of a sex worker—incurs six months to three years imprisonment and up to $1,000 in fines, unless threat, force, or fraud is used, or if the potential sex worker is under 18: then it is prosecuted as sex trafficking (201.300). Nevada also has a vagrancy statute (NRS 207.030) that makes it a misdemeanour to "be a pimp".

Nevada has several laws designed to combat sex trafficking that blur the lines between trafficking and prostitution. The crime of "facilitating sex trafficking" (NRS 201.301.2) involves facilitating, arranging, providing, or paying transport of a person to induce that person to engage in unlawful sexual conduct or prostitution. Notably, the crime is helping to transport any sex worker, not just doing so by force. If the person is over 18, the penalty is one to six years in prison; if under 18, it is three to 10 years. Convicted sex traffickers are required to register as sex offenders.

Under state law, anyone arrested for prostitution must submit to an HIV test (NRS 201.356.1). Despite advances in HIV treatment, which can render the virus undetectable and therefore untransmittable, any sex worker engaging in legal or illegal prostitution who tests positive for HIV is liable to be charged with a felony offence (NRS 201.358).

Workers' Rights in the USA and Nevada

No workers' rights accrue due to prostitution being illegal in most states. No positive workers' rights accrue from working in a brothel in Nevada, bar the fact that working is not considered to be a crime.

Sexual Harassment

Feminist legal activism has meant that robust sexual harassment laws operate in the USA; but, as Schulhofer (2017) notes, these operate in narrow circumstances, and, in our study, we have not found them to be utilised by victims who have experienced sexual violence while sex-working.

While brothel employees could, theoretically, file complaints, there have been no known cases where EEOC (Equal Employment Opportunity Commission) complaints or civil lawsuits have been taken against brothel owners or customers. Also, in contrast to Aotearoa New Zealand, there are no special protections or avenues for brothel workers, only the same protections that apply to all workers. There has been concern that legal brothel workers, who are classified as independent contractors, are not protected by employment law. However, as determined by a number of court cases, many adult industry contract workers meet the conditions of an employee and are, therefore, covered by discrimination law (Gwin, 2024).

Sexual Violence Laws and the Concept of Consent

United Kingdom

The Law in the Legal Systems of the UK

Sexual offences were only unified in the early part of this century, in the distinct legal systems of the UK. Prior to this, laws concerning rape and sexual assault had developed in a fragmented, piecemeal manner, governed largely by the common law. Moving away from the historical understanding of rape as requiring force, consent became part of the common law in the last century, and in statute since the 1976 (Sexual Offences (Amendment) Act, 1976 in England and Wales, where rape was defined as sexual intercourse without consent. The law, however, failed to provide a clear dividing line between 'real consent' and 'mere submission', leaving it to juries to give consent its 'ordinary meaning' (as per *R v Olugboja* [1981]). This left considerable space for interpretation and, it has been argued, for the utilisation of rape myths to fill the gaps between common sense understandings and facts presented (Ellison & Munro, 2010; 2013). Moreover, as Temkin and Ashworth (2004, pp. 336–337) note, without "a clear indication of what is meant by lack of consent, sexual acts obtained by abuse of trust or coercion other than violence may well go unpunished". Thus, while consent models seek to move beyond understanding sexual offences as a crime of violence and recognise them as a violation of sexual autonomy, the operation of the law means the reality is that, most often, only cases of 'real rape' (Estrich, 2018, pp. 1092,1170), i.e. a violent attack perpetrated by a stranger, make it through what is a well-documented process of attrition.

This focus on 'real rape' remains the case, despite recent reforms which have sought to provide a clearer and more expansive statutory definition of consent in the legal systems of the UK. Sustained feminist campaigning inspired a series of governmental reviews of sexual offences, which focused primarily on legal reform. The most prominent, *Setting the Boundaries* (Home Office, 2000), stated that by "setting clear boundaries for society as to what is acceptable and unacceptable behaviour", reforms could bring coherence to the law, reflect changes in society, encourage victims to come forward and bring cases to court, and educate police and prosecutors towards a better understanding of the ambit of consent' (Home Office, 2000, p.18, p.18). These reviews led to the creation of Sexual Offences Acts in each jurisdiction, broadly similar in the sense that each contains a series of distinct sexual offences, all centred around the concept of consent.[5]

England and Wales

The Sexual Offences Act (SOA) 2003 created a series of distinct sexual offences: (s1) rape (s2) assault by penetration; (s3) sexual assault; and (s4) causing a person to engage in sexual activity without consent, the cornerstone of which is the concept of consent.[6]

Following a number of common-law jurisdictions, the SOA 2003, for the first time, creates a statutory definition of consent. Section 74 states "a person consents if he [or she] agrees by choice, and has the freedom and capacity to make that choice". This general definition of consent

[5] The commentary that follows is based around the law in England and Wales. The intention is not to be Anglocentric but, rather, to attempt to offer a clear statement of the law, in recognition of the fact that the SOA 2003 preceded and modelled reform in the other jurisdictions and that much academic debate has concerned the cases in English courts. On the substantive issues, the legal systems on this issue are largely similar, unless otherwise stated (see Appendix 1 for distinctions).

[6] The commentary that follows is based around the law in England and Wales. The intention is not to be Anglocentric but, rather, to attempt to offer a clear statement of the law, in recognition of the fact that the SOA 2003 preceded and modelled reform in the other jurisdictions and that much academic debate has concerned the cases in English courts. On the substantive issues, the legal systems on this issue are largely similar, unless otherwise stated (see Appendix 1 for distinctions).

is joined by a set of exhaustive (Temkin & Ashworth, 2004, p. 335),[7] rebuttable (s.75) and irrebuttable (s.76) evidential presumptions about consent and reasonable belief in consent, which are designed to give some indication of situations where consent is not present.

Section 75 outlines evidential presumptions about consent, including whereby, if circumstances are proved, consent cannot be provided if the victim was: unable to resist because of the use of violence or fear of violence, unlawfully detained, asleep, unconscious, had a physical disability or was too affected by substance. Section 76 outlines conclusive presumptions of consent vitiation, including whereby the defendant intentionally deceived the complainant, either about the nature and the purpose of the act or about the true identity of the perpetrator.

The maximum sentences for these offences are life (Section 1 [rape] and 2 [sexual assault by penetration], and Sect. 4 [causing sexual activity without consent] if it involves penetration) and 10 years (Sections 3 [sexual assault] and 4 [causing sexual activity without consent - without penetration).

Scotland

Sexual offences in Scotland are legislated under the Sexual Offences (Scotland) Act (SOSA) (2009). The first three sections of the SOSA, contained within Part 1, pertain to rape (Sections 1), sexual assault by penetration (Sections 2), and sexual assault "and other sexual offences" (Sections 3). Across these offences, there is understanding that a crime is committed if the victim does not consent and the perpetrator does not reasonably believe the victim is consenting. Consent is more specifically covered under Part 2 of the SOSA and is defined as 'free agreement'. Conditions, whereby an individual does not provide free agreement (noted in Sections 13), include where someone is incapacitated through alcohol or where someone is mistaken, through deception by the other,

[7] This means that only Parliament can add to the list of circumstances. There has been debate as to whether it should be non-exhaustive as per other jurisdictions (e.g. Canada and Australia) (Temkin and Ashworth 2004, p. 335), which means that case law could help develop the law beyond the stated examples. Doubt has also been expressed with regard to the current hierarchy of the presumptions.

"as to the nature or purpose of the conduct". Section 13 (e) also references where free agreement is not given due to the perpetrator impersonating a person known personally to the victim. Part 6 (and Schedule 2) of the SOSA outlines penalties for sexual offences, with the maximum sentences for rape and sexual assault by penetration being listed as "life imprisonment and a fine"; the maximum penalty on conviction on indictment for sexual assault is life imprisonment *or* a fine, or both.

Northern Ireland

Consent is not directly defined in The Sexual Offences (Northern Ireland) Order 2008. Its meaning is to be inferred by reading ss.9 and 10, which outline circumstances in which consent is absent. These are the same as the rebuttable and irrebuttable presumptions in the 2003 Act in England and Wales.

Consent in the UK: Concepts of Consent, Deceptions, and Conditional Consent

The reforms described in the previous section have achieved some positive changes. The definition of consent introduced in the Sexual Offences Acts puts the onus on the defendant to demonstrate a reasonable belief in consent, as opposed to the victim having to demonstrate an active denial of consent. Submission is no longer part of consent: belief in consent now has to be reasonable; and judicial directions now operate in an attempt to counter jury stereotypes and preconceptions with regard to sexual norms (Elvin, 2008, p. 530). Many commentators note, however, that despite the intention that statutory definition would help to clarify, and help to broaden out, the operation of consent, achieving a common understanding remains elusive and rape continues to be interpreted in law in a restricted manner.

Judicial guidance is minimal and circular, repeating statutory wording (Temkin & Ashworth, 2004, p. 336). There is currently remarkably little case law on the meaning of consent in sex offences; and the cases that have been decided—in particular, around if and specifically how deception operates to preclude consent, and the ambit and operation of presumptions—has led to even more confusion. This has, in turn, led to calls for further statutory reform (Criminal Law Reform Network Now (CLRNN), 2023; Murray & Beattie, 2021, p. 16).

In an effort to synthesise what is a voluminous and, at times, complex academic debate, a series of contradictory judgments on the scope of what forms of deception can constitute rape, and on the emerging concept of conditional consent, reveals a lack of clarity in the current law. A conflict has emerged between restrictive (Laird, 2014; Rogers, 2013) and expansive approaches (see, for e.g. Herring, 2005; Murray & Beattie, 2021), revealing differing perspectives on where it is appropriate to draw the line in order to constitute the legal 'wrong of rape' (Gardner & Shute, 2000). This is crucial for our research, as our study shows that many forms of unwanted sexual contact fall within this legal grey area.

Restrictive

Before the 2003 Act reforms, the common law distinguished between deception in inducement (deception used to induce another into having sex) and deception in ad factum (deception to the nature of the act or regarding identity) (*R v Clarence* [1889]). The law only recognised the latter as deceptions capable of violating consent (*R v Clarence* [1889]). This approach was confirmed by the Court of Appeal (COA) in the 1995 case of R v Linekar (1995), which considered whether the non-payment of a sex worker could be rape. According to the COA, Linekar's deception related neither to his identity nor to the nature of the act, but to the collateral matter of payment and, thus, did not negate consent. The COA stated that "The sex worker knew that she was engaging in sexual intercourse with the appellant and consented to it", and reaffirmed the previous common-law restrictive view: "[it] is the absence of consent and not the existence of fraud which makes something rape" (COA in Linekar, at 75; and see Syrota, 1995, p. 338).

Some later decisions would appear to support presumptions in the 2003 Act, in reiterating a limited set of deceptions (nature of act, identity) as undermining consent. For example, R v Dica (2004) (failure to disclose HIV status was not considered rape, as B was not deceived as to the 'nature' of the sexual act); *R (Monica) v DPP* (2018) (judicial review upheld the CPS decision not prosecute a rape case where consent to sex was obtained by an undercover police officer and this deception was considered insufficiently connected to the nature and purpose of sexual activity); and R v Lawrence (2020) (appeal allowed against a conviction of rape where consent relied on the assurance that the accused had undergone a vasectomy and the COA stated that B was not deceived as to the "sexual intercourse itself" but only as to the "broad circumstances" surrounding it).

Expansive

In contrast to these cases, the 2003 Act's more affirmative definition of consent, and a number of subsequent decisions, suggest a more expansive approach. The discussion of deceptions ad factum mentioned in s.76 of the 2003 Act refers to conclusive evidential presumptions (Temkin & Ashworth, 2004, p. 338) rather than to the general definition of consent (s.74). These presumptions state categorically where consent is absent, but do not exclude situations where there is no free agreement (Murray & Beattie, 2021). The SOA introduced a more general meaning under s.74, which, as a number of academics argue, allows for a wider recognition of deceptions that undermine free agreement[8]: a person consents if they agree by choice, and have the freedom and capacity to make that choice. This "offers a richer recognition of the right to make decisions about one's sexual conduct" (Murray & Beattie, 2021, p. 571). Cases such as R v Jheeta (2007) confirm this approach: deceptions in the form of anonymous, threatening texts from someone posing as a police officer did not pertain to the nature or purpose of

[8] This is also the view of the Scottish Law Commission (2006).

sexual intercourse (s.76), but also did not preclude a charge under s.74, as the threats rendered the victim not 'free' to make her own decision.

This broader understanding of consent was also affirmed by the case of Assange v Swedish Prosecution Authority (2011). In connection with proceedings relating to charges faced by WikiLeaks founder Julian Assange in Sweden, the High Court had to decide if two separate complaints by women, that the accused penetrated each of them without a condom, despite their consent relying on his agreement to wear one, would also constitute a criminal offence under English law (in order to fulfil the dual criminality test). Assange argued that this was not a known offence under English law because the deception did not go to the nature of the act. The High Court disagreed, finding that each complainer was deceived about a sufficiently important aspect of the act so as to negate her consent under s.74 of the SOA (*Assange*, at 86). The case's importance lies in the observation that s.74 operated separately from s.76. It has also been described as an authority for an emerging concept of conditional consent (Doig & Wortley, 2013, p. 291).

Assange has been followed by increased media reporting of the crime of 'stealthing' (Bond 2023; Stonehouse, 2021) and a number of successful cases, including one in Scotland[9] and an unreported case involving a sex worker, this second example being one to which we now briefly turn our attention. In 2019, Lee Hogben from Bournemouth was found guilty of rape and two counts of assault by penetration, and sentenced to 12 years in prison. Consent for sexual intercourse was given by the victim, on the condition that a condom was used; these terms were agreed upon beforehand and also clearly stated on her website. The accused removed the condom and continued to have sex with the victim despite her protests, assaulted her, and left without paying. While the case also involved other acts of physical violence, the prosecuting lawyer, Jodie Mitchell, in press reports noted: "Hogben went beyond what was consented to by removing the protection, which the complainant will say was a condition of intercourse" (Aspinall, 2019).

[9] https://www.thescottishsun.co.uk/news/10663712/guilty-rape-stealthing/. Interviews with prosecutors in Scotland revealed that, while there was no similar guidance in Scotland, they would follow *Assange*; and this case, as reported in the *Scottish Sun*, suggests stealthing is covered by the SOA Act.

Subsequent legal judgments appear to confirm the approach in *Assange* and suggest that it is possible for someone to consent to sexual intercourse on the condition that their partner does not ejaculate inside them (*R (on the application of F) v DPP and A* [2013]) or on the condition that their partner is a cisgender man (*R v McNally* [2013]).[10]

Importantly, the dicta from *Assange* is reflected in and informs new Crown Prosecution Service guidance, which reflects an expanded notion of conditional consent:

- There must be ostensible consent at the relevant time, usually at penetration,
- There must be a deception, other than one which falls within Sections 76 of the Sexual Offences Act, 2003, or a condition upon which the complainant agreed to the act,
- Prosecutors should avoid defining the 'concept' of conditional consent by reference to the topic or subject matter of the condition or deception in question, as these cases are no more than examples of the need to apply all relevant context when deciding issues of free choice under Sections 74,
- A condition or deception is an important part of the context but not all of it. Whether consent was absent may well depend on other contexts,
- The evidence relating to 'choice' and the 'freedom' to make any particular choice must be approached in a ['] *broad common-sense way*,' [Lord Judge CJ in ***F***], and
- The imposition of conditions embodies personal sexual autonomy which Sections 74 was intended to provide. Their contextual importance derives, in part, from the fact they represent positive choices made by a participant to sexual acts about which another participant can be in no doubt.

[10] The case of *McNally* is controversial. Treating a trans person's gender identity as deceptive has been described as transphobic (Sharpe, 2018). A careful discussion of this issue is not possible in the space permitted but it should be noted that suggested reforms which create a new category of deceptive relations, would offer a more satisfactory legal solution, as this would allow for the defence of a reasonable excuse to be utilised (see Gibson, 2019).

(Crown Prosecution Service, 2021a; original emphasis)

While this CPS guidance suggests a "developing concept of conditional consent", it also notes the "absence of clear authority as to how far the concept extends" (Crown Prosecution Service, 2021b). Moreover, reference to "broad common sense way" and "contextual" approaches does not seem to be particularly helpful given the current uncertainty that exists in this area of law.

Is Payment an Issue of Conditional Consent?

The question of whether the concept of conditional consent extends to non-payments is unclear. It would seem that the new statutory definition of consent, which includes freedom and capacity to consent, coupled with the case of *Assange*, which recognises a richer sense of sexual autonomy, could also apply to other conditions that are important to sex workers, such as payment (Kotiswaran, cited in Mirren, 2019; Palmer, 2023). However, while arguments for a more expansive reading post-2003-Act are compelling, courts and legal personnel may be reluctant to extend the law beyond stated law in Linekar, and thus law reform is required to clarify this grey area.

Fraud

The Linekar case describes non-payment as fraud, and while criminal fraud charges could apply in these cases (especially in Scots law, which has a broader test), in practice this has not been charged. Civil claims have also not been pursued, likely due to the quasi-illegal status of sex work and the principle *ex turpi causa non oritur action* (from a dishonourable cause an action does not arise) (see *Pearce v Brooks* [1866]).[11]

---

[11] A carriage had been hired for a woman in which to undertake prostitution business. Action has been taken for payment of rental of the carriage. It is held that the owners knew the underlying immoral purpose and that, therefore, the claim was unenforceable: "Anyone who

Charging and treating deceptions, whether around payment or condom use, as either criminal fraud or civil cases do not address the sexual nature of the crime. The previous crime of procurement (Sexual Offences Act, 1956, Part 1, Sections 22–31: "It is an offence for a person to procure a woman, by false pretences or false representations, to have unlawful sexual intercourse in any part of the world"), abolished by the 2003 SOA, would have addressed this, and reformers must have assumed new definition s.74 would cover these cases. That it has not has instigated calls for (de-gendered) reinstatement of the previous procuring offence, or a new offence of inducing sexual activity by deception (such as a series of 'deceptive sexual relations crimes' that would mirror the main sexual offences [Gibson, 2023]). This would help clarify the law, overcome the binary between expansive and inclusive approaches to deception, and offer more justice options to victims and prosecutors.

Aotearoa New Zealand

Sexual offences are contained in Part VII of the Crimes Act 1961. Sexual violation is the most serious sexual offence, defined in Sections128 as the act of sexual connection without consent and without a reasonable belief in consent. Depending on how the sexual connection is effected, sexual violation amounts either to rape (Sections 128 (2) (where there is penetration of a person's genitalia by a penis)) or unlawful sexual connection (Sections 128 (3)). The crime of sexual violation is liable to imprisonment for a term not exceeding 20 years.

Additionally, Sections 129A (1) renders sexual activity induced by threats a crime, punishable by imprisonment for a term not exceeding 14 years. In Connolly v R (2009), a former police officer was found guilty of this crime, as he had made improper use of his powers to make express or implied threats that induced a sex worker to have a sexual connection with him.

contributes to the performance of an illegal act by supplying a thing with the knowledge it will be used for that purpose, cannot receive the price for that thing so supplied".

The Meaning of Consent

In terms of defining consent, there is no clear statutory definition. Sparse judicial interpretations state that consent should be "full, voluntary, free and informed" to be "real, genuine or true" consent (legal consent) (R v Cook (1986)). Similarly, as Jackson notes, a model direction frequently used by judges in directing juries states: "consent means true consent if it is freely given by a person who is in a position to give it" (Bishop et al., 2018, at CRI128.4). The New Zealand Police website states "[a] person consents to sexual activity if they do it actively, freely, voluntarily and consciously without being pressured into it" (New Zealand Police, n.d.).

As previously noted, Sections 17 of the PRA states that the fact that a person has entered into a contract to provide commercial sexual services does not, of itself, constitute consent for the purposes of the criminal law, if he or she does not consent, or withdraws his or her consent, to providing a commercial sexual service. The Crimes Act is silent on the meaning of consent, providing only a legal definition of what it is not (see s.128A, below). Section 128A provides a list of non-exhaustive and rebuttable presumptions similar to those under 2003 SOA in England and Wales. The statute also notes that this section does not limit the circumstances in which a person does not consent to sexual activity.

As with the reforms in the UK, these definitions are circular (consent is defined as "true consent freely given"), self-referential and fail to answer the fundamental question of what consent is (Jackson, 2020). The latter two subsections of s.128A would appear to limit the scope of deceptions to the common-law position, permitting deceptions ad factum only as per the previous common law (following cases of *Clarence* and *R v Linekar*, which are cited with authority in Aotearoa New Zealand). While 'mistakes as to identity' remains narrow (Sections 127 (6)),[12] the interpretation of 'mistaken about its nature and quality' (Sections 128A (7)) has been subject to some extension in recent years, beyond a misunderstanding of the act's sexual nature as it was ruled in the case of KSB v

[12] Mistakes as to identity are restricted to the actual identity of the other person, or are interpreted narrowly. In R v Papadimitropoulos (1957), where consent was obtained by a fictitious marriage ceremony, it was held that mistakes as to the status of a person were not contemplated by the provision.

Accident Compensation Corporation (2012). The New Zealand Court of Appeal held that a non-disclosure of HIV was sufficient to constitute rape.[13]

In addition, and of considerable importance to our research, a recent case, R v Campos (2021), involving a sex worker has introduced the notion of conditional consent into Aotearoa New Zealand law, following the English case of *Assange*. In this case, Mr Campos eventually agreed to wear a condom when the victim explained that he was required to do so by law, but, in a second encounter during the booking, Mr Campos removed the condom and ejaculated inside the victim. A District Court (Wellington) jury held that, where condoms/prophylactic devices are removed without a sex worker's consent, this should be classified as sexual violation by rape under the Crimes Act 1961, s.128A. The offender received a sentence of three years and nine months' imprisonment, and both the decision and the sentence were later upheld by the Court of Appeal (*Campos v R* [2022]).

The decision has been hailed as "a long-awaited extension of the law and an affirmation that these practices undermine an individual's dignity, sexual autonomy and security" (Goh, 2021). This wider construction of consent appears to be gaining ground in a number of jurisdictions (see, for e.g. *DPP v R (Yeong) (a pseudonym)* (2022), although there are criticisms that this approach goes too far (for example, Noakes, 2022).

This means that cases involving condom refusal/ removal could potentially be charged as sexual violation (rape as per *R v Campos*), indecent assault, or breach of Sections 9 (requirement to use a prophylactic). All are criminal charges, but penalties vary widely, from discharge without conviction, to a fine (maximum penalty of a fine of $2,000), to imprisonment.

[13] The majority approved the dicta of the Canadian Supreme Court in *R v Cuerrier* (1998) at 47, per McLachlin J., that the deception went to the nature of the sexual act and differed from other statuses "in a profoundly serious way that merits the criminal sanction" (*R v Cuerrier*, at 72). This is a departure from previous case law; and common-law jurisdictions now all point in different directions, raising important issues of the interaction between criminal law and public health policy (Weait, 2007).

Non-payment as Rape

The question remains whether *R v Campos* can be extended to cases involving non-payment, given the restrictive authority of *R v Linekar*. It should be noted that a 2015 case in Australia (R v Livas, 2015) did recognise as rape a case in which Mr Livas pretended to pay a sex worker $850 with an envelope containing folded-up paper. The offender pleaded guilty to one offence of sexual intercourse without consent and was sentenced to 25 months' imprisonment. The judge Penfold J stated: "it must be clearly understood that something that looks like a consent to sexual intercourse, if obtained by fraudulent activity as this one clearly was, is not a consent".

United States

Rape and Sexual Assault Legislation

Historically, rape and sexual assault were considered a serious felony under common law (judge-made law) in the States of America. Rape was defined as sexual intercourse by a man, with a woman, not his wife, by force and against her will. To prove sexual assault, the American criminal justice system required evidence of force through corroborating evidence and evidence of a victim's resistance (Estrich, 1987). Beginning in the 1970s, reformers have sought to address the limitations in approaches to sexual violence, through a series of statutory reforms, which include definitional changes of rape and sexual assault that eliminated or modified corroboration and resistance requirements (Bachman & Paternoster, 1993; Clay-Warner & Burt, 2005; Horney & Spohn, 1991; Spohn & Horney, 1993; 1996).

Reforms operated at the state level, meaning that there are significant differences in the laws relating to rape and sexual offences across the United States. Because the legal definition of sexual assault varies by state, it can have an impact on formal reporting of victimisation (Kahn et al., 2003; Weiss, 2011) and public perceptions of the severity of sexual crimes (Pinchevsky et al., 2024). Statutes also vary nationally in how consent is defined and the interpretation, with regard to the importance of force and fear in undermining consent in the crime of rape, highlights difficulties in interpreting sexual assault statutes. California statutory provisions use an affirmative consent model, whereas Pennsylvania legislation only describes non-consent in relation to forcible compulsion and incapacitation (Blanco, 2018).

Currently, sexual assault laws in the USA do not recognise a conditional consent standard, as established as a result of the case of *Assange* in England and Wales (Blanco, 2018) and in the Aotearoa New Zealand case of *R v Campos*. Conditional consent standards are essential for protecting against unwanted sexual contact such as stealthing, and, in the absence of common-law development in this area, statutory reform would seem necessary. California has implemented such a law (California Penal Code 261 PC)[14] and there are calls for other states to follow. Note, however, that its statute only provides civil penalties (financial compensation), not criminal sanctions (Hernandez, 2021). Blanco (2018) discusses the importance of adopting a conditional consent standard into pre-existing sexual assault laws, as opposed to the creation of new, stealthing-specific, legislation that could, she argues, overly criminalise sexual conduct. The American Law Institute's recent draft Model Penal Code[15] seeks to establish an affirmative consent standard and recognise the impact of coercion, but conditional consent remains restricted to the current common-law position with regard to deception (Schulhofer, 2017).

[14] 'Consent' is defined to mean positive cooperation in act or attitude, pursuant to the exercise of free will. The.

person must act freely and voluntarily and have knowledge of the nature of the act or transaction involved (California Penal Code § 261.6).

[15] Due to the federally fragmented nature of USA law reform, the American Law Institute (ALI) is necessary. It is an unofficial, self-appointed group of leading lawyers, professors, and judges. Its mission is to promote uniformity and sound standards in American law. One of the most successful ALI products is its Model Penal Code (MPC), which it completed in 1962, more than 60 years ago. The MPC does not have the force of law, but states have widely enacted it. See: https://www.ali.org/publications/show/sexual-assault-and-related-offenses/

USA, Nevada

In the state of Nevada, the term sexual assault is used and defined as the subjection of another to sexual penetration,[16] or the forcing of another to sexually penetrate themselves or another or a beast, "against the will of the victim or under conditions in which the perpetrator knows or should know that the victim is mentally or physically incapable of resisting or understanding the nature of his or her conduct" (NRS 200.366.1.).

Here, non-consensual sexual touching that falls short of penetration—such as groping—is not rape. In these cases, possible charges would be for open and gross lewdness (NRS 201.210) or lewdness with a minor (NRS 201.230), depending on the victim's age.[17]

The law in Nevada is less nuanced than that in the other case-study jurisdictions and goes into significantly less detail about the specifics of different 'types' of sexual violence, or the meaning of consent. In interpreting the phrase "against the will of the victim", Nevada courts have developed a 'totality of the circumstances' test (*McNair v State* [1992]). In a jury trial, the jury must determine whether "(1) the circumstances surrounding the incidents indicate that the victims had reasonably demonstrated their lack of consent and (2) it was reasonable from the point of view of the perpetrator to conclude that the victims manifested consent" (McNair v State (1992)). This approach to consent continues to place the victim's actions as central to the analysis of consent/non-consent.

Case law has established that it is not necessary to prove overt force and physical force (Dinkens v State, 1976), which ruled that there is no consent where the victim is induced to submit to the sexual act through fear of death or serious bodily injury (*State v Denton* [1966]; *State v Thomas* [1973]).

---

16 'Sexual penetration' is defined (NRS 200.364.9) as "cunnilingus, fellatio, or any intrusion, however slight, of any part of a person's body or any object manipulated or inserted by a person into the genital or anal openings of the body of another, including sexual intercourse in its ordinary meaning. The term does not include any such conduct for medical purposes".

17 Under NRS § 200.481, Nevada law defines the crime of battery as "any willful and unlawful use of force or violence upon the person of another". A simple battery that does not cause injury is treated as a misdemeanour. The punishment includes up to six months imprisonment and fines of up to $1,000. Domestic violence is a separate crime.

Deception

Nevada's Supreme Court ruled, in *McNair v State*, that the language of Nevada's sexual assault statute "is sufficiently broad and explicit to encompass conduct ... occurring as a result of fraud and deceit" (Christopher & Christopher, 2007, p. 92), but also confirms the currency of the narrow common-law interpretation of rape by deception. This means that Nevada has one of the most restrictive definitions in the jurisdictions we examined, in relation to any recognition of rape by deception. It follows the narrow common-law approach, which only recognises deception in ad factum (i.e. relating to the sexual nature of the act and the identity of the accused) (Licea, 2022). This is similar to the English case of *R v Linekar*.

In this case (of *McNair v State*), the victim was a medical patient who was penetrated under the pretext of medical treatment. The court considered whether fraud and deceit were sufficient to vitiate the victim's consent in law. The court found that the physician's deception vitiated the victim's consent because the victim was "not in a position to exercise an independent judgement concerning the act of sexual penetration" [57].

This common-law approach to rape by deception would not accommodate the experience of sex workers who consent to sex based on fraud, such as non-payment or reduced payment, as, following the reasoning in Linekar, this deception does not relate to the nature of the act but to the circumstances surrounding it.

Conclusion

The purpose of this chapter has been to sketch the laws that operate in relation to sex work and sexual violence. In the next chapter, we document sex workers' experiences of setting up the conditions of consent and we consider what they do when these conditions are breached. We also consider, in subsequent chapters, the extent to which the 'law' informs these sex workers' experiences and responses to unwanted sexual contact.

References

Abel, G., Healy, C., Bennachie, C., & Reed, A. (2010). Five: The Prostitution Reform Act. In G. Abel, L. Fitzgerald, C. Healy, & A. Taylor (Eds.), *Taking the crime out of sex work* (pp. 75–84). Policy Press. Retrieved June 20, 2024, from: https://doi.org/10.51952/9781847423351.ch005

AQ Thailand. (2022). NZIPT 505589. Retrieved February 24, 2024, from: https://hyimmigration.co.nz/wp-content/uploads/2023/05/rem_20220729_505589.pdf

Armstrong, L. (2017). From law enforcement to protection?: Interactions between sex workers and police in a decriminalised street-based sex industry. *British Journal of Criminology, 57*(3), 570–588.

Armstrong, L. (2021). "I can lead the life that I want to lead": Social harm, human needs and the decriminalisation of sex Work in Aotearoa/New Zealand. *Sexuality Research and Social Policy, 18*(4), 941–951. https://doi.org/10.1007/s13178-021-00605-7

Aspinall, G. (2019). A British man has been convicted of rape after removing a condom during sex. *Grazia Magazine*. Retrieved June 20, 2024, from: https://graziadaily.co.uk/life/in-the-news/stealthing-conviction-rape/

Assange v Swedish Prosecution Authority. (2011). EWHC 2849 (Admin). Retrieved July 4, 2023, from: https://www.supremecourt.uk/cases/docs/uksc-2011-0264-judgment.pdf

Bachman, R., & Paternoster, R. (1993). A contemporary look at the effects of rape law reform: How far have we really come? *Journal of Criminal Law and Criminology, 84*(3), 554–574. https://scholarlycommons.law.northwestern.edu/cgi/viewcontent.cgi?article=6785&context=jclc

Barbagallo, C., & Cruz, K. (2022). Dancers win at work: Unionization and Nowak v Chandler Bars Group Ltd. *Studies in Political Economy, 102*(3), 354–375. https://doi.org/10.1080/07078552.2021.2000208

Bennachie, C., Pickering, A., Lee, J., Macioti, P., Mai, N., Fehrenbacher, A., Giametta, C., Hoefinger, H., & Musto, J. (2021). Unfinished decriminalization: The impact of Section 19 of the Prostitution Reform Act 2003 on migrant sex workers' rights and lives in Aotearoa New Zealand. *Social Sciences, 10*, 79. https://hdl.handle.net/2381/25205339.v1

Bishop, S., Dawson, B., Hall, E., Murray, I., Northwood, B., O'Sullivan, J., Sheat, C., & van Echten, A. (2018). *Garrow and Turkington's Criminal Law in New Zealand*. Retrieved June 20, 2024, from: https://www.lexisnexis.com/en-nz/products/legal-content-library/criminal/garrow-and-turkingtons-criminal-law-in-new-zealand?srsltid=AfmBOoolV2h0G__I3mA6n5XV4yOY1iUB8GVj75POcE9d3ho_Q0sYvMD1

Blanco, M. (2018). *Sex trend or sexual assault?: The dangers of 'stealthing' and the concept of conditional consent*. Retrieved December 13, 2023, from: https://www.pennstatelawreview.org/wp-content/uploads/2018/12/123-Blanco-FINAL.pdf

Blunt, D., & Wolf, A. (2020). Erased: The impact of FOSTA-SESTA and the removal of Backpage on sex workers. *Anti-Trafficking Review, 14*, 117–121. https://doi.org/10.14197/atr.201220148

Bond, K. (2023). What is stealthing—and what to do if you think it has happened to you. *Cosmopolitan*. Retrieved June 20, 2024, from: https://www.cosmopolitan.com/uk/reports/a45246257/what-is-stealthing/

Brents, B. G., & Hausbeck, K. (2005). Violence and legalized brothel prostitution in Nevada: Examining safety, risk, and prostitution policy. *Journal of Interpersonal Violence, 20*(3), 270–295. https://doi.org/10.1177/0886260504270333

Brown, K., Grace, S., & Redman, S. (2024). Policing vulnerability: The care and control of sex workers through designated police officers. *British Journal of Criminology*, Open access.https://doi.org/10.1093/bjc/azae026

Campos v R. (2022). NZCA 311. Retrieved July 5, 2024, from: https://www.openlaw.nz/case/2022NZCA311

Christopher, R. L., & Christopher, K. H. (2007). Adult impersonation: Rape by fraud as a defense to statutory rape. *Northwestern University Law Review, 101*, 75.

Civic Government (Scotland) Act. (1982). Retrieved May 4, 2024, from: https://www.legislation.gov.uk/ukpga/1982/45/contents

Clay-Warner, J., & Burt, C. H. (2005). Rape reporting after reforms. *Violence against Women, 11*(2), 150–176. https://doi.org/10.1177/1077801204271566

Connolly v R. (2009). HC CHCH CRI 2008–409–014401. NZHC 2473. Retrieved July 11, 2024, from: https://www.nzlii.org/nz/cases/NZHC/2009/2473.pdf

Consumer Guarantees Act (CGA). (1993). Retrieved June 20, 2024, from: https://www.legislation.govt.nz/act/public/1993/0091/latest/dlm311053.html

Crimes Act. (1961). Retrieved June 20, 2024, from: https://www.legislation.govt.nz/act/public/1961/0043/latest/DLM327382.html

Criminal Justice and Police Act. (2001). Retrieved June 20, 2024, from: https://www.legislation.gov.uk/ukpga/2001/16/contents

Criminal Law Reform Network Now (CLRNN). (2023). *Reforming the relationship between sexual consent, deception and mistake*. http://www.clrnn.co.uk/media/1031/clrnn3-deception-report.pdf

Crown Prosecution Service (CPS). (2021a). *Rape and sexual offences—Chapter 6: Consent*. Retrieved June 20, 2024, from: https://www.cps.gov.uk/legal-guidance/rape-and-sexual-offences-chapter-6-consent

Crown Prosecution Service (CPS). (2021b). *Rape and sexual offences—Chapter 3: Case building*. Retrieved June 20, 2024, from: https://www.cps.gov.uk/legal-guidance/rape-and-sexual-offences-chapter-3-case-building

Dalziel, L. (2003). *Prostitution Reform Bill—in committee*. Retrieved June 13, 2024, from: https://www.parliament.nz/en/pb/hansard-debates/rhr/document/47HansD_20030514_00001525/prostitution-reform-bill-in-committee

Decriminalise Sex Work. (2024). *What is SESTA/FOSTA?* Retrieved June 20, 2024, from: https://decriminalizesex.work/advocacy/sesta-fosta/what-is-sesta-fosta/#What-Is-SESTA-FOSTA

Dinkens v State. (1976). 92 Nev. 74, 546 P.2d 228. Retrieved July 5, 2024, from: https://casetext.com/case/dinkens-v-state-11/case-details

Director of Public Prosecutions (DPP) v Yeong (a pseudonym). (2022). (Victoria, Australia). Retrieved July 5, 2024, from: https://jade.io/j/?a=outline&id=944275

Doig, G. A., & Wortley, N. (2013). Conditional consent? An emerging concept in the law of rape. *The Journal of Criminal Law, 77*(4), 286–291. https://doi.org/10.1350/jcla.2013.77.4.848a

Ellison, L., & Munro, V. E. (2010). A stranger in the bushes, or an elephant in the room? Critical reflections upon received rape myth wisdom in the context of a mock jury study. *New Criminal Law Review, 13*(4), 781–801.

Ellison, L., & Munro, V. E. (2013). Better the devil you know? 'Real rape' stereotypes and the relevance of a previous relationship in (mock) juror deliberations. *The International Journal of Evidence & Proof, 17*(4), 299–322.

Elvin, J. (2008). The concept of consent under the Sexual Offences Act 2003. *The Journal of Criminal Law, 72*(6), 519–536.

Estrich, S. (1987). *Real rape: How the legal system victimizes women who say no.* Harvard University Press.

Estrich, S. (2018). Is it rape? In P. Searles (Ed.), *Rape and society* (pp. 183–193). Routledge.

Feis-Bryce, A. (2017). Policing sex work in Britain: A patchwork approach. In *Policing the Sex Industry* (pp. 19–37). Routledge.

Fernandez, F. L. (2016). *Hands up: A systematized review of policing sex workers in the US* (PhD thesis, Yale University).

Gardner, J., & Shute, S. (2000). The wrongness of rape. In J. Horder (Ed.), *Oxford essays in jurisprudence* (pp. 193–218). Clarendon Press.

Gibson, M. (2019). Deceptive sexual relations: A theory of criminal liability. *Oxford Journal of Legal Studies, 40*(1), 82–109. https://doi.org/10.1093/ojls/gqz031

Gibson, M. (2023). Deception, consent and the right to sexual autonomy. In Criminal Law Reform Now Network (Eds.), *Reforming the relationship between sexual consent, deception and mistake* (pp. 48–55). Retrieved June 10, 2024, from: http://www.clrnn.co.uk/media/1031/clrnn3-deception-report.pdf

Goh, B. (2021). *Full, free and informed: Assessing the scope of conditional consent*. Retrieved June 20, 2024, from: https://www.equaljusticeproject.co.nz/articles/full-free-and-informed-assessing-the-scope-of-conditional-consent2021

Gwin, C. (2024). It's time to sue for what we want: New legal tools for strippers. In B. Barton, B. Brents, & A. Jones (Eds.), *Sex work today: Erotic labor in the twenty-first century* (pp. 275–284). NYU Press.

Harris, K. (2021). Survivor of attempted sexual assault says migrant sex workers are targeted due to NZ law. *The New Zealand Herald.* Retrieved September 1, 2022, from: https://www.nzherald.co.nz/nz/survivor-of-attempted-sexual-assault-says-migrant-sex-workers-are-targeted-due-to-nz-law/3H434JHI2SEANQCRWH2PDDBUSA/

Hernandez, J. (2021). California is the 1st state to ban 'stealthing', nonconsensual condom removal. *NPR.* Retrieved June 13, 2024, from: https://www.npr.org/2021/10/07/1040160313/california-stealthing-nonconsensual-condom-removal

Herring, J. J. W. (2005). Mistaken sex. *Criminal Law Review,* pp. 511–524. https://ssrn.com/abstract=1287130

Home Office. (2000). *Setting the boundaries, reforming the law on sex offences.* Retrieved June 22, 2024, from: https://lawbore.net/articles/setting-the-boundaries.pdf

Horney, J., & Spohn, C. (1991). Rape law reform and instrumental change in six urban jurisdictions. *Law & Society Review, 25*(1), 117.

Indecent Displays (Control) Act. (1981). Retrieved May 4, 2024, from: https://www.legislation.gov.uk/ukpga/1981/42

Jackson, D. (2020). Six mistakes of law about consent. *New Zealand Women's Law Journal*, Volume IV. Retrieved June 20, 2024, from: https://www.womenslawjournal.co.nz/edition-four-2020

Kahn, A. S., Jackson, J., Kully, C., Badger, K., & Halvorsen, J. (2003). Calling it rape: Differences in experiences of women who do or do not label their sexual assault as rape. *Psychology of Women Quarterly, 27*(3), 233–242. https://doi.org/10.1111/1471-6402.00103

KR v Mick Costello and others. (2022). 4111660/2021. Retrieved May 20, 2024, from: https://drive.google.com/file/d/1apU0R0bB0_3mry6qciAuLH0pckXdnwyW/view

KSB v Accident Compensation Corporation. (2012). NZCA 82. Retrieved July 5, 2024, from: https://armstrongthompson.co.nz/wp-content/uploads/2012/03/KSB-v-ACC-Court-of-Appeal.pdf

Laird, K. (2014). Rapist or rogue? Deception, consent and the Sexual Offences Act 2003. *Criminal Law Review, 1*, 492–510.

Licea, R. (2022). How to expand rape by deception and protect consent. *University of Massachusetts Law Review, 17*(2), 1.

McNair v State. (1992). 20127 Supreme Court of Nevada. Retrieved May 20, 2024, from: https://justis.vlex.com/#vid/895599504

Mirren, F. (2019). How sex workers who are sexually assaulted are being failed by the justice system. *I News*. Retrieved Febraury 24, 2024, from: https://inews.co.uk/opinion/how-sex-workers-who-are-sexually-assaulted-are-being-failed-by-the-justice-system-328027

Murray, K. L., & Beattie, T. (2021). Conditional consent and sexual offences: Revisiting the Sexual Offences Act 2003 after Lawrance. *Criminal Law Review, 7*, 556–574.

National Police Chiefs' Council (NPCC). (2024). *Sex work national police guidance*. Retrieved June 20, 2024, from: https://www.npcc.police.uk/SysSiteAssets/media/downloads/publications/publications-log/national-crime-coordination-committee/2024/npcc-sex-work-guidance-v2---february-2024.pdf

Noakes, S. (2022, December). 'Stealthing'—an analysis of 'Campos v R' [2022] NZCA 311. *New Zealand Law Journal*, 395–399.

NR v MR. (2014). 2014, NZHC 863. Retrieved May 20, 2024, from: https://defamationupdate.co.nz/wp-content/uploads/case-database/2014/NR-v-MR-2014-NZHC-863.pdf

Obscene Publications Act. (1959). Retrieved June 20, 2024, from: https://www.legislation.gov.uk/ukpga/Eliz2/7-8/66/contents

Palmer, T. (2023). Freedom to negotiate. In Criminal Law Reform Now Network (Eds.), *Reforming the relationship between sexual consent, deception and mistake* (pp. 74–83). Retrieved May 20, 2024, from: http://www.clrnn.co.uk/media/1031/clrnn3-deception-report.pdf

Pearce v Brooks. (1866). LR 1 Ex 213. Retrieved July 5, 2024, from: https://www.scribd.com/doc/46735334/Pearce-v-Brooks-1866-Lr-1-Ex-213-Exch

Pinchevsky, G. M., & Hayes, B. E. (2022). Understanding college students' perceived help-seeking knowledge and awareness about sexual misconduct policies and procedures. *Journal of Interpersonal Violence, 08862605221081 9*. https://doi.org/10.1177/08862605221081935

Pinchevsky, G. M., Augustyn, M. B., Kennedy, A. H., & Rennison, C. M. (2024). Perceptions of sexual violence terms used in statutes throughout the United States. *Violence Against Women, 30*(15–16), 3991–4011. https://doi.org/10.1177/10778012231188088

Policing and Crime Act. (2009). Retrieved June 20, 2024, from: https://www.legislation.gov.uk/ukpga/2009/26/contents

Prostitution (Public Places) (Scotland) Act. (2007). Retrieved June 20, 2024, from: https://www.legislation.gov.uk/asp/2007/11

R (Monica) v DPP. (2018). EWHC 3508 (QB). Retrieved February 24, 2024, from: http://www2.bailii.org/ew/cases/EWHC/Admin/2018/3508.html

R (on the application of F) v DPP and A. (2013). EWHC 945 (Admin). Retrieved December 13, 2023, from: https://www.judiciary.uk/wp-content/uploads/JCO/Documents/Judgments/f-v-dpp-judgment.pdf

R v Campos. (2021). NZDC 7422. Retrieved July 5, 2024, from: https://www.districtcourts.govt.nz/all-judgments/2021-nzdc-7422-r-v-campos/

R v Clarence. (1889). 22 QB 23. Retrieved July 5, 2024, from: https://www.oxbridgenotes.co.uk/law_cases/r-v-clarence

R v Cook. (1986). 2 NZLR 93 (CA). Retrieved July 5, 2024, from: https://plus.lexis.com/api/permalink/32a11bdc-1f56-40ae-b9fb-956c42dd68c4/?context=1001073

R v Cuerrier. (1998). 2 SCR 371. Retrieved July 5, 2024, from: https://www.hivlegalnetwork.ca/site/wp-content/uploads/2014/02/2.Cuerrier1998summary.pdf

R v Dica. (2004). EWCA Crim 1103. Retrieved June 10, 2024, from: https://www.globalhealthrights.org/wp-content/uploads/2014/06/UK-2004-R-v-Dica.pdf

R v Jheeta. (2007). EWCA Crim 1699. Retrieved May 24, 2024, from: https://ipsaloquitur.com/criminal-law/cases/r-v-jheeta-harvinder-singh/

R v Lawrence. (2020). EWCA Crim 971. Retrieved May 14, 2024, from: https://files.justice.org.uk/wp-content/uploads/2020/09/06165908/Y-R-v-Lawrence-002.pdf

R v Linekar. (1995). QB 250. Retrieved May 24, 2024, from: https://ipsaloquitur.com/criminal-law/cases/r-v-linekar-gareth/

R v Livas. (2015). ACTSC 50. Retrieved June 10, 2024, from: https://jade.io/j/?a=outline&id=369436

R v McNally. (2013). EWCA Crim 1051. Retrieved July 5, 2024, from: https://justis.vlex.com/#vid/793830081

R v Olugboja. (1981). 4875/A/79. Retrieved from: https://justis.vlex.com/#vid/792562701

R v Papadimitropoulos. (1957). HCA 74. Retrieved July 5, 2024, from: https://www8.austlii.edu.au/cgi-bin/viewdoc/au/cases/cth/HCA/1957/74.html

Rogers, J. (2013). The effect of 'deception' in the Sexual Offences Act 2003. *Archbold Review, 4*, 7–9.

Sanders, T., Vajzovic, D., Brooks-Gordon, B., & Mulvihill, N. (2020a). Policing vulnerability in sex work: The harm reduction compass model. *Policing and Society, 31*(9), 1110–1116. https://doi.org/10.1080/10439463.2020.1837825

Sanders, T., Scoular, J., & Campbell, R. (2022). Sex work, hate crime and the criminal law. *The Journal of Criminal Law, 86*(2), 109–125. https://doi.org/10.1177/00220183221086679

Schulhofer, S. (2017). Reforming the law of rape recommended citation. *Law & Inequality: A Journal of Theory and Practice, 35*(2), 335–352. https://scholarship.law.umn.edu/cgi/viewcontent.cgi?article=1577&context=lawineq

Scottish Government. (2024). *Prostitution—challenging and deterring men's demand: Strategic approach*. Retrieved June 20, 2024, from: https://www.gov.scot/publications/scotlands-strategic-approach-challenging-deterring-mens-demand-prostitution-supporting-recovery-sustainable-exit-those-involved-prostitution/

Scottish Law Commission. (2006). *Discussion paper on rape and other sexual offences (Discussion 131)*. Retrieved June 20, 2024, from: https://www.scotlawcom.gov.uk/files/3012/7892/7070/dp131_rape.pdf

Sexual Offences (Amendment) Act. (1976). Retrieved July 5 2024, from: https://www.legislation.gov.uk/ukpga/1976/82

Sexual Offences Act. (1956). Retrieved July 5, 2023, from: https://www.legislation.gov.uk/ukpga/Eliz2/4-5/69/contents

Sexual Offences Act. (2003). Retrieved July 5, 2024, from: https://www.legislation.gov.uk/ukpga/2003/42/contents

Sexual Offences (Scotland) Act. (2009). Retrieved July 5, 2024, from: https://www.legislation.gov.uk/asp/2009/9/contents

Sharpe, A. (2018). *Sexual intimacy and gender identity 'fraud': Reframing the legal and ethical debate.* Routledge.

Spohn, C., & Horney, J. (1993). Rape law reform and the effect of victim characteristics on case processing. *Journal of Quantitative Criminology, 9*(4), 383–409. https://doi.org/10.1007/BF01064110

Spohn, C., & Horney, J. (1996). The impact of rape law reform on the processing of simple and aggravated rape cases. *The Journal of Criminal Law and Criminology, 86*(3), 861. https://doi.org/10.2307/1143939

State v Denton. (1966). 101 Ariz.455, 420 [92 Nev. 78] P.2d 930. Retrieved June 20, 2024, from: https://law.justia.com/cases/arizona/supreme-court/1966/1654-0.html

State v Thomas. (1973). 9 Wash.App. 160, 510P.2.d 1137. Retrieved December 13, 2023, from: https://www.courtlistener.com/opinion/1117007/state-v-thomas/

Stonehouse, R. (2021). Stealthing: 'I didn't realise it's rape until it happened to me'. *BBC Newsbeat*. Retrieved June 20, 2024, from: https://www.bbc.co.uk/news/newsbeat-57618003

Syrota, G. (1995). Rape: When does fraud vitiate consent? *The University of Western Australia Law Review, 25*(2), 334–345. https://research-repository.uwa.edu.au/en/publications/rape-when-does-fraud-vitiate-consent

Temkin, J., & Ashworth, A. (2004). The sexual offences act 2003: (1)—Rape, sexual assaults and the problems of consent. *Criminal Law Review,* pp. 328–346. https://ora.ox.ac.uk/objects/uuid:8f9f81d6-e99c-47c5-a8c7-71a952b4cc6d

Weait, M. (2007). *Intimacy and responsibility*. Routledge.

Weiss, K. G. (2011). Neutralizing sexual victimization: A typology of victims' non-reporting accounts. *Theoretical Criminology, 15*(4), 445–467. https://doi.org/10.1177/1362480610391527

3

Negotiating Consent: Setting Boundaries in the Sexual Contract

Gillian Abel, Cherida Fraser, Barbara G. Brents, Teela Sanders, and Jane Scoular

Introduction

Sex workers construct and maintain boundaries between their sex-worker life and their private life, which provides a form of emotional protection (Abel, 2011; Brewis & Linstead, 2000; Day, 1994). Some sexual acts are

G. Abel
University of Otago, Dunedin, New Zealand

C. Fraser
NZPC: Aotearoa New Zealand Sex Workers' Collective, Wellington, New Zealand

B. G. Brents
University of Nevada, Las Vegas, Nevada, USA

T. Sanders (✉)
University of Leicester, Leicester, UK
e-mail: teela.sanders@leicester.ac.uk

J. Scoular
Strathclyde Law School, University of Strathclyde, Glasgow, UK

T. Sanders et al. (eds.), *Voicing Consent*, Palgrave Advances in Sex Work Studies,
https://doi.org/10.1007/978-3-031-77715-8_3

only seen as relevant in their private lives and so, when engaging in sex in their working life, they need to ensure that the boundary between these two lives is protected. Sex workers typically adopt what Anderson (2004) has proposed as a negotiation model of consent, which requires verbal communication with a client prior to engaging in sex, to establish exactly what activities they are consenting to and what the boundaries are of the sexual transaction. In most cases, clients respect this boundary and commercial sex is completed without any non-consensual events (Comte, 2014). Sometimes, however, things do not go according to the negotiated contract. This chapter looks at how sex workers use formal and informal laws when negotiating and maintaining boundaries and how this differs between legislative environments.

Learning to Negotiate

Clients have different expectations of what they will get when they book a sex worker. Sometimes these expectations are influenced by stigmatised understandings of sex work and sex workers. Sex workers in our study talked of the burden of challenging stereotypes, such as the idea that a client cannot "rape an escort" (Sophia, UK, independent). Anna, who worked on the street in the UK, noted that some clients do not accept they are sexually assaulting sex workers, and claimed that this behaviour equates to failure to accept the conditions of consent. The inability of the client to see the sex worker as a person, or accept their full humanity, means that the breach is not registered as non-consent: "They don't understand that, they just think—A lot of clients just see you as a piece of meat. They don't see you as somebody's daughter. They've got no respect for us" (Anna, UK, street-based).

Some clients think that they are entitled to anything they like given that they are paying for a sexual service. Chrissie and Tess were very clear that a commercial sexual encounter *required* their consent:

> I think being a sex worker, men think that they don't have to have as much respect for you or uphold your boundaries because they're paying you, so they feel they're in a position of power, when I don't see it that

> way. I think if anything I have more power because I need to consent to what you're doing. But I think that some men, whereas they might not do it to a non-sex-working woman, a girlfriend, a date or something, they're more likely to do it to a sex worker, because they think that we just have to take it. (Chrissie, USA, various)
>
> Then you get some people who think, because they've paid you, they can do what they like, they can spend all day and all night: 'You've got to do this, you've got to do that'. They don't realise you haven't got to do anything, do you know what I mean? You haven't got to do anything. (Tess, UK, street-based)

Some respondents stated that, while most clients 'were okay', other clients considered the sex worker's consent was not important, that money could in some way obviate consent, or that because they were members of a stigmatised population, they were not entitled to sexual autonomy. Linda notes that "others may need to learn this", in reference to societal attitudes that sex work is work and that sex workers are capable of not consenting to certain activities:

> It's all about awareness isn't it, really? You know, like people never used to wear a seatbelt until it was aware. People never knew not to smoke on buses until it was aware. It's about making things aware to people and then maybe things will change. (Linda, UK, street-based)

Criminalisation in any of its forms fosters stigmatising attitudes to sex workers. They are positioned as being less valued by society, morally corrupt, without rights and 'disposable' (Armstrong, 2019; Benoit et al., 2018; Krüsi et al., 2016). This can serve to validate clients' actions when they overstep the boundaries. Sex workers, therefore, look to reframe clients' expectations and assert their power by setting the tone of how the booking will proceed, backed up by formal laws (official legal statutes on sexual violence) and informal workplace rules or norms (norms developed through the culture within a brothel and/or learned experience as a sex worker). This can be difficult, especially if there is no one to guide them on what to expect and how to deal with clients. Some new sex workers do not even know that they can set boundaries. Few people coming into sex work have the skills and knowledge to effectively negotiate what they want to happen in a commercial sexual transaction; nor do they know of any informal norms in the sex industry. Queen talked about the "gross" things she did when she first started sex work because she was unaware that she could set boundaries. With time and experience, she felt a 'power shift' in her work relationships, as she learnt how to assert herself with clients:

> Like at the start, when I first did the job, I did stuff that was gross and it was only being around other women [that helped me understand I could set boundaries] … But I did all that stuff because I didn't know you could say no … That's why we need to be able to communicate with each other. … At the start I probably would have been, 'What would you like me to do?'. Now it's like, 'Sit down, this is what's going to happen'! It's something that only comes with experience, but I probably gave that out and that's what I'm reluctant to say; it's like, are you giving out that you'd allow somebody to do something to you? And I guess you sort of do if a client comes in and you're going, 'What do you want me to do? Are you happy?' And now I'm like, 'Fuck off'. So, I guess the shift changes between having an air of authority about you; you've got to keep that and that's something that happens over time and experience. (Queen, UK, various)

Negotiation skills are, therefore, essential to the safety of sex workers—and, as Queen said, this is most effectively learnt through communication between sex workers. The legislative environment within which sex workers operate has a part to play in enhancing negotiating skills and thus creating a safer environment. Sex workers in this study who worked in brothels in both Nevada and Aotearoa New Zealand (ANZ) learned from others with whom they worked, as well as from managers/madams, about how to negotiate effectively, take control and so prevent unwanted incidents. This, then, cemented in clients' minds that there was an informal brothel norm that would not tolerate boundary crossing:

> The information from our managers was so helpful that we all learned ways, and even off the other girls, sharing our techniques and stuff to manage that better. But, of course, there are times when they don't want

> to hear it; the customer doesn't want to hear that you're not fine with something. Yeah. ... 'Cause obviously a lot of people that come to a place will return to a place, and they begin to expect a sort of environment. Yeah, and so we got less of those customers ... because the girls had been taught and encouraged to stand up for them being in control of the situation, and our clientele would come to know that, and we'd get less of the ones that don't agree. (Jane, ANZ, brothel)

Sex workers in the Nevada legal brothels who we interviewed spoke about undergoing some training before starting. This training was usually around effective negotiation with a client. Here, the madam sometimes assigns 'big sisters' to a new worker and often they sit in and assist the first few negotiations. The new worker learns how to clearly state what they are willing and not willing to provide as part of their service. Teaching negotiation skills within the brothel thus provides a uniformity that sets the culture (or norms) of the brothel:

> I learned how to negotiate through a combination of my madam, the other working ladies here, as well as just the experience of doing it all the time. So, right, when I got here, being brand new, my madam walked me through the entire process from when a client walks into the bar, to when you negotiate, to when you go back to the bedroom, to when you walk them back out. Everything was discussed and trained. And then the madam will set you up with a big sister, which is a more experienced working lady, and then she'll shadow you for your first two weeks or so to even come into negotiation with you to show you how the seasoned girls do it. And then I've learned my own little take on the negotiation as time has gone on. I've added my own flavour to it. But they definitely give you all the resources necessary to have a good negotiation with clients. (Abigail, USA, Nevada legal brothel)

Sex workers' negotiations with clients are mediated by power relations (Shannon et al., 2008). Commercial sex transactions are safer when sex workers have greater power in their negotiations with clients (Platt et al., 2018). The brothel-based workers in our study learnt from others prior to engaging in commercial sex, which gave them a sense of power and control in the negotiation process. In time, they adapted their negotiations to better fit their personal boundaries of consent.

Working collectively creates a supportive environment for sex workers; they have the power to refuse unwanted services and avoid violence (Brents & Hausbeck, 2005; Krüsi et al., 2012; Perkins & Lovejoy, 2007; Pyett & Warr, 1997, 1999; Sanders & Campbell, 2007) and this, in turn, works to foster their health and their human rights (Goldenberg et al., 2015). Our survey clearly showed that most sex workers in all participating countries strongly agreed that they feel safer when there are others nearby (Fig. 3.1).

An inability to communicate with other sex workers, on the other hand, increases vulnerability (Atchison et al., 2015). Sex workers in the UK and USA (excluding the legal Nevada brothels) are unable to work collectively, as, in these jurisdictions, it is legally construed as a trafficking-like situation. Sophia (UK, independent) recalled a time when there were brothels in the UK who would "teach them the game". She felt she would be safer in this environment, but it became more difficult to get advice when the law changed, and brothels were shut down. It was

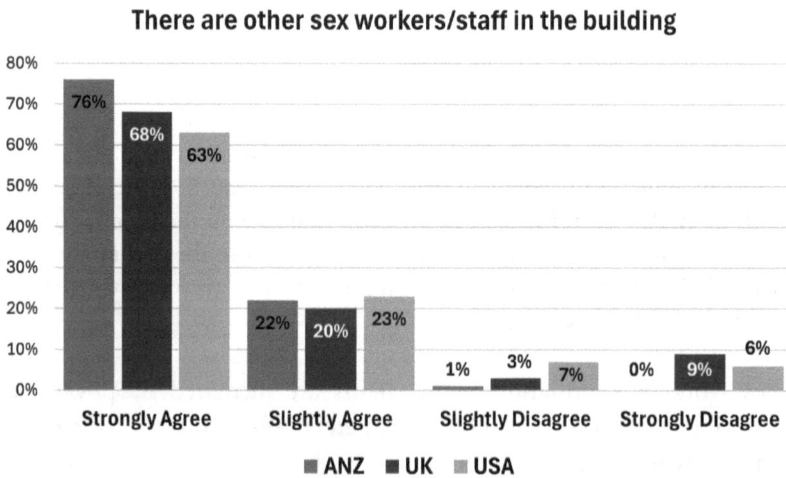

Fig. 3.1 Feeling safer if others are in the building when a client wants something that has not been consented to

also difficult to get advice from other workers without putting themselves at risk of being seen as trafficking each other:

> You're learning all the time. Because my mate's done it. She's 36 and she started when she was 20, so she's got 16 years' experience on me. She has helped a lot, because you can't really help each other because then it's seen as a thing. I don't know, but, if anything happens, I'll message her and she'll say, 'This is what I do'. But it used to be that when you'd work in brothels there'd be a madam. That's how you'd start; that's how she started. There'd be a madam and she'd teach you the game, and it was all really safe, and then all the good brothels got shut down. (Sophia, UK, independent)

As Sophia acknowledged, there is a danger when sex workers do not have the ability to learn effective negotiating skills from others. Working independently means that the potential for breaches of consent is greater (Abel & Fitzgerald, 2012). This is somewhat alleviated in ANZ because sex work is decriminalised. Independent sex workers can work with others from their own home or rented premises. They, therefore, still can learn from more experienced sex workers. In addition, there is a publication called *Stepping Forward* (written and distributed by the NZPC—Aotearoa New Zealand Sex Workers' Collective), for new sex workers, which gives tips on handling clients, managing risk, and other useful information. Independent sex workers in ANZ, therefore, do have power in the negotiation process, backed up by a good knowledge of formal law (see the following section on 'setting the boundaries'). In countries like the UK, however, where sex work is only legally possible if sex workers are entirely independent, and in the USA, where it is only possible to work legally in a certain area of Nevada, there is little choice, and acquiring skills in negotiation is almost entirely a 'learning experience'. Some US independent workers said that they had no formal initiation into sex work but that they learnt on the job through "trial and error" (Cody, USA, independent). Cody had been working for five or six years before she "was introduced to the sex worker community": "Many of the women ... taught me about more formal types of screening and that there were blacklists you can join. That was astounding to me; I had no idea" (Cody, USA, independent).

Nancy (USA) and Tess (UK) both thought that they had to do whatever the client wanted when they first started working:

> In my early years I was unable to tell somebody that certain things weren't okay, I wasn't able to voice myself. But in later years I basically verbally tell people upfront, 'X, Y and Z is okay, this is not'. (Nancy, USA, independent)
>
> When I started this job if a client said, 'Do this', I'd just do it, because I thought, 'They're paying and that's what you do'. And then you just learn what you will and won't do, and you have to just do it yourself. (Tess, UK, street-based)

The issue of experience is particularly important. Many independent sex workers in the USA and UK spoke about how they had engaged in risky practices when they first started working because they thought that they did not have a choice in the matter. Unlike brothel-based sex workers, they had no knowledge of sex work or the possibility of setting boundaries, which translated into little power in their negotiations. While independent sex workers talked about eventually getting to a place where they became more confident in negotiating their boundaries, this skill only came with time. The legislative environment that prevented them from communicating with other sex workers put them in a risky position during this initial learning period. Through (often many) unconsented experiences, they identified ways to set consensual boundaries and manage clients who attempted to violate those boundaries. In doing so, they developed their own informal norms on how to work that suited them.

Setting the Boundaries

In this study, most sex workers reported that their negotiations of consent took place prior to sexual encounters commencing. These discussions were important in establishing boundaries. The discussions functioned to manage clients' expectations and establish the terms of the sexual contract—for example, outlining the services they were willing to offer and those that they would not consider providing. The associated costs were communicated, as well as the location (if they were not working in brothels), timing, and duration, alongside safety features such as condom use and dental dams. These negotiations formed the basis of the commercial arrangement. They established exactly what sex workers were prepared to consent to and their non-consent to all other activities. However, negotiations were more easily accomplished in some venues than in others, and this was clearly linked to the legislative environment.

There were two things that were always discussed in the negotiation process: payment and condom use. Payment is crucial to sex work as it is work—sex workers rely on payment to survive. The negotiated price is the first condition of consent, as argued by Carrie: "The payment is so significant to what I'm willing to do, and you know, even just seeing you, it's like it's payment for my time, you know, and if you don't get paid you wouldn't be here" (Carrie, ANZ, independent). A USA illegal escort also indicated, in our survey's free-text box, that they placed most importance on getting paid:

> There's a saying, 'Chalk it up to the game', which basically means, you win some, you lose some in this unregulated industry due to the illicit nature of it. But that is why most SWs [sex workers] prefer to get their payments upfront. I personally will walk away from a date if not paid upfront. (Survey respondent, USA)

It could be argued that if full payment for the service is not received it negates the conditions of consent, which some sex workers argued was an offence: "Sex work is, you know, a job, and not paying for that service is a crime" (Sheryl, ANZ, independent). Sex workers who work in brothels seldom have to negotiate or accept direct payment from clients; payment is taken by management prior to the service. Independent sex workers are more susceptible to underpayment as they work on their own and must do their own payment negotiations. Independent workers in Aotearoa New Zealand can be paid by direct credit into their bank accounts. The client takes a screenshot of the deposit on their smart phone and shows this to the sex worker on their arrival, as proof of payment.

Sophia worked online as a webcam model in the UK and took deposits from clients prior to providing a session. She argued that she ran the risk of losing clients this way, but reasoned that this was a lesser threat than losing out on payment. She indicated that she would not experience such difficulties, and would be better able to maintain her safety, if sex work was decriminalised:

> The only way we're going to be completely safe is decrim. The way I keep myself safe now is asking for personal info and taking deposits. I've just told my mate that's what she needs to do, and she's started taking deposits. But it's hard because you feel like you're losing a lot of business, but you're only losing the business of people who would do something. So I get a lot of texts where they go, 'I'm not paying a deposit'. And it's like, 'Well, it's on my profile, and the only reason you wouldn't pay a deposit is if you're a rapist'. (Sophia, UK, independent)

Street-based sex workers are particularly vulnerable to non-payment for services, as they rely on cash from the client, often once they've completed the sexual service. When they or their clients are criminalised, they cannot take the time to negotiate for too long before getting in the car, in case they are spotted by police (Amnesty International, 2016b; Krüsi, 2014; Landsberg et al., 2017; Östergren, 2006). Clients also try to negotiate the price down, knowing that sometimes the sex worker might be desperate. A UK street-based sex worker provided the following free-text comment in our survey:

> They are always trying to pay you less — I just tell them to go to someone else — I'm not doing it for that, but when you are desperate to score they will try and pay you less. And it's worse since they stopped the managed area zone because there are dodgier people about. There's been fake money going around lately. It's one or two groups of men but they try to pass it on. (Survey respondent, UK)

Respondents also explicitly defined condom use as a condition of consent to sexual services. Condoms signify the professional nature of sex work and are one of the boundary markers between private and work sex (Day, 1994). It offers a physical and psychological barrier (Sanders,

2002) between sex workers' public and personal lives and is mandatory in legal brothels. Not wearing a condom, or removing a condom, was seen as a reason to reject a client, although some interviewees did mention times when they were pressured or where other sex workers might be vulnerable to accepting for financial reasons:

> Some girls are so desperate and it's sad to say and I'm not calling them, I'm not saying I'm better than them, because I'm not, but it's sad. They just need educating on the dangers of doing it without a condom, you know? (Anna, UK, street-based)

In ANZ, Sect. 9 of the Prostitution Reform Act (PRA) deals with safer sex practices and stipulates that sex workers and clients need to take all reasonable steps to ensure a prophylactic sheath or other appropriate barrier is used if services involve vaginal, anal or oral penetration (Prostitution Reform Act, 2003). If anyone contravenes Sect. 9, they may be liable, on conviction, to a fine of up to NZ$2000. This law is a useful tool, as sex workers can draw on it in negotiating condom use with clients (Abel, 2014). There have been some arguments, however, that this section be removed from the PRA as it can be used to entrap sex workers. As argued in Chapter 2, police may also prosecute the non-use or removal of a condom by a client under this section, when the action may be better aligned with rape given that condom use is a condition of consent. Nevertheless, as Kat argues below, the existence of this section does provide physical and mental protection. It also placed her in a position of power when negotiating with clients, as she could draw on the law to reinforce condom use:

> I know that some people want to remove that law, but I completely disagree with that because I think that it has, it has a place and it's important, and it gives sex workers lots of power as well. Like, you know, you can have it in the room and be like, 'Well actually, it's against the law to not use a condom', you know. ... And I think it protects us, not just physically, but I think mentally as well, knowing that that's, that's protecting you. I think that's a really big thing for pretty much everyone, you know, like, to know that they can quote that law or just use it whenever they, you know, whenever they need to, and they can get rid of a client cause

they're like, 'You don't want to use that law, then see you. Like, my health is more important than you getting off'. (Kat, ANZ, various)

Some ANZ sex workers in this study had experienced stealthing. One of them had successfully taken this to court, not under contravention of Sect. 9, but as a rape charge under the Crimes Act (see Chapter 2 discussion on *R v Campos* (R v Campos [2021] NZDC 7422)). This was possible because Sect. 17 gives sex workers the right to withdraw consent. The importance of this case clearly played an important communicative role in helping other sex workers understand that they can and should report stealthing:

And because I'd seen it and me and my girlfriend were in the motel room reading about it, and I'd read about it like two days before, and I was like, and when I jumped back, I guess, yeah, like when I jumped back, I was just like, 'Oh my God, no way'. ... Having that news and having my friend and think about all the times that I hadn't reported fellows, and how that makes me sick thinking about what they would have done, or what they have done since to me. (Erihapeti, ANZ, independent)

It seemed that some brothels in ANZ "took care to make sure that new people knew about the laws around it [sex work] and just helpful information" (Jane, ANZ, brothel). Kat indicated that management were supportive of her being able to work within the parameters of the legislation set out in Sects. 16 and 17 of the PRA and "say no to a client, and you can choose whatever service you want to do. You can change your mind halfway through a booking" (Kat, ANZ, various). Section 17 was included in the PRA to combat the assumption that payment equals consent, and it has bolstered sex workers' understanding that they can say 'no'. These ANZ sex workers perceived that the law was on their side and would, if necessary, protect their rights; and their knowledge of the law translated into power in setting the boundaries of their service.

Non-use of condoms is illegal in Nevada brothels and these sex workers, like their ANZ counterparts, drew on this formal law when it came to condom negotiation.

> A lot of times, guys will try to bribe you to take off the condom. I personally cannot be bribed. I've started letting people know that in my negotiations: 'There's no amount of money you can offer me to take off the condom. It is illegal for us to remove it, and to keep pushing is not only frustrating but it's also illegal'. That is one we have to deal with a lot here. (River, USA, various)

Sex workers in these Nevada brothels, did not talk about their rights, but they knew that they had backup if clients did not stick to the agreed boundaries of the service. Jessica had a "three strikes then you're out" policy which was backed up by the informal norms of the brothel:

> I go over that [setting boundaries] before anything goes on or begins, and I let them know. They usually ask before this what my do's and don'ts are, and I tell them what my don'ts are and I let them know that first I give them a warning. (Jessica, USA, various)

All clients received the same preamble. Roxanne described her negotiations as a "process" and she made sure there was no contact between her and the clients before negotiations were mutually agreed:

> I take him back to my room, and the whole time he should not be trying to touch me. He should not be trying to do anything. We haven't agreed to anything yet. … I figure out what they can pay. They figure out what my prices are for time and certain activities. I have a pricing menu. … So that's how they know what I'm consenting to and they're also consenting to those activities. And we just have like a 10 to 15 minute conversation about it, and I make sure that I'm not sitting on their lap or anything, like I'm sitting on a chair; he's sitting on the bed usually. So I make sure that we're not feeling up on each other before things are agreed upon. (Roxanne, USA, Nevada legal brothel)

Some sex workers said they were also careful to not offer services that their workmates did not consider acceptable so that they did not raise clients' expectations that this was a service that other sex workers in the brothel would provide:

> I mean certain things I just knew that I wouldn't be okay with, but I think you definitely also learn from your surroundings. So, for example, in the brothel I would see what was sort of, some things were frowned upon. Like, for example, okay, this isn't something I would have provided anyways, but men ejaculating on a woman's face. That was like something brothel workers would not like if other brothel workers were doing, because then you would all feel like, well, 'We all have to provide this'. (Chrissie, USA, various)

While it appears that brothels offer the most safety for sex workers, many in legal or decriminalised settings make the decision not to work under a system of management, for a variety of reasons—including not wanting a proportion of their earnings going to management, wanting more flexibility in when and for how long they work, and wanting to set their own prices (Abel & Ludeke, 2021a). Talia elaborated:

> I like working independently because I am in control of pretty much everything to do with the business. So, I set my own hours, I set my own days, I set my own rates. I can decline a customer readily, just by the way that they're communicating over the phone with me. I get to choose what locations I work from. (Talia, ANZ, brothel)

Independent workers usually advertise online for clients and generally they stipulate the services that they offer in their adverts. This means that clients can make a choice based on who will provide the experience that they are looking for, and so avoid conflict because of unmet expectations. By offering some clarity around price and services, adverts were described by our study participants as helping to reduce space for uncertainty, manage clients' expectations, and avoid time wasters. It allowed sex workers to establish clear boundaries with regard to services they did not want to undertake. Sex workers can work independently by themselves in the UK, and those who advertised online pointed to detailed profiles that outlined services that they were willing to offer, or, as one sex worker noted, "try":

> On my AdlWork [online platform] it's the longest because I have to explain everything in great detail. So, on my AdlWork profile, there

should be no questions for them to ask, and most of my clients have said, 'I have no questions after reading it'. So, there's a section on there that says escort services, and it says, 'In a 30-minute booking this is what's included', 'In an hour or more booking this is what's included' and 'In an overnight this is what's included.' (Sophia, UK, independent)
I just tell them straight up. Usually it has it on my advert, if I've got an advert up, it will tell them what I do, don't do, things I might try. And then I'll have the set list of prices as well, so then there's none of that awkwardness. (Emily, UK, various)
The online stuff, it is stated quite clearly and it's just beforehand and, you know, it's whether or not you can afford to say, 'I want you to do this'. And I'm going to say, 'No'. And he's going to say, 'Okay, I don't want the booking'. And I'll go, 'Fine, fuck off'. I'm in a very lucky position where I know there's more clients. (Queen, UK, various)

Most independent sex workers, like Paul for example, negotiated with individual clients in addition to what was mentioned in the adverts:

> A lot of the information is on my online profile, and then there's obviously a little bit of about what they would like to be involved in the session and whether that's something that I want to do ... It's usually text based before meeting, either email or messages on the site or WhatsApp ... It's much easier for me to do things by text. (Paul, UK, independent)

When clients requested services that workers were not comfortable with providing or sought a lower price, a common reaction was to refuse or terminate discussions before meeting them. As Abuya shows, sex workers' ability to challenge clients is based on experience:

> ...if [they] deviate from this, hang up and move on to next one. Yes, my profile is very detailed, if they call me and ask me things that I don't do I just hang up, but I know that a lot of girls are under pressure to do things that I know that, the girls, they don't want to. It doesn't bother me because I'm like, 'Okay maybe just ... move on to the next one'. It doesn't bother me; it doesn't really make me scared or anything because you cannot be everybody's favourite. They're so obvious when they call you and they're not going to respect you, so why would you consider it? (Abuya, UK, independent)

In the USA, outside of legal brothels, the criminalised environment made it very difficult to provide too much information, both in online advertising and in-person negotiations, and this had implications for safety. Workers could potentially be entrapped by police and arrested for sex-work-related activities and so some thought that the less said the better. Some free-text comments in the survey spoke about this: "I don't like to list my services. It's incriminating" (Survey respondent, USA), and "Since it's not legal to sell sex, I don't allow any discussion of what I will or won't do, but I don't allow clients to do just whatever they want" (Survey respondent, USA). And one participant indicated that decriminalisation would make negotiations much easier and consequently safer: "Decrim would allow me to post more specific services, or talk about services, before meeting with a client. So everyone is understanding what's going to happen and no one will be confused or angry or underpaid" (Survey respondent, USA).

Cody said that she did try providing some information online but tended to do most of the negotiation once she is face-to-face with the client:

> Ultimately, I try to be, without being incriminating, open [on the website] that I do provide intimacy and a safe place for exploration. But I'd really wait until we're face to face to negotiate specific boundaries, and I try to adhere to an informed, enthusiastic consent model. (Cody, USA, independent)

These sex workers had relatively little power in negotiations when compared to sex workers who were working legally. They learned with experience how to set clear boundaries and benchmarks around which clients were acceptable, how to manoeuvre out of difficult situations, and how to remove individuals.

Workers in the USA and UK did not discuss formal law nor did they think that they could (or would) report any breach of boundaries. For instance, Chrissie (USA, various) said "There was really nowhere to report … You're breaking the law with what you're doing. You're not going to want to go to the law for help" and Abigail (USA, Nevada legal brothel) claimed that "[outside of work] there aren't very many resources communicated to us … I wouldn't really know what to do if I was sexually assaulted". These sex workers relied solely on their own informal norms developed through experience. In contrast, ANZ and Nevada brothel-based sex workers drew on the law to maintain power in their negotiations, as well as the informal policies and workplace culture within brothels, and their fellow sex workers They went through the negotiation process that they were taught, which had the backup of the brothel management.

Maintaining the Boundaries

At times, clients directly violate the terms of consent by engaging in acts that are explicitly identified as non-consensual prior to the start of the booking. Clients sometimes engaged in acts and behaviours that were not formerly discussed or failed to explicitly give a 'warning' or make requests about engaging in certain acts during sexual services. Some sex workers, like Cody and Jessica, firmly enforced their boundaries and argued that they would warn a client and then terminate a booking if they overstepped what had been consented to:

> Obviously, boundary pushers exist and boundary violations happen, as much as I don't want them to. But they also happen outside of sex work as well. It's a human experience. But if it's through writing — we're not actually in the same room together — I try to give them [boundary pushers] a written warning like, 'Hey, I'm not comfortable discussing that with you' or 'Please review my website; I've detailed that restriction. This is your one and only warning'. … If they pursue the conversation, I cut it off, and if they've already paid a deposit I say, 'I'm happy to return your deposit to you but I'm no longer interested in moving forward with booking the reservation'. If the boundary pushing happens in person, I will say no, which is a full sentence but I will say, 'No, I don't do that'. I really resent having to say why, so I try to just leave it at that: 'We're not doing that today, let's move on'. But if they continue to press the issue, I de-escalate and end the session as quickly as possible and remove them from my space or I try to safely exit from their space. (Cody, USA, independent)

> Sometimes there's not much you can do to prevent it [boundary pushing]. Sometimes they're just that type of people. That was the plan to do something like that. … If they don't listen to what I'm saying, and then after the warning, I'm going to firmly say it again, and sternly instill it in them. (Jessica, USA, various)

There is a level of security within brothels that is not possible to achieve in other locations for sex work (Abel, 2010; Brewis & Linstead, 2000). This provides such sex workers with an advantage over independent sex workers when it comes to maintaining the boundaries set in the negotiations. Most brothels have panic buttons in the rooms that, when pressed, bring security guards or other workers and managers rushing in: "There's one [panic button] under the massage table now, and one at the door, and you just pull it" (Alice, ANZ, various). There are also people in other rooms who could hear the sex worker if they called out:

> If there's a struggle going on, or something's going on, the lady next door to you is going to hear something. It's just more likely because you're working with a bunch of people, whereas when you're working independently, it's just you in a hotel room. And everybody kind of minds their business. (Jessica, USA, various)

Brothel norms help sex workers to maintain control when a client does attempt to breach the boundaries. Clients learn what they can expect in a particular brothel and this reduces breaches. In ANZ, when Chanelle had a bad experience at a strip club, she moved to a brothel where she found more supportive management, which enabled her to keep her boundaries:

> We've got amazing clientele at my place that we're at. I think it's just 'cause of the level of respect that they do have to have, and 'We won't have them if they do step out of line', and it's really, really nice, actually. They're all pretty good. I've only had like a couple of dudes that tried to push my boundaries, but very light pushing of boundaries … It's really good, and we're able to say, 'Hey, look, like we can end this booking now?', and we know that our boss will come in and be like, 'No, that's it'. So, it's really nice just to know you've got the back-up and we're also

> in a quite safe place to be like, 'Hey, like, yeah, you can't do that to me'. (Chanelle, ANZ, various)

Clients in brothels may still try and push the boundaries but having firm boundaries within a safe environment, as well as knowledge of formal laws or informal norms, gave the brothel-based sex workers in our study the confidence to enforce their negotiated conditions:

> It goes really well in negotiations and then I feel like the line of consent tries to be crossed more once you get back to your room or get back to your suite or wherever you're going. That's when they want to cross that line. ... and you have to just tell them, 'Hey this is not what we agreed upon. This wasn't in your price range. This wasn't anything I'm comfortable with'. (Cielo, USA, Nevada legal brothel)
>
> I feel like I'm pretty privileged so I'm able to have firm and clear boundaries, whereas if you're working on the street or barely scraping by, your boundaries might be more fluid. Not because you want them to be, but because they have to be. (Chrissie, USA, various)

Some sex workers provide a girlfriend experience, which gives the client an illusion of a genuine reciprocal connection. Abbey said that this sometimes created the context for boundary pushing, but she was prepared to lose a client rather than give in:

> They're like, 'Oh my god, you're giving me the girlfriend experience and actually making me feel like your boyfriend — let's not use condoms'. It's called experience. You don't get the full enchilada. ... 'It's not on the menu, sir' ... Especially with some long-term clients... I actually fired one because he wanted to text me all the fricking time. And I'm like 'Are you going to pay me? If this is a fetish chat, that's sexting and it's this much per minute'. ... you have to maintain boundaries: 'Just because I'm friendly, doesn't mean we're friends'. (Abbey, USA, independent)

Other sex workers use tactics like distraction or threats of ending a service to ward off boundary crossings:

> I like to redirect their energies into something that I'm more interested in doing [when boundaries are pushed] and often that usually works. If it's a situation where they are truly getting stuck on something that we didn't pre-negotiate, then I'll actually be like, 'Yeah, actually that's not my jam. If that's what you're interested in then I'd be happy to transfer you to somebody else that might be a better fit for you'. And oftentimes they usually drop it because when they see my boundaries can't really be broken in that regard, usually they realise that I am actually the one in control of the situation. (Sebastian, USA, various)

Some interviewees recognised that others may be more pressured to accept conditions (both the price and/or sex acts) when they are less experienced or when their own circumstances mean the money is more important than their safety or boundaries. Interviewees talked about how compromises to expectations and boundaries were part of the job. For instance, Paul talked of times when he had let things happen but also of other times when he was confident to say no. In part, this is an assessment of the likelihood of violence (relative size of the client, the levels of physical isolation) but he also talks of the power that regular clients hold—because of their relative rarity and the security they afford ("I didn't want to disrupt the relationship because regular clients are like gold"). A lot of decisions ended up being made in situ:

> It's not happened very often. It depends on the client and how comfortable I feel. It depends on the situation at the time. There has been times where I've just let it happen and then broached the subject afterwards and said, 'Look, that was not appropriate', and then there's been other times where I have felt confident enough in the moment to say something there and then. (Paul, UK, independent)

Paul argued that sometimes "we have to compromise on the job, just for the satisfaction of your customer or the client"; and, similarly, Abbey would weigh things up as to whether she felt comfortable enough to offer a service that had not been pre-arranged:

> I'm not great at maintaining boundaries. ... It has happened that somebody has paid for XYZ and then in the middle decided that they want to

> sprinkle in some extra shit and I just let it happen. Because I don't want to kill the mood; I don't want to lose the client potentially as a long-term client. And also depends on my comfort level because this person wants this extra thing that we never discussed. Is it a big deal to me, is it not a big deal? How much of a safety risk is it, is it not? (Abbey, USA, independent)

Similarly, a brothel-based sex worker in ANZ talked of unwanted sexual contact such as "a finger in your butt", which she positioned as inevitable and part of the job. This could be solved by asking for more money, as it was a service that she would offer if pre-negotiated:

> I couldn't tell you how many times someone's like licked or kissed or whatever, and there's, you know, an expectation that we laugh it off or whatever … Unfortunately, that's the reality of that job, but I think I manage it pretty well now. But yeah, if someone does that, I will say, 'Okay, so that's my extra price'. … Stuff that I offer anyway. Like, you know, like, they might just all of a sudden, like, put a finger in your butt or something, and I was, like, 'Wow, okay. Like, you could have asked. Like, I do offer it anyway'. (Kat, ANZ, various)

For some sex workers in our study, therefore, boundaries were hard, while for others they were fluid, if it fitted with what they were willing to provide.

Conclusion

This chapter raises two important issues for sex workers and their ability to effectively negotiate consensual commercial sex. Firstly, information and communication are important for effective negotiation and, therefore, key contributors to the health and safety of sex workers. Negotiation sets the boundaries of consent. Clients sometimes have unrealistic expectations of what sex workers will provide in a booking and do not always acknowledge that sexual consent for services needs to be given. Significantly, sex workers who are new to the industry are better placed to get the information they need to keep safe from peers, whether this be other sex workers or sex worker organisations, if they are operating in decriminalised or legalised settings. This chapter highlighted that sex workers in Aotearoa New Zealand and in Nevada brothels were far better prepared to undertake negotiations with clients and communicate the boundaries of what they were and were not prepared to provide in a service. They were also better able to maintain boundaries as they had the security of having others nearby to intervene if necessary. This contrasted with sex workers who were criminalised and who had to learn by experience. They were more vulnerable to unwanted sexual contact, especially when they were new to sex work. Learning by experience means learning through bad experiences and trying to prevent these in the future by acting differently. The harms caused by these experiences may, however, prove too damaging. Criminalisation, in any of its forms, does not allow appropriate communication in order to protect new sex workers from harm.

Secondly, formal statutory law and informal rules and norms are important in informing the level of power sex workers have in their negotiations with clients. Hertogh (2009) has argued that rather than official law, unofficial law sometimes plays a more important role in people's lives. In this chapter, we looked at sex workers' knowledge and perceptions of formal law as it pertains to sex work, and also what they consider important regardless of the law; in other words, how they develop norms or a way of negotiating which works for them. It is evident that sex workers are more aware of their legal rights in a decriminalised environment. On the face of it, sex work in ANZ is seen as an occupation like any other, although still stigmatised (Abel & Ludeke, 2021b). ANZ sex workers' discourses were subtly different from their counterparts in other countries. Most of the interviewed ANZ sex workers had a good knowledge of the contents of the PRA —in particular, the sections of the Act that were relevant to their interactions with clients and brothel operators, i.e. Sections 9, 16 and 17. They used this knowledge as a tool in their negotiations with clients: the fact that they were citing the law gave them more power in the negotiation process. Knowledge of the law, however, does not necessarily translate into action to achieve justice. Although sex work has been decriminalised for over 20 years in ANZ, some sex workers are still hesitant to report violations of consent.

However, perceptions of the law and what it could do for them are slowly changing in the wake of some successful convictions for non-consensual acts committed against sex workers. People's views of the law are often shaped by the way they believe "officials understand and apply the law" (Hertogh, 2023, p. 306). Media confirmation of a successful court case in ANZ affected other sex workers' legal consciousness because they then felt that they could rely on the enforcement of the law. Certainly, some sex workers we interviewed felt more empowered in their negotiations by the news. This does not necessarily follow that they would report a non-consensual act to the authorities, but they believe that they could and, most importantly, they believe that they could get justice.

Legal brothel workers in Nevada that we interviewed understood that they were 'legal' and could report violations to the police and they also understood that condom use was mandatory in the brothels. However, other than that, they did not articulate knowledge of any other formal sex work, workplace, or sexual violence law that may protect their rights in commercial sex transactions. The law in Nevada currently does not explicitly recognise conditional consent or explicitly recognise the ability of consent to be revoked at any time. The sex workers in the Nevada brothels relied on informal norms, which stems from brothel culture, to reinforce their rights in negotiation and get justice when boundaries were crossed.

Independent sex workers in the USA and UK had very little knowledge of formal law and most—particularly USA illegal sex workers—perceived that there was nothing that the law could offer. They accepted that they could have bad experiences in a commercial sex transaction and that, through these experiences, they would develop their own informal norms to prevent future boundary crossings.

In conclusion, negotiating power is vital for the health and safety of sex workers. In this chapter we identified two conditions that contributed to increased negotiating power: (1) the ability to communicate with other sex workers to gain knowledge on how to set conditions of consent; and (2) the knowledge and belief that the law, whether this was formal law or informal norms, would back them up if the conditions of consent were breached.

References

Abel, G. (2010). *Decriminalisation: A harm minimisation and human rights approach to regulating sex work* (PhD thesis, University of Otago). Christchurch.

Abel, G. (2011). Different stage, different performance: The protective strategy of role play on emotional health in sex work. *Social Science and Medicine, 72*(7), 1177–1184.

Abel, G. (2014). A decade of decriminalization: Sex work 'down under' but not underground. *Criminology and Criminal Justice, 14*(5), 580–592. https://doi.org/10.1177/1748895814523024

Abel, G., & Fitzgerald, L. (2012). "The street's got its advantages": Movement between sectors of the sex industry in a decriminalised environment. *Health, Risk and Society, 14*(1), 17–23.

Abel, G., & Ludeke, M. (2021a). Brothels as sites of third-party exploitation? Decriminalisation and sex workers' employment rights. *Social Sciences, 10*(3), 1–15.

Abel, G., & Ludeke, M. (2021b). Business like any other? New Zealand's brothel industry post-decriminalisation. *Culture, Health & Sexuality, 24*(9), 1243–1256.

Amnesty International. (2016b). *The human cost of 'crushing' the market: Criminalization of sex work in Norway*. Retrieved July 7, 2024, from: https://www.amnesty.org/download/Documents/EUR3640342016ENGLISH.PDF

Anderson, M. J. (2004). Negotiating sex. *Southern California Law Review, 78*, 101–138.

Armstrong, L. (2019). Stigma, decriminalisation, and violence against street-based sex workers: Changing the narrative. *Sexualities, 22*(7–8), 1288–1308. https://doi.org/10.1177/1363460718780216

Atchison, C., Benoit, C., Burnett, P., Jansson, M., Kennedy, M. C., Ouellet, N., & Vukmirovich, D. (2015). The influence of time to negotiate on control in sex worker-client interactions. *Research for Sex Work, 14*, 35–36.

Benoit, C., Jansson, S. M., Smith, M., & Flagg, J. (2018). Prostitution stigma and its effect on the working conditions, personal lives, and health of sex workers. *The Journal of Sex Research, 55*(4–5), 457–471.

Brents, B. G., & Hausbeck, K. (2005). Violence and legalized brothel prostitution in Nevada: Examining safety, risk, and prostitution policy. *Journal of Interpersonal Violence, 20*(3), 270–295. https://doi.org/10.1177/0886260504270333

Brewis, J., & Linstead, S. (2000). 'The worst thing is the screwing'(1): Consumption and the management of identity in sex work. *Gender, Work & Organization, 7*(2), 84–97.

Comte, J. (2014). Decriminalization of sex work: Feminist discourses in light of research. *Sexuality & Culture, 18*(1), 196–217. https://doi.org/10.1007/s12119-013-9174-5

Day, S. (1994). What counts as rape? Physical assault and broken contracts: Contrasting views of rape among London sex workers. In P. Harvey & P. Gow (Eds.), *Sex and Violence: Issues in Representation and Experience* (pp. 172–189). Routledge.

Goldenberg, S. M., Duff, P., & Krüsi, A. (2015). Work environments and HIV prevention: A qualitative review and meta-synthesis of sex worker narratives. *BMC Public Health, 15*(1), 1–15.

Hertogh, M. (2009). What's in a handshake? Legal equality and legal consciousness in the Netherlands. *Social & Legal Studies, 18*(2), 221–239.

Hertogh, M. (2023). Relational legal consciousness in the punitive welfare state: How Dutch welfare officials shape clients' perceptions of law. *Law & Society Review, 57*(3), 293–316.

Krüsi, A. (2014). *The social and structural production of violence, safety and sexual risk reduction among street-based sex workers* (PhD thesis, University of British Columbia).

Krüsi, A., Chettiar, J., Ridgway, A., Abbott, J., Strathdee, S., & Shannon, K. (2012). Negotiating safety and sexual risk reduction with clients in unsanctioned safer indoor sex work environments: A qualitative study. *American Journal of Public Health, 102*(6), 1154–1159.

Krüsi, A., Kerr, T., Taylor, C., Rhodes, T., & Shannon, K. (2016). "They won't change it back in their heads that we're trash": The intersection of sex work-related stigma and evolving policing strategies. *Sociology of Health & Illness, 38*(7), 1137–1150.

Landsberg, A., Shannon, K., Krüsi, A., DeBeck, K., Milloy, M., Nosova, E., Kerr, T., & Hayashi, K. (2017). Criminalizing sex work clients and rushed negotiations among sex workers who use drugs in a Canadian setting. *Journal of Urban Health, 94*(4), 563–571.

Östergren, P. (2006). *Sex workers critique of Swedish prostitution policy*. Retrieved 7 July 2024, from: http://www.petraostergren.com/upl/files/115326.pdf

Perkins, R., & Lovejoy, F. (2007). *Call girls: Private sex workers in Australia*. University of Western Australia Press.

Platt, L., Grenfell, P., Meiksin, R., Elmes, J., Sherman, S. G., Sanders, T., Mwangi, P., & Crago, A. L. (2018). Associations between sex work laws and sex workers' health: A systematic review and meta-analysis of quantitative and qualitative studies. *PLOS Medicine, 15*(12), e1002680.

Prostitution Reform Act 2003. Retrieved July 7, 2024, from: http://www.legislation.govt.nz/act/public/2003/0028/latest/DLM197815.html

Pyett, P., & Warr, D. (1997). Vulnerability on the streets: Female sex workers and HIV risk. *AIDS Care, 9*(5), 539–547.

Pyett, P., & Warr, D. (1999). Women at risk in sex work: Strategies for survival. *Journal of Sociology, 35*(2), 183–197.

R v Campos (2021) NZDC 7422. Retrieved July 5, 2024, from: https://www.districtcourts.govt.nz/all-judgments/2021-nzdc-7422-r-v-campos/

Sanders, T. (2002). The condom as psychological barrier: Female sex workers and emotional management. *Feminism and Psychology, 12*(4), 561–566.

Sanders, T., & Campbell, R. (2007). Designing out vulnerability, building in respect: Violence, safety and sex work policy. *The British Journal of Sociology, 58*(1), 1–19.

Shannon, K., Kerr, T., Allinott, S., Chettar, J., Shoveller, J., & Tyndall, M. (2008). Social and structural violence and power relations in mitigating HIV risk and drug using women in survival sex work. *Social Science and Medicine, 66*(4), 911–921.

4

Defining Violation: Sex-Worker Experiences of Unwanted Incidents

Barbara G. Brents, Chris Wakefield, Jane Scoular, Teela Sanders, and Gillian Abel

Introduction: Legal Consciousness and Naming Sexual Assault

Research suggests that sex workers are often effective at enforcing boundaries with clients, particularly in managing the risk of unwanted contact (Comte, 2014). However, what happens when these boundaries are

B. G. Brents
University of Nevada, Las Vegas, Nevada, USA

C. Wakefield
Whitman College, Walla Walla, Washington, USA

J. Scoular
Strathclyde Law School, University of Strathclyde, Glasgow, UK

T. Sanders (✉)
University of Leicester, Leicester, UK
e-mail: teela.sanders@leicester.ac.uk

G. Abel
University of Otago, Dunedin, New Zealand

T. Sanders et al. (eds.), *Voicing Consent*, Palgrave Advances in Sex Work Studies,
https://doi.org/10.1007/978-3-031-77715-8_4

breached and how do sex workers understand and label these violations? Decades of research on sexual harassment and assault in the population generally reveal that individuals do not uniformly interpret or label such events when they happen. The process of understanding an incident as problematic involves multiple factors:

1. assessing the severity of the violation;
2. weighing possible next steps;
3. choosing whether and whom to tell;
4. evaluating the likelihood of being taken seriously;
5. anticipating the repercussions of reporting, such as stigma or further violence; and
6. considering what constitutes appropriate remediation or justice.

Although developed to describe civil actions, the 'naming, blaming, and claiming' framework (Felstiner et al., 1980) helps illustrate how these harassment and assault decisions are influenced by a range of factors, including an individual's social position, worldview, and relationships with others and institutions (Calavita & Jenness, 2013; Chua & Engel, 2019; Felstiner et al., 1980). These processes are closely interconnected, but recognising and addressing unwanted contact begins with naming the issue.

Legal consciousness, or the ways people experience, understand, and act in relation to the law (Chua & Engel, 2019), plays a pivotal role in how individuals label and react to violations. As the #MeToo movement has highlighted, acknowledging a violation of consent has been fraught for the non-sex-working population. About 60% of female rape survivors do not identify their experiences as rape (Wilson & Miller, 2016). Victims of sexual violence often struggle with labelling their experiences, feeling powerless and confused about whether the incident constitutes a sexual offence or even an unacceptable act (Peleg-Koriat & Klar-Chalamish 2022). Factors like shame, guilt, and isolation can hinder this labelling process. Those who blame themselves for their situation are less likely to view the incident as harmful (Coates & Penrod, 1981; Felstiner et al., 1980), although this relation may be more complex than some research has suggested (Calavita & Jenness, 2013).

There is a crucial distinction between legally defining unwanted contact as a crime and labelling it as wrong or injurious. 'Rape acknowledgment' refers to a survivor's recognition of their victimisation as rape (Wilson & Miller, 2016), while 'rape consciousness' involves comparing their experience with legal definitions and cultural expectations of rape (Oberweis et al., 2021). Despite legal reforms, a rape consciousness persists where many still perceive rape in traditional terms, as requiring force; and cases involving strangers or physical injury are often seen as more credible. Women especially, but all individuals who are 'out of place' sexually or seen as too sexual, are less likely to be protected by rape law. The fear of such perceptions can discourage survivors from labelling their experience as rape due to fears of disbelief or further psychological damage (Ahrens, 2006; Patterson et al., 2009).

Gash and Harding (2018) argue that these cultural understanding of legality—defined by Ewick and Silbey (1998, p. 22) as the "meanings, sources of authority, and cultural practices that are commonly recognised as legal, regardless of who employs them or for what ends"—often undermines victims' experiences. The prevailing legal rules of evidence and conventional ideas about what constitutes a lack of consent can significantly affect victims' interactions with professionals and legal authorities. In essence, rape law, by restricting the options available for legal recourse and healing, restricts the way individuals name and understand their experiences.

Sex Workers and Double Legal Consciousness

Sex workers occupy a complex position regarding legality when it comes to interpreting violations of consent. In criminalised settings, nearly every aspect of their work falls under the shadow of illegality. For instance, as discussed in Chapter 2, there are unclear legal prohibitions and laws that obscure how they advertise, negotiate, and provide services. In the UK, while advertising is less restricted, collaboration among workers remains illegal. In the USA, the spectre of arrest haunts every aspect of their work.

At the same time, sexual assault is illegal in all jurisdictions. Even with their precarious legal standing, sex workers may still refer to formal laws when confronted with sexual violence. They encounter similar barriers to reporting as do non-sex workers, such as rape consciousness, not being believed, and being retraumatised, but these are further exacerbated by stigma and discrimination.

Inspired by W.E.B. Du Bois's concept of double consciousness—used to describe the dual identities Black Americans navigate in terms of their Black identity and the identity imposed by white society—sex workers too exhibit a form of double *legal* consciousness. This concept illustrates how sex workers (1) manage their work (i.e. their professional identities as entrepreneurs, service providers, and contract negotiators), while (2) confronting societal and legal frameworks that often stigmatise, marginalise, and criminalise their sexuality and, indeed, their very existence. Du Bois captured this tension by describing it as "always looking at oneself through the eyes of others, of measuring one's soul by the tape of a world that looks on in amused contempt and pity" (1903, p. 3). Similarly, sex workers view their negotiations and any violations both through their own business sense and through a lens clouded by legal scrutiny and societal disdain, measuring actions and experiences in relation to the law.

In other words, sex workers face two kinds of legal consciousness that may interact differently in various legal contexts. First, they have, what we term here, a transactional legal consciousness, which involves their understanding and interpretation of how the law relates to their boundaries and consent within the context of individual transactions between themselves and their clients. This concept highlights the unique consent-based negotiations that occur in each professional interaction. But second, sex workers also face a legal system that measures whether they are 'out of place' sexually and legally, as individuals, which can cloud their naming of any violence they experience. This double consciousness places them in a fundamentally different position compared to those experiencing sexual violence in their personal lives, complicating how we might understand their legal consciousness around sexual violence.

This chapter investigates how varying legal frameworks and norms related to prostitution and sexual violence influence how sex workers recognise and describe instances of unwanted contact. We examine two angles of view on this naming and labelling process: (1) survey data from each country on incidents of unwanted contact; and (2) interview data on sex workers' perceptions of incidents that violate the rule of law.

Survey—Distributions of Unwanted Sexual Incidents

What types of unwanted contact do sex workers most frequently encounter? To answer this question, we begin by examining our survey results; here, respondents were asked about the different types of unwanted contact that they had experienced as sex workers, but, importantly, we did not explicitly frame these incidents as crimes. This analysis focuses on responses from individuals who had experienced actual incidents ($n = 483$) and excludes attempted incidents.

As discussed previously in this book, our recruitment strategies limit the ability to generalise these findings to all sex workers. The survey is not able to compare to representative samples among non-sex workers or examine, in detail, incidents of sexual violence outside of participants' sex work experiences (for example, one respondent confided, in the context of an interview, that "I have never been raped while I was doing sex work, but I was raped when I [worked a non-sex-work job] by someone that I hired" [Sebastian, USA, various]). The survey, in conjunction with the interviews, provides a comprehensive insight into the range of events that sex workers experience and their perceptions of these events. It is important to reiterate that we are describing sex workers' experiences of specific events, not the frequency of these events as representative of the broader sex-worker population.

Our survey asked participants to indicate what had happened that *they had not given permission for* in the last 12 months while sex working, along with stating the last time such an incident had happened. Specifically, we asked, "In the last 12 months while you were selling sexual services, how often have any of these things happened to you, without your permission?" We presented participants with a list of potential incidents but did not label them in legal terms. Respondents could select from the following options:

- "The client did not pay you at all";
- "The client paid you less than was agreed";
- "You were paid in fake money";
- "Someone penetrated your vagina or anus, with their penis";
- "Someone penetrated your vagina, mouth or anus with their fingers or an object";
- "You agreed to sex, but the other person would not stop when you asked them to";
- "Someone physically assaulted you before or during sex (e.g. you were hit, kicked or punched)";
- "Someone had sex with you when you were too drugged or drunk to agree to it";
- "Someone threatened or harassed you into having sex with them"; and
- "Someone removed or damaged a condom during sex (sometimes called stealthing)".

We followed that up with, "The LAST time something happened to you in sex work without your permission, what was that?", allowing respondents to choose from the same options.

Survey—Incidents in the Past Year

Figure 4.1, shows the distribution of the kinds of incidents experienced among those who indicated that they had experienced some form of unwanted incident at least once in the past year. These items may not be mutually exclusive events so could be combined by the respondent; for example, one incident of unwanted contact could include penetration, refusing to stop when asked, and a payment problem such as non-payment.

While laws and policies often emphasise physical assault and unwanted penetration, sex workers in our study reported a wide variety of incidents of unwanted contact. Unwanted penetration and assault are crimes in all surveyed locations. However the most common form of incident that sex workers reported concerned issues with payment. In the past year, 44% (213 out of 479) of respondents had experienced

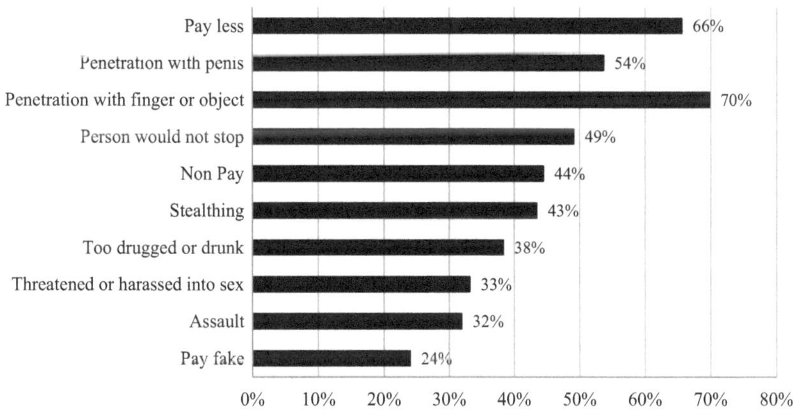

Fig. 4.1 Distribution of incident types reported by individuals experiencing unwanted contact in the last year (number of reports, multiple responses allowed)

non-payment for services, and 66% (301 out of 459) had encountered clients paying less than the agreed amount. Combining all payment-related problems within the last year reveals that 75.57% of sex workers (365 out of 483 respondents) reported at least one issue. However, it should be noted that non-payment (and, likewise, 'stealthing') is a legal offence only in Aotearoa New Zealand.

A less frequent, yet significant, category concerned clients attempting to access services without prior negotiation or failing to adhere to agreed terms. These incidents were experienced by a significant proportion of respondents and were reflected in several of our categories involving unwanted penetration. For example, 54% of respondents experienced unwanted penetration with a penis while providing services. Additionally, a substantial number of sex workers reported unwanted penetration by a finger or object, although fewer respondents (331 out of 483) answered this question, potentially inflating its percentage. Respondents more often skipped this question than they did others, by a margin of more than 100 respondents, which could inflate the proportion of reported incidences among those who responded. About the same number of respondents reported penetration with a finger or object (231) as those reporting penetration with a penis (241) or a client not stopping when being asked to (222). Nearly half of the respondents (49%) reported at least one incident where a client did not stop despite requests, and this was the most common incident after being paid less and unwanted penetration. As sex workers explained in interviews, several incidents often occurred in contexts where the client overstepped negotiated terms, such as during services initially agreed to involving only oral sex or an erotic massage. Based on interviews, as we see below, being paid less than negotiated, the client not stopping, and unwanted penetration may be a part of the same incident for many sex workers.

'Stealthing', reported by 43% of respondents, involved clients secretly removing condoms, posing a serious health risk. Condom use is mandated in Aotearoa New Zealand under the Prostitution Reform Act for oral or vaginal sex, with substantial fines for non-compliance. In Nevada's legal brothels, the public health code requires condom use, holding the brothel accountable for violations.

Notably, even the least common outcomes were reported by a third or more of the respondents. Assault, experiencing sex while under the influence, and threats used to compel sexual activity were each reported as having occurred in the last year by over 100 respondents. Also notable was the fact that, despite being less frequently experienced, the sex workers we interviewed often discussed their most violent experiences first when describing unwanted contact, reflecting prevalent stereotypes about 'real rape', as discussed in the following sections.

Survey—The Last Time an Incident Happened

Figure 4.2, focuses on the most recent incidents experienced by respondents. This focus on the 'last time' provides a slightly different picture compared to the broader trends of incidents experienced over the course of a year (discussed in Fig. 4.1). For instance, certain behaviours might have become normalised over time and so not be reported as frequently when reflecting on the past year. However, these same behaviours may be recalled more readily when considering the most recent incident. On the other hand, some events are perhaps more likely to appear across the long

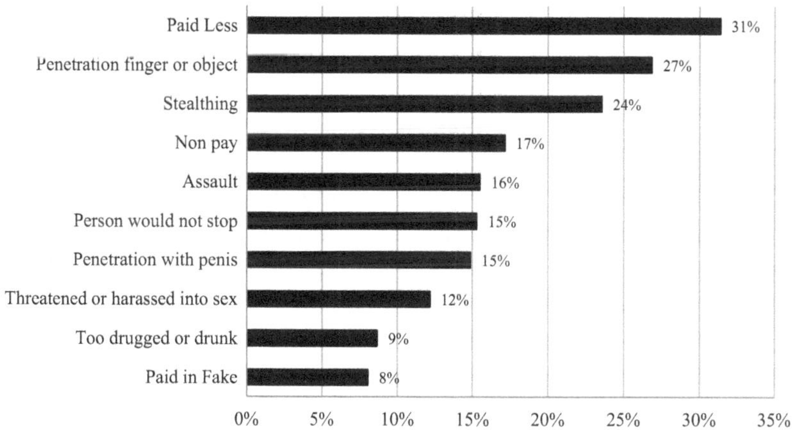

Fig. 4.2 Distribution of incident types reported by individuals experiencing unwanted contact the last time it happened, all sites (number of reports, multiple responses allowed)

term, even though they are or may be one-time events or highly infrequent ones. Seasonal or cyclical trends that affect the incidence of certain behaviours, making some more prevalent at different times of the year, thus impacting the 'last time' responses differently than those reflecting the entire year.

Figure 4.2 highlights that, while physical violence often dominates policy, law, and popular discourse, payment issues and stealthing were more frequently cited concerns in our survey. Nearly half of all sex workers, 48.6% (235 out of 484 responses), had experienced some sort of payment problem the last time that there was an incident.

In addition to payment issues, Fig. 4.2 also supports a higher percentage of incidents involving penetration with a finger or an object, with this being the second most common item reported as respondents' last incident.

Furthermore, a full quarter of respondents identified stealthing—secret removal of a condom as a part of their most recent encounter, marking it as the third most common issue and worthy of note, despite its lower ranking in lifetime-experience reports. The incidence of assault also notably ranks higher in the 'most recent' data than it does in the 'lifetime' data.

Figure 4.2 captures a more 'average' set of events than does Fig. 4.1, where the less frequent reports likely represent rarer occurrences, and the most frequent reports indicate events most likely to happen. Focusing on the most recent incident provides insights into the typical challenges faced by sex workers, beyond the most extreme or sensationalised cases, potentially offering a clearer view of their daily occupational realities.

Figure 4.3, compares the distribution of 'last time' incidents across each of our sites. The distribution is notably similar across all sites. However, these findings should be interpreted with caution as they only represent distributions among individuals who reported incidents and do not suggest a higher frequency of any event at any site. Additionally, as previously stated, more than one type of incident could occur during any given 'last time' incident.

Despite the overall similarity, certain differences are worth noting. For example, in Aotearoa New Zealand (ANZ), incidents of penetration with a finger and stealthing are higher in relation to other incidents in that country. In the UK, the prevalence of incidents involving clients drugging or threatening workers stands out. Conversely, in Nevada's legal brothels, the rarity of these threats and a higher distribution of payment issues is significant.

Given that this project emphasises cross-national comparison, subtle variations in the data may be significant, although we need more in-depth data analysis. Our sampling strategy focused on individuals who have experienced harm, naturally highlighting higher incidences of harm. Further, it is not surprising to find that legal frameworks do not drastically reduce the occurrence of unwanted contact in sex work. This is consistent with criminological research, which suggests that violence is rarely deterred by the threat of punishment; rather, the chance of being caught is a vastly more effective deterrent (National Institute of Justice, 2016). This is especially evident when considering that legal reforms have not reduced cases of sexual violence among the non-sex-working population (Spohn, 2020). Decriminalisation alone does not eliminate sexual violence or solve all workplace issues. However, what does change with decriminalisation and legal variations, as our interviews below will show,

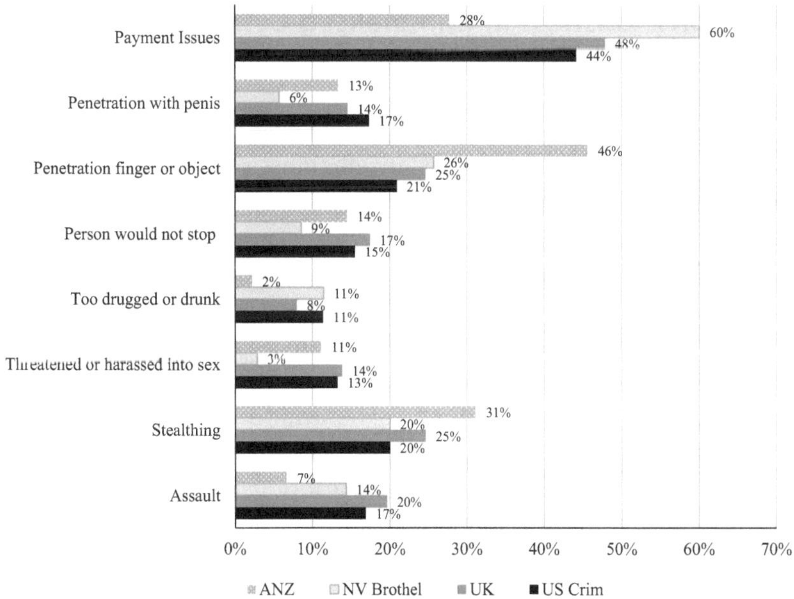

Fig. 4.3 Distribution of incident types reported by individuals experiencing unwanted contact, per cent of all respondents the last time this happened, by site

is how workers perceive these events, along with their ability to report and manage them.

Rape Consciousness—'With the Law'?

We now turn to our interviews to examine the perception of events and the naming process, and to better understand the incidents behind our survey responses. We asked sex workers to describe incidents "that others might see as a crime or sexual violence while working".

Rape Consciousness in Criminalised Contexts

As discussed in Chapter 3, many sex workers in criminalised contexts in the USA and UK have only a general understanding of sexual violence and sex work laws in their local jurisdictions, though this knowledge may be inaccurate and lacks detail. They do not believe the law offers them much protection in specific instances. Legal alienation is defined as a cognitive state of psychological disconnection from official state law and the justice system (Hertogh, 2018, p. 55). Ewick and Silbey (1998) found that marginalised individuals are more likely to adopt an 'against the law' dimension of legal consciousness. In this orientation, the legal system is perceived as something to be avoided because it is seen as a product of arbitrary power, capricious, and potentially dangerous to invoke. In this form of consciousness, legality is not seen as conditionally appropriate or useful but is condemned outright (Ewick & Silbey, 1998, p. 192). Our data supports this view, showing that participants in criminalised contexts must balance a view of the law as adversary with their attempts to prevent and manage sexual violations. One USA respondent, when asked about experiences with crime, responded, "So all of it [sex work] is technically a crime. Do you mean, like, a sexually violent crime?".

However, in their initial responses to questions about crime or sexual violence, participants frequently emphasised the most severe incidents involving injury. This pattern in how they thought about their own experiences reflects a typical kind of rape consciousness, where recognition of an experience as rape hinges critically on legality (Oberweis et al., 2021; Wilson & Miller, 2016). Their rape acknowledgement reflects enduring societal and cultural views that equate 'real rape' with visible force and injury (Estrich, 1987). In other words, in this respect, their legal consciousness is 'with the law.'

For example, two UK street sex workers responded to questions about crime and sexual violence this way:

> Yeah, definitely. Basically, I was left for dead by a client. He ended up getting two life sentences for it. Basically, he picked me up and I can't

> really remember a lot of it still now, but basically, beat me with a baseball bat and he left me in a lay-by. (Anna, UK, street-based)
> I was assaulted by a guy, violence … I ended up in the hospital. … and my case was in the newspapers too. Now that guy's in jail for a few years. (Stephanie, UK, street-based)

In both these cases, sex workers defined these incidents as clear-cut instances of violence because they were able to get justice for violent incidents by going to the police. These reflected "real rape" in the eyes of the law. Even in Aotearoa New Zealand, many sex workers talked first about a past violent incident, in answering whether they had ever experienced a crime or sexual violence. For example:

> I got attacked like eight years ago... He, like, strangled me and when I was knocked out, he'd bring me back and strangle me … But he'd just finished attacking one of the other girls before me. Yeah, and I didn't know. Got caught trying to pick up another girl. And he'd just got out of jail, too, after six years. They ended up calling the police and the police got him, and he went back to jail for six more years or something and got killed inside. (Athena, ANZ, street-based)

Many sex workers brought up these kinds of incidents involving injury, force, or lack of an ability to consent, especially in first responses, regardless of how frequently or often this incident may or may not have occurred. Anna, Stephanie, and Athena, like several of the interviewees, immediately followed their accounts of sexual violence by telling the interviewer how the violations they experienced were verified in criminal justice institutions by convictions. While their experiences of reporting and other post-violation actions are the subject of Chapter 5, the fact that they brought up independent verification so prominently in their stories and naming of violation underscores the role of legal validation, through convictions, in shaping sex workers' perceptions of sexual violation.

For Anna in the UK, this external verification was critical in her seeing the violation described above, involving her being left for dead, as the most serious, given that the police often disbelieved her other reported incidents:

> And then there's been other times when I've been attacked and that, and the police has just not been interested. I've even had the police turn round and say it's an occupational hazard … No means no. And no matter what I do, it don't give any man any right to come and — I'm still somebody's daughter, I'm still somebody's sister. Just because I do what I do, don't give no man no right to overstep the boundaries. (Anna, UK, street-based)

Anna's quotes above and earlier reflect the complicated ways sex workers draw on sexual violence law in naming violations in a criminalised context. On the one hand, she was 'with the law', relieved that the law eventually supported her claims (Ewick & Silbey, 1998) as she noted above. She asserted rape stereotypes around injury, physical force, and the eventual conviction. On the other hand, she was "against the law", explaining how the police had told her "It's just part of the job". She rejected their definition of events just because she was a sex worker. To add another layer of complexity, she added that she was someone's daughter and sister. That could have been to just emphasise that she was no different than anyone else. But it also may have reflected a discourse based on the historical roots of rape law, that violations were only violations if the woman belonged to a man in a patriarchal system—a wife, daughter, or sister of a man.

It is worth pointing out that the recruiting process for sex workers from the UK and Aotearoa New Zealand for our study resulted in netting individuals who were much more likely to have experienced sexual violence and reported it to some authority. In general, the UK interviewees had worked in the industry longer, more than 10 years, and many (five of 15) worked on the streets. Eight out of these 15 interviewees talked about an incident that involved physical force. Of those, seven had reported incidents to the police, with three of the perpetrators having then been convicted. All three of these convictions were for incidents that included injury to the sex workers. In addition to force and injury, two UK interviewees first described experiences of unwanted penetration outside the services that were negotiated, and the rest described stealthing, stalking, and online recording. One said she had not experienced any incident of unwanted contact.

Five out of the 14 USA sex workers we interviewed brought up force or the inability to consent, in response to our question about incidents. However, none of these interviewees had experienced positive outcomes with law enforcement; none had been able to use this as a route to verify their concerns. Most did not work on the streets, and none had successful experiences in reporting any injuries through the legal system. Incidents that happened within legal brothels were handled by management.

Cases where sex workers had successfully reported, and perpetrators were convicted of an event, as discussed above, did not reflect the experiences of most sex workers from the fully criminalised context (the USA) in our sample. Only 7% (37 of 512) of respondents who had experienced a violation had reported it to the police. In criminalised contexts, very few situations were verified by legal institutions, or even witnesses, but respondents still described violations that included injury, lack of consent or force; they just used a different word to describe the injury—trauma. Unlike non-sex workers, who may have been confused or struggled to label the experiences, they clearly labelled the situation as wrong. Like Linda and Emily in the UK or Cody in the USA, many had a mental dialogue concerning what they thought the law could do. They emphasised injury but also emphasised the "but" or "just" in naming the kind of injury the law might see as evidence:

> It's all just trauma, trauma, trauma, but it's fine. Yeah, just the usual, being robbed, beaten, you know, and worse. I've had, god, I've had loads of knives at my throat. And I just see it as experience, as well as trauma. It's experience but it makes me who I am today; it makes me extra cautious. (Emily, UK, various)

> Yeah, but I have been attacked a few times, badly, but you've got instinct and try and go somewhere kind of safe. (Linda, UK, street-based)

Some were a bit resentful, like Nancy, who got no results after reporting an incident to the police. She still ultimately emphasised the injury: a traumatic memory:

> We ended up making the whole night of it, we seen a show, we had dinner and then the next morning — and I had a lot to drink — and the next

> morning when I woke up, he was having his way, so that happened when I was passed out … [But the incident] just basically faded away and I moved on with my life. I mean, it's still a traumatic memory, but nothing happened, nothing happened with courts. (Nancy, USA, independent)

In criminalised contexts, these respondents were trapped by the laws and stigma against sex work and alienated from the laws around sexual violence. At the same time, far from seeing this in terms of self-blame, and therefore as not harmful, in the same way as non-sex workers might do, some made pragmatic judgements about the severity of their experience to inform future actions. They labelled the experience as traumatic and strategised actions to take in the future to prevent this harm. Their interpretation of their experiences accepted that they were, in a sense, out of place in engaging in sex for pay, outside of rape laws, but they did not accept that they should be outside the law (Ewick & Silbey, 1998). We see this as a complicated relationship to legal consciousness, where they are both 'with the law' and 'outside the law'.

Rape Consciousness in the Decriminalised Context

In Aotearoa New Zealand, where sex work is decriminalised, sex workers' responses to interviewers' question about crime and sexual violence initially mirrored those from other regions, in highlighting injury where it happened. However, they distinctively emphasised how the law affirmed their boundaries of consent as legitimate. Among the 11 sex workers interviewed in Aotearoa New Zealand, seven reported experiencing some level of force, including one significant case of physical injury. However, every one of these respondents who reported incidents they could not control to the police had been successful in getting a conviction.

Sex workers in Aotearoa New Zealand also consistently labelled both severe and less traumatic incidents as sexual assaults. This contrasts sharply with sex workers in the USA and UK, who often relied on external validation and grappled with self-blame and pragmatic judgements when naming violations. Talia, an Aotearoa New Zealand sex worker with 11 years of experience in both brothels and independent settings, described a series of encounters that she unequivocally defined as "assaults". Unlike her counterparts in criminalised locations, Talia did not depend on legal outcomes to validate her experiences; she confidently reported these incidents, either to her employers or directly to the police, as harmful:

> I would say for the entire time that I've been a sex worker, there's been elements of sexual violence present in my experiences. Um, so, the things that stand out the most while working at [two brothels] were the customers doing — So, they push on you, they slap you, they bite you, they spread your legs apart and forcefully lick the vagina. That sort of thing is stuff that I did not report to the police, but [I reported them to the brothel management] where events had happened. And then, changing from that and working independently, there's sexual violence still, but it's not, I guess, as frequent as what I think it is at the brothels. Um, and I think that's just that at the brothel, the customer thinks he can get away with it a lot more. Maybe he's tried it on other girls, and they've allowed it. It just seems that they'll repeat the pattern if they're not turned away after the first incident at the door. It seems to recur. Um, so, yeah, I found I was assaulted a lot more while working at brothels than what I have been while working independently. Um, and in saying that, last year, I took three different assaults to the police, two of which I can't discuss because they're current cases. (Talia, ANZ, brothel)

Talia clearly defined these incidents as assaults but blamed brothel management for not handling them as they should. Now that she is working independently, she can be more proactive in both defining these incidents and then reporting the perpetrators to the police.

This proactive stance is indicative of a unique legal consciousness among Aotearoa New Zealand sex workers, shaped by their more positive relationship with law enforcement. At least regarding the sex workers we interviewed, this relationship fosters a 'with the law' rape consciousness, supporting their ability to assert their rights and pursue justice should they want to. The success of their legal actions likely reinforces this alignment, as seen in the high rate of conviction for their reported cases. Such a legal environment empowers them to identify and address sexual violations without the hesitation observed in jurisdictions where sex work remains criminalised.

Naming Violations in a Transactional Context

Sex workers operate within a framework of double consciousness that profoundly influences their understanding of legality and how they acknowledge sexual assault. Unlike non-sex workers, whose experience of assault is deeply tangled with personal relationships, sex workers often view such incidents through the professional boundaries of their work. This work-related, transactional view allows them to define and respond to violations with a set of norms that differ markedly from those governing their personal lives. This transactional view allows them to minimise the confusion and shame that often accompany the recognition and acknowledgment of violations.

Day (1994) found that, for London sex workers, the definition of rape in work versus personal relationships varied significantly. In their professional capacity, the notion of rape included not just physical assault but also breaches of contract such as bounced cheques or the non-consensual removal of a condom. This broader definition contrasts with their narrower view of rape in personal relationships, which was seen as requiring physical coercion. We consider this their 'transactional legal consciousness'.

For example, Aotearoa New Zealand sex worker Carrie described her experience with legal proceedings in a stealthing and assault case, showing how her professional identity influenced her perception of the incident:

> The way I kind of perceive it is that in one way it's not personal. You know that client didn't rape me. He raped Carrie [her sex work name], which is a manifestation of his attitudes towards women and towards sex workers. It's not personal. You know, it could have been anyone in that situation. I was the one that showed up. And so having that kind of barrier makes a really big difference as opposed to men that have raped

> me in my personal life. That really hurts because it's like, 'Oh, I thought you liked me. I thought we had a good thing going', and, you know, that's really different. That's really upsetting. But with this, it's like you can detach it because it's business. (Carrie, ANZ, independent)

Similarly, Queen, a UK worker, felt that, in her professional life, she was much better at identifying violations of consent:

> I'd look back at previous relationships where I could go, 'Actually, that was assault', but I didn't know it was assault. Now that I'm a sex worker, I'm like 'Fuck, that was assault', do you know what I mean? Now that I've been in sex work, it's weird, I actually understand consent so much better than when I was in relationships, to be honest with you. (Queen, UK, various)

These ways of categorising violations are indicative of a double legal consciousness where sex workers navigate two realms: their business operations underpinned by contractual legality and a personal identity that is often alienated from the protections offered by the legal system, especially in regions where their work is criminalised. This alienation from formal legal recourse does not prevent them, however, from using their own legal consciousness to name and label incidents effectively, particularly in contexts where the legality of their actions is ambiguous. They often view these incidents through a lens of professional necessity rather than personal violation, which empowers them to label events as violations more decisively, especially when those acts are unambiguously criminal. This becomes clear in the data we have regarding stealthing and non-payment.

'Stealthing', Professional Boundaries and Rules of Consent

Survey Results on Stealthing

While sex workers frequently emphasised incidents involving violence, force, or coercion in interviews, our survey revealed that non-consensual removal of condoms, or stealthing, is a more prevalent issue, especially in Aotearoa New Zealand, where 7% of respondents reported assault compared to 31% who reported stealthing (see Figs. 4.3 and 4.4). However, non-consensual condom removal is a significant issue for sex workers across *all* contexts; Fig. 4.4 illustrates that a similar percentage of respondents across all sites reported stealthing as part of their most recent incident.

We should note that stealthing in the Nevada legal brothel category included respondents who worked predominantly, but not exclusively, in legal brothels. Their reports of stealthing did not necessarily occur in these brothels, and it may be that, for a number of these respondents, stealthing occurred while they were working independently.

Comparisons with non-sex-worker populations reveal that stealthing is a widespread issue generally. Reported rates among sex workers may be similar to, or only slightly higher than, those reported by non-sex workers. Various studies highlight that more than 10% of women in non-clinical settings report stealthing over their lifetimes (Gómez-Durán & Martin-Fumadó, 2024), with rates in specific groups, such as Australian sexual health clinics, reaching 32% for women and 19% for MSM (men who have sex with men) (Latimer et al., 2018). Other studies using different sampling methods find rates ranging from 7.9% to 43% for women, and from 5.0% to 19% for men (Davis et al., 2024). When

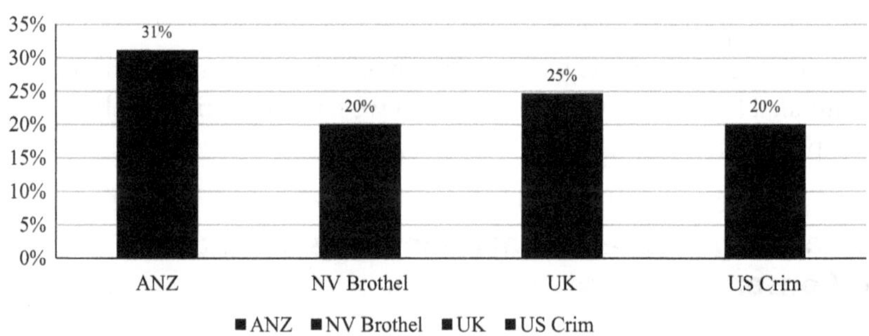

Fig. 4.4 Stealthing—respondents indicating stealthing the last time it happened, by site

compared to the highest rates found in certain clinical or specific demographic studies (up to 43% for women), the rate among sex workers seems less of an outlier.

Sex workers, due to the nature of their work, are at a higher-than-average risk of experiencing stealthing. But their professional boundaries and direct health risks lead to heightened vigilance and potentially higher reporting accuracy. This contrasts with the non-sex-working population, where individuals may not as readily identify or report stealthing. Research finds that non-sex-working women often react with confusion, self-blame, shame, or embarrassment upon discovery of this type of incident (Lévesque et al., 2021) and may not classify stealthing as sexual assault because they had consented to sex, considering it instead as "rape adjacent" (Brodsky, 2017).

Our interviews support the idea that sex workers have a broader legal consciousness around stealthing. Despite the legal ambiguity in some areas, the sex workers we interviewed consistently recognised stealthing as wrong. They name these incidents as violations, mostly naming them as violations of their stated rules. However, their interpretations of it within the criminal context varied depending on the local legal status of sex work.

Stealthing in a Criminalised Context

In regions where stealthing is not explicitly illegal, sex workers still view it as a violation. Yet, their descriptions reflect a use of the law and rape consciousness as benchmarks. For instance, two of the 15 UK respondents and two of the 14 USA respondents mentioned a stealthing incident in their interviews.

Sophia, a UK sex worker, was adamant that a client had broken her condition of consent, aligning her understanding of stealthing with rape consciousness, including her stress on the lack of physical evidence:

> He took the condom off and tried to put it in my arse, which I don't do. Those are the two things I've never done. They're basically the two biggest noes, so I just kept saying no. I said no more than five times; I don't know how many times because I weren't counting … I was injured

> mentally, but there were no proper marks because it didn't even go all the way in because I was making that much of a fuss. So, I wasn't physically injured, but mentally it did affect me. (Sophia, UK, independent)

In the USA, Jessica, who currently worked in legal brothels, recounted a stealthing incident while working illegally that had left her feeling profoundly violated—yet, she did not define it as rape:

> I've never been raped, I've never been beat on … but I have had my own share of things that were not OK, or I felt violated … One experience I will say that I think was the worst that I've had, that I felt violated … So, I always go to check myself, to make sure nothing's inside that's not supposed to be — and there was. So that's why I started flipping out, and he just stuck to his story that he done it and the condom stayed on, and he didn't do anything wrong. (Jessica, USA, various)

Cody, from the USA, provided a typical insight into understanding sex workers' legal consciousness in criminalised contexts:

> I definitely have experienced things that fit under a penal or criminal statute. I've experienced types of harm that don't really fit into any category. But among those things, definitely is sexual violence. The most direct definition is a physical violation of my sexual boundaries. But, also, I see stealthing on here and then the denial of your conditional consent, which is payment, I've experienced that as well. (Cody, USA, independent)

In all of these situations, individuals felt wronged, and some (like Cody) considered such incidents to be sexual violence. Unlike non-sex workers, who may struggle with recognition and reporting of stealthing, due to confusion and self-blame, sex workers explicitly name these acts as clear violations of the boundaries they have meticulously set. However, they were unable to rely on any legal protections regarding stealthing, effectively placing them 'outside' of rape law. While sex workers in criminalised contexts articulate a clear understanding of violations like stealthing, through a nuanced legal consciousness, they often find themselves navigating a legal vacuum.

Stealthing as a Legal Violation in Legalised and Decriminalised Contexts

In Aotearoa New Zealand and Nevada's legal brothels, there are statutes in place explicitly addressing stealthing; however, in both jurisdictions, these are classified under health regulations. In Nevada, these are administrative, not criminal, codes, and are enforced against brothels. In Aotearoa New Zealand, these are part of the Prostitution Reform Act (PRA), which mandates safer sex practices, such as the use of barriers for vaginal, anal, oral, or any activity that could transmit sexually transmissible infections (STIs), with violations subject to a $2000 fine. Workers we interviewed in Aotearoa New Zealand and Nevada's legal brothels benefit from the legal recognition of stealthing, even at this limited level. Recent court rulings in Aotearoa New Zealand have resulted in convictions for stealthing as a sexual assault crime.

Sex workers in Aotearoa New Zealand described stealthing as a critical violation of the conditions they set out in transactions. They identify stealthing as a health issue, but more importantly, they see it as a violation of their specifically stated rules. Additionally, the respondents were more capable than those in criminalised contexts of aligning these violations of their consent with legally recognised harms. In interviews, nine out of 11 Aotearoa New Zealand sex workers mentioned experiencing incidents of stealthing; all but one had previously reported these incidents, and two cases had, so far, led to successful prosecutions. Meanwhile, sex workers in Nevada's legal brothels did not report experiencing stealthing. However, they emphasised that stealthing crossed boundaries and referenced the law when discussing how they prevented incidents.

An example of the seriousness with which sex workers define stealthing comes from Carrie in Aotearoa New Zealand, who took an incident of forced anal penetration with a finger followed by stealthing, to the police. Law enforcement officers initially wanted to pursue the more severe crime of forced penetration, but Carrie insisted on focusing on the stealthing incident:

> The next man [police] that I dealt with, um, he was really interested in pursuing the non-consensual thing in the arse incident, but I went, 'No,

> no, I want to talk about the stealthing incident. I want to set that precedent'. ... And he talked about like, 'Oh, you know, the stealthing incident, if that breaches Section 9, that's a $2000 fine, but a non-consensual finger in the arse is like a $3000 fine or something', and I'm like, 'It's about the principle. This is the violation that means the most'. (Carrie, ANZ, independent)

Recently, courts in both England and Wales and Aotearoa New Zealand have recognised stealthing as sexual assault, marking a pivotal shift in how such violations can be legally acknowledged. In England and Wales, the High Court held that consent was conditional on a condom being worn (Assange v Swedish Prosecution Authority, 2011). As a result, current CPS guidance (Crown Prosecution Service, 2021) encourages recognising conditional consent. In the USA, meanwhile, Maine and California have established laws that frame the non-consensual removal of a condom as a form of sexual assault, illustrating evolving legal consciousness around consent and sexual violence. While in criminalised settings it remains less likely, it is still possible for these laws to be applied to sex workers.

In Aotearoa New Zealand, successful prosecutions of stealthing as sexual assault involving sex workers have not only increased sex workers' awareness of their legal rights but also validated their experiences in the eyes of the law. This legal acknowledgment plays a critical role in how stealthing violations are named and addressed. District Court Judge J. Harrop's ruling in *R v Campos* ([2021] NZDC 7422), stated that the client had "put her employment and income as a sex worker at risk" (p. 5 [14]) and "A sex worker who is raped is no less a victim than any other woman ... there have been significant consequences from your deliberately having sex without a condom on a basis that she did not consent to and that you knew she did not consent to" (pp. 5–6 [16]). As the appeals court said, "The victim consented to protected sex. She never consented to unprotected sex" (Stevens, 2022). This, along with similar rulings in those Australian states where sex work is legal, has helped to reinforce the concept of conditional or contextualised consent specifically for sex workers, empowering them to define stealthing as rape or sexual assault.

This evolving legal landscape empowers sex workers like Jane and Talia from Aotearoa New Zealand, who use the law to define violations of their consent. Jane, with six years of experience in managed brothels, recounted a stealthing incident that she unequivocally considered rape because the client had broken her rules:

> So, some people would describe it as stealthing. Um, some people would call it just rape and, you know, there are some people who wouldn't call it anything at all. Um, for myself, I think rape's the correct term. I was working and they decided to take the condom off, even though I'd previously let them know that's not something I was interested in. Yeah, and so went to court for all of that and he's now a convicted rapist. (Jane, ANZ, brothel)

Jane's case highlights how the legal process supported her understanding of the incident and validated her feelings of violation:

> [Jane:] Well, I don't know if they normally ask you what you want to charge against. Like do they normally ask you if it's, 'Do you think this person sexually assaulted you?' I don't know. I just went to an interview, said all of that, and the next time I saw a thing about court, it was rape, and I was like, 'Well, I'll run with that'. Yeah.
> [Int:] Yeah, did that surprise you in a way? Did you feel like it might ... have been a lesser charge?
> [Jane:] Yeah, it surprised me, yeah, being in the work that I did, that I didn't have to say a word and they saw it for what it was.

Similarly, Talia brought "three different assaults" to the police, emphasising that the stealthing violated her established rules:

> He decided that he was going to ignore my rules and he put his mouth on my vagina without a dental dam. So that's one I have taken to the police and, um, he ended up pleading guilty to indecent assault. (Talia, ANZ, brothel)

The court's response to Jane's case, where the charge was framed as rape without her having to prompt or argue for it, illustrates a growing alignment between individual experiences of violations and legal responses, which is a key aspect of legal consciousness.

Carrie's insistence on focusing the legal proceedings on the stealthing incident, despite police interest in a different assault, highlights her determination to name and address the specific violation that mattered most to her. Carrie's action to set a legal precedent emphasises the active role sex workers are taking in defining what constitutes a violation in their work context, pushing the boundaries of legal recognition.

Not all sex workers, however, initially defined stealthing as assault. Chanelle, for instance, shared her early experience:

> I was quite new. I was about 19 at the time. I guess I knew it was an assault but not enough to really recognise that this had happened to me. I guess I did a lot of disassociating and that sort of thing when I was working there, so I kind of like, kind of brushed it [stealthing] off. I did tell the manager that was on at the time, but I was kind of told just to go back on the floor, 'cause I wasn't like fully in tears or anything else. It was just like, 'Hey, this happened. I'm pretty sure it shouldn't have happened', but yeah, no, 'Okay, fine, off you go'. And I was like, 'Okay, cool'. But yeah. (Chanelle, ANZ, various)

These narratives underscore the significant role of legal consciousness and legal alienation in how sex workers perceive and address incidents of stealthing. As legal frameworks evolve, they influence sex workers' ability to assert their rights and receive recognition and support from the legal system. This shift is crucial for understanding the dynamics of naming and labelling stealthing violations within the broader context of legal consciousness.

Naming incidents within the setting of work affords sex workers greater clarity than non-sex workers. But it also highlights the marginalised position within the legal system of those in criminalised contexts. Here, the concept of double consciousness becomes relevant. Sex workers operate within dual spheres of legality—engaging as professionals making contracts and as individuals frequently positioned outside protective legal boundaries due to the criminalised nature of their work.

As laws continue to evolve, they have the potential to recognise and validate the experiences of sex workers, shifting the legal landscape to better support their rights and acknowledge their professional boundaries. This shift in legal consciousness is essential for a deeper understanding of the dynamics of naming and labelling violations like stealthing.

Non-Payment as Rape

While stealthing potentially affects both sex workers and non-sex workers, issues related to being underpaid or not paid at all are unique to sex workers. Our survey indicates that payment problems are one of the most reported incidents relating to unwanted contact, with 75.57% of sex workers (365 out of 483 respondents) experiencing at least one form of payment issue.

Survey Results on Payment Issues

Figure 4.5, compares payment issues across our sites. Payment issues are prevalent across all countries but are a larger percentage of the array of issues in USA's and UK's criminalised sectors, compared to Aotearoa New Zealand and Nevada's legal brothels. Interestingly, however, being paid less is reported more frequently in Nevada legal brothels than anywhere else. This discrepancy could be attributed to the smaller sample size at this site, where small variations in responses can significantly impact percentages. In Nevada, terms are negotiated, and payment is made to the brothel before services are provided, suggesting that clients may push for more services once payment has been secured. Additionally, brothel workers' frustration with splitting payments 50/50 with the house could be influencing these reports.

In the USA's criminalised settings, a significant proportion of workers report payment issues, with the UK closely following. Aotearoa New Zealand shows the lowest rates, yet it remains a concern in all areas.

Figure 4.6, shows how sex workers feel non-payment should be labelled. Even though sex workers view their work as work, allowing

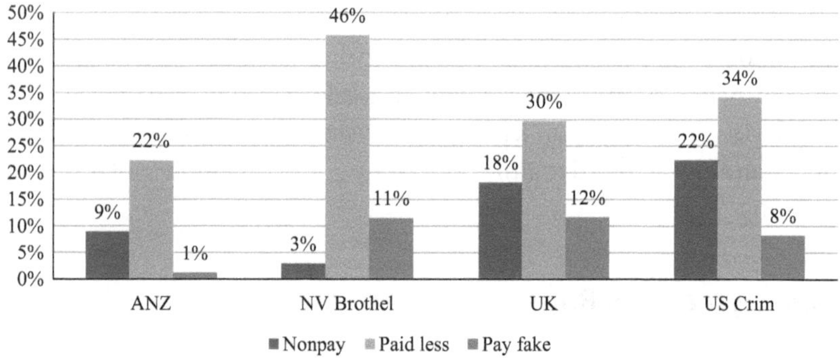

Fig. 4.5 Per cent of respondents who experienced a payment issue the last time it happened, by site

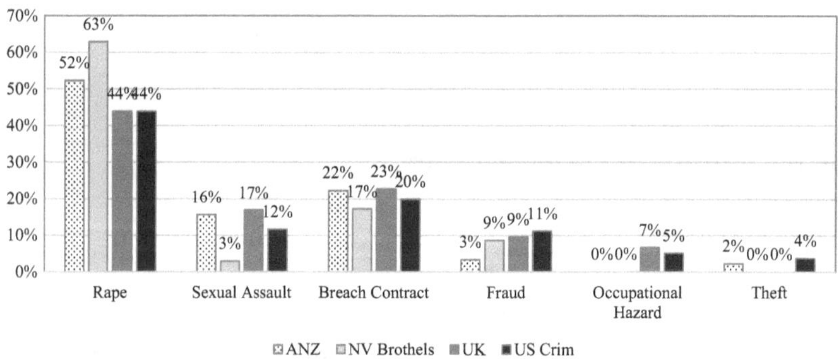

Fig. 4.6 Per cent of respondents who indicated that "if a sex worker has sex with a client, but they do not pay, it should be treated as...", by site

them to name violations to their contracts distinctly, non-payment is seen far less as a breach of contract, fraud, or theft, but as rape or sexual violence. Comparing countries, about two-thirds of respondents across all sites define non-payment as rape or sexual assault (ANZ 68%, Nevada brothels 68%, UK 61%, and USA criminalised 56%), while between one-quarter and one-third (ANZ 27%, Nevada brothels 26%, UK 32%, and USA criminalised 35%) see it as a workplace violation of breach of contract, fraud or theft.

In Nevada's legal brothels, a higher percentage of workers view non-payment as rape, possibly reflecting a broader trend in managed settings or influenced by the smaller sample size. Notably, only respondents in the USA and UK criminalised markets refer to non-payment as an occupational hazard, a categorisation entirely outside legal frames, which is significant given the larger sample sizes in these regions.

The above findings are important as we consider legal reforms related to non-payment in sex work. Should sex work be treated uniquely, as in Aotearoa New Zealand, or should it be regarded similarly to any other job, with sex viewed just like any other service? Understanding how sex workers perceive non-payment in their workplace is crucial for shaping these legal discussions.

Non-payment in Criminalised Contexts

UK sex workers like Paul, Halley, Sophia, and Harrison may have viewed non-payment as a violation of conditional consent, but, often, did not align these experiences with legally recognised harms. In the USA, difficulties with payment platforms due to FOSTA/SESTA and other anti-sex-work policies make existing problems with non-payment worse. Anti-trafficking measures restrict the use of credit cards for transactions related to sex work. Conversely, sex workers in Nevada's legal brothels, like those in other managed settings, are better positioned to secure payment from clients beforehand.

The interviews show a clear consensus among sex workers that non-payment is a severe violation—a form of violence. For instance:

> One time on the job, I was outsmarted, yes. At the end, the client didn't pay me and he absconded with my money and I wasn't able to contact him. Would I consider that an act of violence? Yes, I would. (Halley, UK, independent)

Harrison described a client who complained that his services were too 'pricey' and refused to pay:

> So that was violence, the only one. I was like, 'No, you don't short-change me; I will say that I was raped'. Well, actually, that was actually sexual violence at that moment. (Harrison, UK, independent)

Jessica described being given fake money:

> So I was really upset about it, because I'm like, 'Wow, I just did that for free'. And they just got [one] over on me, because I didn't check the money … Of course you feel violated, because the whole reasoning was to get something in return, so it's like they just got [one] over. (Jessica, USA, various)

Cody described a regular occurrence where police officers would demand services without payment, offering instead information on the next police stings:

> I used to work in a dungeon, which essentially operated like an illegal brothel but most of our clients were seeking full-service fetish-type work. We had cops who came there and they would do the same thing. They expected to have full sessions and not pay or full sessions with partial payment in exchange for insider information about when raids would happen, so that we could prepare ourselves. (Cody, USA, independent)

Anna (UK, street-based) told us that, in her trial, "basically the prosecution made it sound [like] I wasn't raped, I just weren't paid, do you know what I mean?".

Despite recognising these issues as serious violations, sex workers often find themselves outside the protection of the law, or, worse, abused by it.

Non-payment in Decriminalised and Legalised Settings

The stories Aotearoa New Zealand sex workers told us were a significant contrast to those of sex workers in the criminalised USA and UK settings—they had the backing of the law when they were not paid. Brothel workers (both in Aotearoa New Zealand and Nevada's legal brothels) and Aotearoa New Zealand independent sex workers can be paid via direct credit into their employer's or their own bank accounts. Illegal workers in the USA have few platforms available to take payment thanks to bills like FOSTA SESTA. Yet even brothel workers in decriminalised and legalised settings still experience the issue of underpayment. Respondents in Aotearoa New Zealand described how the client will take a screenshot of the deposit on their smartphone and show this to the sex worker on their arrival as proof of payment. There have been some instances in Aotearoa New Zealand specifically, however, where the client has reversed the transfer straight after taking the screenshot as banks provide a small window of possibility to do this; brothel workers, as opposed to independent workers, are less likely, though, to experience these problems. For sex workers working in legal brothels in Aotearoa New Zealand and Nevada, laws addressing payment are similar to those for other businesses. For independent workers in Aotearoa New Zealand, issues of non-payment can be taken to the small claim disputes tribunal as a civil case, but they need to know the legal identity and address of the client. If there is evidence of deception, for example, a doctored screenshot, the police can charge as fraud. However, non-payment is not formally regarded as a sexual violation.

Four respondents from Aotearoa New Zealand described incidences of non-payment, and each account provides some insights into why sex workers consider non-payment as rape. Eripaheti, an independent sex worker for two years, described some fake bank transfers and described it as "a theft of time and money; and it's pre-meditated, so that is pretty violent". The other three had the backing of the law to verify their interpretation of the non-payment.

Christine, who had worked in various sectors including street work off and on for 30 years, described an incident from the street 20 years ago, starting with a clear statement: "I've been raped". She described having provided services to a guy in his car; when he refused to pay, she gathered an unopened condom wrapper and his registration and told nearby police and he got a seven-year prison sentence. The police, who were nearby, reinforced her evaluation of the situation. Neither she nor the police, saw physical violence as being necessary for this to be defined as assault, although they may have considered the stealthing that was also involved as comprising an important component:

> [Int:] Were you injured? Did you have…?
> [Christine:] No, no, he just slapped me in the face, but there was no mark until the next day, and I said, 'Yeah, well it was what he done'. (Christine, ANZ, various)

Hunu, a trans-female, street-based sex worker, recounted how one client tried to get out of paying:

> He gave me some money and then like as he got to the ATM, he, like he thought that he could be a cunt and be like, 'Oh my gosh, oh no, this money's gone out of my account. Oh no, who's kind of, like, used my account?' (Hunu, ANZ, street-based)

Hunu had no qualms about defining this as a crime: "I did call the police on him, and I got them to come up actually to the ATM and I was like, 'No, motherfucker, you get my money out'…". She added that the police officers who assisted were "awesome" in validating her read of the situation:

> The other chick [police officer] was like, 'No, dude, like you can't expect her to fucking make you come and then not like pay her. What the hell, and then give her some more money. What the fuck'. She was like, 'Why don't you give her tip while you're at it?', you know? I was like, 'Fucking hell. Wow, you're awesome. I've never met anyone like you'. (Hunu, ANZ, street-based)

In contrast, Sheryl was confused initially regarding her experience, but the law helped her to eventually define this as violence. Sheryl was working independently in a house she rented by the hour and described a case of underpayment: "With my case that I went through the court system with, he underpaid me". She described the case:

> It was a regular client. Um, he underpaid me, so it was different that day. He'd just put the money down and came in and, you know, was quite violent and stuff. … So I didn't even know I had been underpaid or what not. Um, and then it just went from there, so, and then he left. And I sat there for a while thinking, 'Was this right? Was this wrong?' You know,

I knew deep down it was wrong, but I was in shock, I suppose. (Sheryl, ANZ, independent)

Nonetheless, she went to the police and said, "I want to report a sexual assault". The client was convicted and sentenced to 12 months supervision.

Conclusion

This chapter has explored two primary questions: What types of unwanted contact do sex workers most frequently encounter? And how does the law influence their understanding, interpretation, and definition of these incidents? By examining both survey data and interview data, we have gained insights into the complexities of naming and labelling violations in different legal contexts.

Our findings show that payment problems are the most commonly reported incidents of unwanted contact among sex workers who have experienced an incident, with 75.57% reporting at least one issue with payment in the past year. Despite the predominance of payment-related issues, sex workers also encounter a wide range of other incidents that span various levels of severity and types of contact outside of negotiated services.

Despite differences in the legal context, for the most part, sex workers in different locations report a similar range of incidents. However, there are a few differences. In decriminalised settings, sex workers are more likely to report unwanted penetration with an object or finger and stealthing, while those in criminalised contexts report higher instances of assault.

Despite the predominance of other kinds of contact, in interviews, sex workers were all most likely to respond to questions about incidents involving crime and sexual violence with recounts of the most violent of incidents. Their reflections on these incidents reveal how they draw on the law and a broader notion of legality in naming and understanding their experiences.

Three main conclusions emerge from this chapter. The first involves the relation between legal alienation and rape consciousness. Like other marginalised groups, sex workers experience legal alienation, viewing the law as arbitrary and often useless. However, their rape consciousness reflects a more nuanced relationship with the law. Distinguishing between unwanted contact as a violation of one's own boundaries and unwanted contact as a legally sanctioned crime is important as we move towards possible solutions. Interviews showed that sex workers' most certain recognition of an experience as criminal sexual violence hinged on injury and, where possible, verification by law enforcement. Thus, they possess a rape consciousness shaped by enduring social, cultural, and legal views that equate 'real rape' with force and injury. In this sense, sex workers are 'with the law', as their understanding of a serious violation is reinforced by legal norms and validation from law enforcement. Therefore, their naming at this level was not that different from non-sex workers, although given a particular accent by cultural views of female sex workers as women 'out of place'. This was consistent across all legal contexts. Given the low level of prosecuting successful sexual assault cases generally, this has implications for how we think about addressing severe sexual violence in sex work.

Second, however, this particular rape consciousness discussed above is not how they view all sexual violations. Unlike non-sex workers, sex workers exhibit a transactional legal consciousness separate from how they see sexual violations in their personal lives (Day, 1994). As we saw in Chapter 3, negotiating boundaries and conditions of consent are key components of their work. Sex workers define violations through these transactional obligations and consent agreements with clients. When clients breach these rules, sex workers see the event as a violation, regardless of whether it aligns with legal definitions of crime. This transactional perspective allows sex workers to minimise the confusion and shame often associated with recognising such incidents in personal contexts. This consciousness is particularly evident in decriminalised contexts, where the law supports and legitimises their transactional boundaries, reinforcing their ability to label and address violations confidently.

Finally, when it comes to defining non-payment, sex workers exhibit a legal consciousness that combines elements of what they believe the law should be with their personal boundaries. Far more sex workers label non-payment as rape or sexual violence, than they do violation of a contract, fraud or theft, reflecting an integration of their professional rules with broader notions of sexual consent and personal violation. In decriminalised settings, where legal frameworks explicitly recognise stealthing (under health codes) and non-payment (under civil codes) as violations (and in the case of stealthing, increasingly, as assault), sex workers are empowered to use these legal definitions to assert their rights and seek justice, leading to a broader and more inclusive understanding of sexual violence.

At the same time, we need to be circumspect about how we advocate for criminal justice solutions to unwanted contact experienced by sex workers. In some ways, we agree with Gash and Harding (2018) that prevailing legal rules of evidence and the conventional ideas about what constitutes a lack of consent can significantly affect victims' understandings of violation and, as we see in Chapters 5 and 6, restrict the options available for legal recourse and healing. This is true across all legal contexts.

The legal context does, however, impact sex workers' understanding and actions. In decriminalised settings like Aotearoa New Zealand, where stealthing and non-payment are recognised by law at some level, sex workers are, as said above, empowered to use legal definitions to name and address violations. This broader legal recognition enables sex workers to have a more expansive notion of violation and a stronger alignment with legal protections. The emerging trend of prosecuting stealthing as sexual violence in Aotearoa New Zealand appears to empower sex workers, giving them greater capacity to recognise these incidents as constituting violations and articulate their experiences accordingly.

References

Ahrens, C. E. (2006). Being silenced: The impact of negative social reactions on the disclosure of rape. *American Journal of Community Psychology, 38*(3–4), 31–34. https://doi.org/10.1007/s10464-006-9069-9

Assange v Swedish Prosecution Authority. (2011). EWHC 2849 (Admin). Retrieved July 4, 2023, from: https://www.supremecourt.uk/cases/docs/uksc-2011-0264-judgment.pdf

Brodsky, A. (2017). 'Rape-adjacent': Imagining legal responses to nonconsensual condom removal. *Columbia Journal of Gender and Law, 32*(2), 183–210. https://doi.org/10.7916/d8708d06

Calavita, K., & Jenness, V. (2013). Inside the pyramid of disputes: Naming problems and filing grievances in California prisons. *Social Problems, 60*(1), 50–80.

Chua, L. J., & Engel, D. M. (2019). Legal consciousness reconsidered. *Annual Review of Law and Social Science, 15*(1), 335–353. https://doi.org/10.1146/annurev-lawsocsci-101518-042717

Coates, D., & Penrod, S. (1981). Social psychology and the emergence of disputes. *Law & Society Review, 15*(3/4), 655–680. https://doi.org/10.2307/3053506

Comte, J. (2014). Decriminalization of sex work: Feminist discourses in light of research. *Sexuality & Culture, 18*(1), 196–217. https://doi.org/10.1007/s12119-013-9174-5

Crown Prosecution Service (CPS). (2021). *Rape and sexual offences—Chapter 6: Consent*. Retrieved June 20, 2024, from: https://www.cps.gov.uk/legal-guidance/rape-and-sexual-offences-chapter-6-consent

Davis, K. C., Hammett, J. F., Chen, W., Stewart, R., & Kirwan, M. (2024). A scoping review of nonconsensual condom removal ('stealthing') research. *Trauma, Violence, & Abuse, 152483802211468*. https://doi.org/10.1177/15248380221146802

Day, S. (1994). What counts as rape? Physical assault and broken contracts: Contrasting views of rape among London sex workers. In P. Harvey & P. Gow (Eds.), *Sex and Violence: Issues in Representation and Experience* (pp. 172–189). Routledge.

Du Bois, W. E. B. (1903). *The souls of black folk*. A.C. McClurg & Co.

Estrich, S. (1987). *Real rape: How the legal system victimizes women who say no.* Harvard University Press.

Ewick, P., & Silbey, S. S. (1998). *The common place of law: Stories from everyday life*. University of Chicago Press.

Felstiner, W. L. F., Abel, R. L., & Sarat, A. (1980). The emergence and transformation of disputes: Naming, blaming, claiming… *Law & Society Review, 15*(3/4), 631–654. https://doi.org/10.2307/3053505

Gash, A., & Harding, R. (2018). #MeToo? Legal discourse and everyday responses to sexual violence. *Laws, 7*(2), 21. https://doi.org/10.3390/laws7020021

Gómez-Durán, E. L., & Martin-Fumadó, C. (2024). Nonconsensual condom-use deception: An empirically based conceptualization of stealthing. *Trauma, Violence, & Abuse, 152483802211417*. https://doi.org/10.1177/15248380221141731

Hertogh, M. (2018). *Nobody's law: Legal consciousness and legal alienation in everyday life*. Palgrave Pivot.

Latimer, R. L., Vodstrcil, L. A., Fairley, C. K., Cornelisse, V. J., Chow, E. P. F., Read, T. R. H., & Bradshaw, C. S. (2018). Non-consensual condom removal, reported by patients at a sexual health clinic in Melbourne, Australia. *PLoS ONE, 13*(12), e0209779. https://doi.org/10.1371/journal.pone.0209779

Lévesque, S., Rousseau, C., & Dumerchat, M. (2021). Influence of the relational context on reproductive coercion and the associated consequences. *Violence against Women, 27*(6–7), 828–850. https://doi.org/10.1177/1077801220917454

National Institute of Justice. (2016). Five things about deterrence. *U.S. Department of Justice Office of Justice Programs*. Retrieved May 24, 2024, from: https://www.ojp.gov/pdffiles1/nij/247350.pdf

Oberweis, T., Henry, D., Griner, S., & Gorislavsky, E. (2021). Making the call: College students' legal consciousness and hypothetical activation of police for sexual assaults. *Violence against Women, 27*(12–13), 2399–2423. https://doi.org/10.1177/10778012211021121

Patterson, D., Greeson, M., & Campbell, R. (2009). Understanding rape survivors' decisions not to seek help from formal social systems. *Health & Social Work, 34*(2), 127–136. https://doi.org/10.1093/hsw/34.2.127

Peleg-Koriat, I., & Klar-Chalamish, C. (2022). Sexual offense victims' responses to the question #WhyIDidntReport? Examining restorative justice as an alternative dispute resolution mechanism. *Conflict Resolution Quarterly, 40*(3), 295–312. https://doi.org/10.1002/crq.21369

R v Campos. (2021). NZDC 7422. Retrieved July 5, 2024, from: https://www.districtcourts.govt.nz/all-judgments/2021-nzdc-7422-r-v-campos/

Spohn, C. (2020). Sexual assault case processing: The more things change, the more they stay the same. *International Journal for Crime, Justice and Social Democracy, 9*(1), 86–94. https://doi.org/10.5204/ijcjsd.v9i1.1454

Stevens, R. (2022). 'Stealthing' case: Convicted rapist loses appeal against jail term after removing condom during sex. *New Zealand Herald*. Retrieved

July 11, 2024, from: https://www.nzherald.co.nz/nz/stealthing-case-convicted-rapist-loses-appeal-against-jail-term-after-removing-condom-during-sex/KYCSBNMHDLWAGOXGMLJTECVSX4/

Wilson, L. C., & Miller, K. E. (2016). Meta-analysis of the prevalence of unacknowledged rape. *Trauma, Violence, & Abuse, 17*(2), 149–159. https://doi.org/10.1177/1524838015576391

5

After the Violation: Sex Workers' Responses to Unwanted Incidents

Teela Sanders, Harriet Smailes, Barbara G. Brents, Gillian Abel, and Jane Scoular

Introduction: Sex Workers Managing Sex Work

Over the past few decades, an increasingly identifiable theme in the literature has been the complex ways in which sex workers manage their business—from broader entrepreneurial approaches (particularly

T. Sanders (✉) · H. Smailes
University of Leicester, Leicester, UK
e-mail: teela.sanders@leicester.ac.uk

B. G. Brents
University of Nevada, Las Vegas, Nevada, USA

G. Abel
University of Otago, Dunedin, New Zealand

J. Scoular
Strathclyde Law School, University of Strathclyde, Glasgow, UK

T. Sanders et al. (eds.), *Voicing Consent*, Palgrave Advances in Sex Work Studies,
https://doi.org/10.1007/978-3-031-77715-8_5

when sex work moved to predominantly being advertised online), to the often intricate personal engagement with clients before, during and after the sexual service (Bernstein, 2001; Day, 2007; Jones, 2015). These strategies of prevention, deterrence, and protection have been described by Sanders (2004a) in ways that demonstrate the complexities of how sex workers look after themselves, particularly in a criminalised setting where self-protection strategies are, in the main, left to the individual. It is already well evidenced how sex workers become managers of their own physical and emotional health and risks (Pyett & Warr, 1999; Sanders, 2004b), and we have continued to document this in Chapter 3. We hope to expand this literature through our focus on asking what actions sex workers take after there is a breach of contract/agreement in the sexual encounter, especially in cases of non-payment and financial discrepancies, condom removal, and non-consensual touching—the most prevalent experiences from this participant group.

We know that sex workers spend much of their working lives setting out boundaries, whether this be through their marketing online or in person through negotiated arrangements. Chapter 3 explored how sex workers negotiated with potential clients prior to sexual encounters. These negotiations established boundaries, helped sex workers distinguish between personal and professional identities (Brewis & Linstead, 2000; Day, 2007), manage expectations with clients, and determine the terms of the sexual contract—for example, outlining the particular services they will and will not offer. Associated costs, location, timing/duration, and safety features such as condom use are typical conditions to be agreed upon in advance. These negotiations form the basis of the commercial arrangement, establishing conditions of consent.

Sex workers emphasised that consent must be ongoing. If an activity breached their boundaries, made them uncomfortable, violated agreed-upon conditions, or turned out to be something they didn't want to do, they had the right to withdraw—just as anyone in a non-commercial context would. Any additional services would need to be negotiated on the spot. What Halley, for example, stated was a common point made by sex workers in all jurisdictions: "If it's something I don't want to do, I politely tell them and if they refuse, I might just have to pick up my things and leave" (Halley, UK, independent).

While Halley demonstrated confidence, this was not always the case for her—nor is it always the case for others. Sex workers' responses to customer breaches evolve with experience. Initially, new sex workers might accept behaviours they hadn't agreed to. Over time, they learn to refuse or react differently in similar situations. We delve into how their reactions change as they become more aware of the power dynamics at play and how to address bad behaviour. By understanding formal government laws, workplace policies and culture, and informal norms, sex workers become more empowered. Ongoing conditional consent, which is just beginning to be recognised in formal legal rulings (see Chapter 2), plays a crucial role in this empowerment.

In Chapter 4, we discussed the types of unwanted contact sex workers experience and how they define boundary breaches. Common experiences like unwanted condom removal, or "stealthing", are considered serious violations. However, interpretations of these breaches vary based on local laws and legal norms, with sex workers in criminalised areas often only recognising serious injury or force as violations.

In Chapter 5, we focus on the actions taken when breaches occur. Guided by a framework of legal consciousness, we explore how sex workers decide on their next steps, influenced by concepts of legal alienation and legal mobilisation (e.g. Hertogh, 2018). Hertogh's approach to "legal alienation" considers alternative forms of redress, such as informal enforcement of boundaries, while others may seek formal legal mobilisation—using legal strategies individually or collectively (Lehoucq & Taylor, 2019). The responses from participants highlight the significant impact of social norms and expectations on how sex workers respond to violations and whether they engage with the law.

Felstiner and colleagues' framework of 'naming, blaming, claiming' (1980) is, therefore, also considered, in order to be able to discuss how, on an individual level, sex workers in this study work through their responses to the violations they experience. This framework acknowledges that individuals must work through stages of identifying a behaviour as harmful (naming—discussed in Chapter 4), holding an individual responsible through some action (blaming), and seeking remedial action from the individual responsible or through another remedy, such as criminal justice (claiming). There is, however, attrition through this process, and, of course, some will not be in a position to even 'name' the harm in the first instance. This has been well reflected through our interviews, as we saw in Chapters 3 and 4, where (particularly less experienced) sex workers may have a much narrower/more limited understanding of what constitutes inappropriate or even illegal conduct. Over time, and through becoming more experienced, sex workers develop an armoury of tools to not just protect themselves and potentially prevent harm, but be more confidently able to respond to crimes/harms through the resolution options they have available to them. These were likely to be individual strategies, rather than those taken by workplaces, which were more closely connected to the legal context of sex work in each jurisdiction. The reality is, as we saw in Chapter 4, that most sex workers suffer in silence and are stuck at the 'naming' stage of understanding the violations that have happened against them. Taken together, *how* sex workers name, blame, and claim and *whether* they invoke the law (either formally or informally)—which is affected by their perceptions and understanding of the 'law'—results in differing actions in response to breaches: 'no action', 'informal action', and 'formal action'. While responses are categorised discretely for the purpose of this chapter, they can, more realistically, be considered as falling along a continuum. It is also worth saying that it is not our intention to suggest that any particular kind of response should be viewed as the 'correct' one.

Sex Workers' Responses to Violations

No Action

As we saw in Chapter 4, non-payment and condom removal were regularly experienced as harmful violations. However, few sex workers enforced any action where they were working in criminalised or semi-criminalised settings, which contrasted with those sex workers we spoke to in Aotearoa New Zealand (where sex work is decriminalised). Cody (USA, independent) described an incident where she was drugged and gang raped when she first started working as an independent escort. She never reported this because, as she said, "It was definitely one of those messy situations where I would never have been considered the perfect victim in order to pursue any legal recourse". In the UK, Linda, who, at the time of the interview, had worked the streets for 25 years, noted: "Yeah, but I have been attacked a few times, badly, but you've got instinct and try and go somewhere kind of safe".

Generally speaking, the sex workers we spoke to in Aotearoa New Zealand appear to be much more aware of their legal rights and of available pathways of action. As explored in Chapter 2, the context of legalisation in Aotearoa New Zealand, notably that sex workers have the same health and employment benefits as any other employee, informed and shaped their legal consciousness in this setting. Also, those aware of the stipulations under the legislation will know that condom use is an essential condition of consent with Aotearoa New Zealand sex workers. Their knowledge of their rights under the Prostitution Reform Act (PRA) empowered them: "… 'Well this directly breaches the PRA, you know, Section 9, up to 1, 3 and 4.' You know, it's not okay. I screamed at him [the client]" (Carrie, ANZ, independent). One participant specifically reflected how having that legislation in place, and being able to say "… 'Well actually, it's against the law to not use a condom' …", is important as it "gives sex workers lots of power" (Kat, ANZ, various). This could suggest, therefore, that the degree to which sex workers feel less able or willing to mobilise the law with respect to clients not using condoms is affected by the legal context in which they work. The way the power in an interaction may also be more on the side of the sex worker from there being legislation in place (to protect their rights) may also prevent such breaches in the future. But still in the Aotearoa New Zealand setting, there was a sense (like in the other case-study jurisdictions) that violations of agreements against sex workers happened so frequently that it would not be possible to tell the police:

> I couldn't tell you how many times someone's like licked or kissed or whatever, and there's, you know, an expectation that we laugh it off or whatever. Um, and I can't be bothered going to the police for every time that happens, 'cause I'd be going in pretty much every booking … Like, that's just, unfortunately, that's the reality of that job, but I think I manage it pretty well now. But yeah, if someone does that, I will say,

> 'Okay, so that's my extra price', and then they're like, 'Pardon?' I'm like, 'Well you clearly want to do it, so you know, you're going to pay for it now'. (Kat, ANZ, various)

Few sex workers reported taking any action when clients had removed a condom. Paul, a trans-male sex worker (UK, independent), considered, when deciding whether or not to take action, if he was engaging with a regular client; he did not want to lose the security of regular work, despite the client not adhering to the conditions that had been outlined: "… someone who just didn't put [the condom] on … I didn't want to disrupt the relationship because regular clients are like gold". Two female sex workers, one of whom worked in a criminalised setting, the other a semi-criminalised setting, told us stories of how condoms have been removed; in both cases, however, they said they did not report such incidents. Regardless of legal context, other factors often were more important: job security and regular income, as well as maintaining relationships with clients. Financial vulnerability and not wanting to jeopardise future income can be considered both as a reason that individuals may be targeted and as a circumstance that shapes legal mobilisation in response to a breach by someone with the power to impact an individual's financial position (Blackstone et al., 2009).

This apparent reluctance to report a breach such as stealthing provides an important example of how decisions and actions taken must all be contextualised by an understanding of the dynamic nature of sex workers' legal consciousness (Blackstone et al., 2009). This is shown throughout the book, in quotes from sex workers reflecting on how they develop an understanding of the formal law through having engaged in criminal processes themselves (see more in Chapter 6), or being exposed to systems and information in different ways. The process through 'naming, shaming, claiming' is not linear, and responses on whether or not to mobilise are not necessarily binary.

Reasons for No Action: Personal Responsibility and Understanding Rights

What is notable in our study is the degree of personal responsibility taken by sex workers when boundaries had been overstepped or conditions not respected by clients. What could be viewed as sexual offences were often excused by sex workers or written off as their lack of experience in handling clients. Learning to say 'no' to establish boundaries came with experience. When boundaries were breached, sex workers understood these, variously, as violations of the terms of agreement, a lack of respect, sexual assault, and violence. Most took incredible amounts of personal responsibility for these breaches—rarely did the respondents explicitly identify their experiences as legally recognisable harms: "It was a very hard learning curve of 'Wow, I have to learn how to not do this again'" (Cody, USA, independent). Chanelle (ANZ, various) recounted a time where she was stealthed. She considered it embarrassing, and felt she should have prevented the incident; moreover, she believed that the formal law could be used against her case:

> It took me a while to tell people, because I was just embarrassed about it, 'cause I was like, 'No, like, how could I let him have done that'. It's actually a little bit embarrassing. And also [there] was the part of it where it's, like, illegal to do that, and I was, like, 'Well, I don't, I don't want anyone to think that I was purposely trying to break the law'. (Chanelle, ANZ, various)

In criminalised settings, unwanted sexual contact was seen as an inevitable part of the job for some sex workers, particularly those who worked in a street environment. Unwanted contact was also positioned as avoidable and a matter of individuals 'just' having to learn from the experience and not let it happen again. In our analysis of the USA interviews, respondents more often treated violations as learning experiences that helped them to develop protective practices that could shield them from future harm. There were accounts of actually learning how to become more empowered when setting boundaries and enforcing them informally. Yet, for many, the way the risks of sexual assault are experienced by the individual/personally is crucial in terms of access to justice. Violations were sometimes understood as an 'occupational hazard' in which no responsibility was laid on the perpetrator; rather, they placed all of it on themselves. Jessica and Abigail reflect on their experiences in the USA:

> Because it's not legalised, and we're doing it illegally, you don't have anybody to call, report. It's not even like they're going to care. Usually, we don't report things, unless like ... I've had a friend that had been strangled, or things like that. (Jessica, USA, various)
> I think you learn through experience how to gauge clients in the bar, and how they're going to interact once you get them behind closed doors, and I hadn't really learned that yet. Even just as women in general, I don't think we really — I don't know how to finish that sentence … And we've been taught since childhood that we need to be the responsible ones and things are our fault. (Abigail, USA, Nevada legal brothel)

The discourse around what to do if clients breach consent in USA legal brothels differed somewhat from the decriminalised Aotearoa New Zealand setting. If things went wrong, the USA sex workers we spoke to tended to believe it was their responsibility to act in response to whatever happened. Their reaction was that *they* needed to reach the alarm sooner, be clearer in their negotiations with clients, and accept that there were consequences to working in the sex industry. The USA sex workers had a strong narrative of individual coping and of accepting the consequences of taking part in an activity that is socially condemned and (outside of Nevada brothels) unregulated and illegal:

> You are selling yourself and yes, you're consenting to it. It's a grey area because it's not rape, it's not something you're not giving over, but it *is* transactional, so there is something in that, that you have to be really mentally be prepared for, to commit to and accept that there might be consequences later on down the road. (Elisa, USA, dancing)

The element of personal responsibility was also linked to how sex workers may have a reliance on their clients and, in particular, may benefit from the regularity of certain clients. Paul explains when he was new to selling sex it was difficult to assert boundaries when feeling inexperienced and when indebted to regular clients:

> ... that was quite early on and I didn't feel comfortable enough at the time to say anything. But yeah, then afterwards I was, like, 'Look, I have said everywhere, all over my profile, that it's always safe. That is a limit that I'll never not want to be safe'. And the client, it was a client I'd seen a couple of times and I think that made it harder than if it was a new client ... (Paul, UK, independent)

While Paul was clear that wearing a condom was a condition of consent and the client should have known this, he did not want to jeopardise that relationship because, as has been noted previously in this chapter, "regular clients are like gold". He did not disrupt that encounter while it was happening, but he did send a text message to the client later, noting that it's "much easier for [him] to do things by text"—"things", in this context, including the communication of boundaries. When, after this story, we asked if he had experienced any sexual violence, he replied, "No". He did not see that incidence as sexual violence.

Sex workers' differing levels of understanding of formal law (gained from both personal experience and the case law) in terms of understanding their legal rights and rights around consent became clear through the interviews. Alongside the quotes already discussed in relation to understanding stealthing and payment rights, it is apparent that an understanding of their rights was something that developed for sex workers—from perhaps considerably less knowledge when they first started working, to a more explicit understanding of thresholds for formal recourse. This can lead sex workers from a state of 'no action' when incidents happen to a greater legal mobilisation:

> I didn't understand what actually pertained meeting this threshold to get a conviction. I thought you can't get a conviction for someone biting you. Now I know you fucking can. I didn't know that, but you can. (Talia, ANZ, brothel)

As Talia engaged with the police on this occasion, her understanding of the law increased, which empowered her both to inform colleagues she worked with in the brothel and act on negative behaviour in the future. But legal processes could still be met with bafflement, disempowering sex workers even if the law was there to assist. Some sex workers discussed themselves, or other workers, not recognising that what had happened to them as sexual assault or rape, as many brushed off the incidents that happen in their sex work:

> I don't understand everything that went on legally. … If I understood, I really understood the process, maybe I'd be able to point out something. But I don't understand it. I just went with it. (Jane, ANZ, brothel)

There was a strong sense of 'legal alienation'—a disconnect of sorts from formal law and the justice system (Hertogh, 2018)—something not uncommon in participants of this project. This type of alienation, sometimes considered more specifically as 'legal meaninglessness' (Genn 1999 in Hertogh, 2011), can be exacerbated by the sex worker not identifying behaviours in a way that would lead them towards some kind of formal legal process. In fact, it has been suggested that perpetrators may target individuals, particularly in the context of sexual violence, whom they believe are less likely to mobilise the law when subjected to incidents and crimes (Blackstone et al., 2009).

This recollection from Jane demonstrates the impact of others on an individual's perception and potential mobilisation of formal recourse following a breach of contract and, in the case above, a breach of the law. With workplace harassment and abuse, the relationships that individuals have outside of their place of work are as important as workplace relationships with regard to being able to act after an event (Blackstone et al., 2009). In fact, closeness with colleagues has been suggested as a predictor for formal legal mobilisation concerning sexual harassment (Blackstone et al., 2009). This is, indeed, evident in this study, where sex workers described developing understanding as a consequence of discussions with co-workers and/or friends or family, and then feeling more confident in potential decisions to pursue formal actions. For example, Chanelle—who, earlier in this section, related having initially felt too embarrassed to tell others she had been stealthed—revealed that, when she did eventually confide in her workplace colleagues about the incident, their support helped her to feel that she could take a different approach in the event of any similar future breaches:

> I think it's because my boss, like, I know she will stand by me, and I know that, like, the girls there will also stand by me. And yeah, I feel like the process would be a lot easier and just having the support there... (Chanelle, ANZ, various)

This is an example of influences on legal consciousness, where the impact of input from others, on what is 'right' and 'wrong', can be considered important in informing an individual's understanding of their rights (Young, 2014). Even if, for example, an individual does not want to, or believe they can, mobilise formal law, developing their own understanding around what they will tolerate is important, as we saw in Chapter 4. In developing this personal understanding, more formal action may, therefore, be taken in the event of a potential future breach. However, while the close structure of the workplace can help to facilitate such mobilisation, it can also sometimes offer challenges to its realisation, even within a legalised context such as Aotearoa New Zealand:

> But yeah, once he'd [perpetrator] left, I — 'cause I had a partner at the time too — I had actually told them [workplace] and then I had phoned him [partner]. He had shot over and only when he arrived, when he was like, 'We're calling the police', that's when I realised we should call the police. I didn't even think, like, we weren't going to call the police until he arrived actually... Um, and the receptionist didn't want to call the police. (Alice, ANZ, various)

This recount of an incident shows the type of uninformed legal alienation (Hertogh, 2018, p. 57) that sex workers experience even in a country that has had over twenty years of decriminalisation. Yet, it was this very legal context that empowered people around Alice to act through informal channels. Brothels in Aotearoa New Zealand provide a more supportive setting for sex workers, meaning that information is more accessible compared to other countries, and that agencies are working together closer and in a more collaborative framework. The fact that, even in this more relaxed legal setting, sex workers still may not fully understand their rights—and be supported to enact them—shows how limited the opportunities for recourse can be for sex workers in partially or fully criminalised jurisdictions. This demonstrates the importance of a combination of providing information to sex workers and supportive structures around the sex workers, which, together, affirm and enable these workers to take action through the mobilisation of formal resolution, if required.

Informal Action

It was the preference of some of the sex workers we spoke with to take some action in relation to breaches, but these fell towards the 'informal' end of the reporting spectrum. Sex workers displayed a number of tactics in this sense, including trying to educate clients about risks and rights and also trying to pass on information to less experienced sex workers, particularly migrants who may be unaware of the cultural and legal norms of the workplace setting. One example of educating clients was recalled by Abbey (USA, independent), where she described a client who had started strangling/choking her. He was autistic and someone who 'watches a lot of BDSM porn'. She was able to immediately stop him and lectured him on how wrong that was, "and he apologised profusely and I was like 'Don't ever do that with a sex worker, don't ever do that with a girlfriend, don't ever do that to a woman'".

How ongoing contact with clients was managed was another example of informal action. Some tried to lead by example when there was a breach, with the interaction quickly being terminated:

> ... 'Service is over, mate because you've took the piss. You took a liberty because obviously, I want you to use a condom, that's why I put the condom on you; if I was willing to do it without a condom, I wouldn't have put the condom on you, so therefore you're taking the piss. So guess what? The service is over'... (Anna, UK, street-based)

Others who were experienced revealed how they would not shy away from physically handling the client to remove him from the situation:

> And then he tried charging at me, charging at my money, and I ended up clipping him by the back of the neck and forcing him out of the room. And lucky being a big girl, like, I had that, 'cause if I was 40 kg or 50 kgs, I don't know. That was, I guess, another thing in making me want to report it, is that like I felt quite lucky in the fact of being bigger in that situation, that that was handled a lot better than him overpowering me. (Erihapeti, ANZ, independent)

This type of response may seem surprising, given the risks posed to sex workers regarding the possibility of physical or sexual assault. However, the above examples demonstrate the impact of different influences on the actions that sex workers take in response to a breach. For some, the view is that "… if I had to choose between being assaulted or not being paid, I'd rather be assaulted" (Carrie, ANZ, independent). This suggests that perhaps some form of action may be taken either way, but the decision around how to mobilise, and for what purpose, is driven by personal priorities, and finance is a very important priority for many.

Sophia (UK, independent) had had experiences of clients removing condoms, but also said she had no intention of ever reporting such incidents, aside from telling sex-worker support groups. It was accepted as part of the job: "There's nothing I can do". Clients would and do often make excuses, she told us—that they "got carried away" or the condom had "fallen off". Sophia talked about clients removing condoms "sneakily": "they won't just take it off in front of you because they don't want the confrontation". Sophia further noted that this rule was difficult to enforce in those situations where a client was intimidating. Additionally, there is the fact that UK-based sex workers mostly operate in a semi-criminalised setting, working alone and outside the law. Notably, the power difference between the female sex worker and the male client when working in an isolated environment indoors is significant, and the risks are considerable when trying to fight back:

> It is bad but there's nothing you can do when there's a six foot five man in front of you in your apartment that you've rented. You can't cause a scene because you've got other clients after him, so there's nothing really you can do other than report it to National Ugly Mugs and put it on ClientEye… There's nothing you can do. I've had it where the client's

> tried and gone in without the condom and I've said, 'Put this on'. 'Oh no, just leave that'. And I'm like, 'No, you need to put it on or I'll leave' and they've already paid you. So they don't want you to leave because they know they're not getting their money back. So that's all you can do really. But if I've got a man saying, 'No, I'm not wearing it' and he's massive, I'm just going to do it because there's nothing I can do. (Sophia, UK, independent)

In the USA, Jessica (various) had, similarly, experienced a stealthing incident but rather than report this to the police, she tried to get more money from the client:

> Everything was fine until the session ended, and I noticed he had pulled the condom off, but he made it look like he was just pulling it off because we were done. But at the same time, it was just too quickly… And I started flipping out on him, and I'm like, 'Well, people charge extra for that… So you need to give me more money'. And then I'm like, 'That's wrong, you don't do that'. I just started going off on him, and then made him give me more money. After that situation, I get very upset when there have been times like that. There's been about probably two times that that's happened in my career. (Jessica, USA, various)

The ways in which sex workers attempted to control the situation and take some form of action—in the form of more informal resolutions—reflects the boundary setting imposed earlier in the interaction with clients, with the ultimate aim of keeping themselves safe while still making money. However, there was a larger and damaging cultural narrative that they had to constantly work against, which presented an everyday threat for many sex workers, particularly those working on the street. The experiences shared by participants, therefore, demonstrate different perceptions and approaches connected with the legal jurisdictions in which they work, but also closely connected with the type of sex work in which they are engaged.

Erihapeti, a mixed race 25-year-old Aotearoa New Zealand sex worker who had been working for about two years, told a story about being robbed at gunpoint after a shift at work. She explained equivocating in the wake of the incident about whether she should have reported it; she had decided not to. However, a subsequent conversation with a girlfriend really changed her mind about whether this had been the right decision:

> I guess I just didn't report it 'cause, I don't know, I never really had heaps of faith in that cops could or would do something. And, um, my girlfriend working, she just, she reined it in on me that that was just not okay. Um, like you need to report it, and then that got me thinking about, I guess, um, yeah, not reporting things and going, 'Fuck, I should of'. And that's when that incident happened last year. Well, as soon as the fellow got out of my room, that was my first thought was like needing to report it. (Erihapeti, ANZ, independent)

In a separate incident (mentioned earlier in this section), Erihapeti recalled dealing with a drunk client who 'just got too handsy' and kept asking for 'natural' sex. Having someone ask multiple times for no condom was nothing new, she said: "We'd gone in to do it, yeah, gone into doggie, and he'd taken off the condom, and I just had real funny feelings in it and then, yeah, I jumped back and then I got real like, 'Get out, get out' ...". She went on to say she was thankful she was bigger than him and able to force him out of the room. But that made it more clear to her that she needed to report this because the opposite scenario could have happened, where he could have overpowered her. However, she found the reporting to be overwhelming and almost gave up, but she kept at it, citing her friend's response to her previous non-reporting as a motivating factor: 'It was just like something you have to do, and yeah, like after hearing my friend just be quite disappointed in me for not reporting the gun incident' (Erihapeti, ANZ, independent). This story is a good example of the decision-making process involved in mobilising the law, which, for Erihapeti, was supported by relying on conversations with others, as well as reflecting on past breaches; against this backdrop, she had decided to formally report the incident rather than to continue treating it as something she 'should' just deal with on her own.

Informal Avenues of Support

So far this chapter has explored the actions that are taken by sex workers when consent has been violated or a condition agreed upon is breached. Knowing that very few sex workers ever report to the police (see Chapter 6), we wanted to investigate if there were any other routes to support—more akin to informal action—that were drawn on when a violation occurred. In support of the interviews conducted, results from our survey data (see Chapter 1 for an overview of our methodology and Chapter 9 for a more thorough discussion) demonstrate the avenues of support sex workers may take, aside from reporting to the police. Table 5.1 suggests that sex workers were more likely to tell another sex worker (39% for all sites) than law enforcement, or friends and family about what happened and find support through their colleagues and peer community. This represented the highest proportion of responses, compared to other avenues for disclosure, although personal relationships emerged as a source of confidence to a similar degree (35%). However, notably, nearly a quarter of the sample told no one at all, confirming the isolating nature of sex work across all jurisdictions. This finding is significant as it points to the fact that a quarter of sampled sex workers experience sexual violations and harms and never tell anyone, suffering in silence and harbouring these violent experiences.

It is a significant finding is that mainstream sexual violence support charities were seldom mentioned by sex workers: 3% of the whole sample (n = 14) referred to telling a mainstream sexual violence charity, such as Rape Crisis, about an incident. There are different possible reasons for this, one being (as has been discussed in Chapter 4) experiences may or may not be labelled as sexual violence by the victim. Those specialist services may be seen as more or less relevant to sex workers' needs. What this may also suggest, however, is that there is considerable work to be done by these services to welcome sex workers into the remit of their support and reduce stigma towards workers who are subjected to sexual harms in their occupation.

While we suspected that specialist support projects would be the preferred route of support for sex workers, these numbers were also relatively low: 12% in ANZ; 22% in the UK; 6% in the USA. The

Table 5.1 'After this happened (last time), who did you tell?'

Who did you tell?	ANZ %	ANZ N	UK %	UK N	USA Crim %	USA Crim N	NV Brothel %	NV Brothel N	All Sites %	All sites N
I didn't tell anyone	17.78	**16**	30.43	**42**	25.00	**55**	14.29	**5**	24.43	**118**
My partner, friend, or family member	35.56	**32**	32.61	**45**	37.73	**83**	22.86	**8**	34.78	**168**
Another sex worker	63.33	**57**	36.96	**51**	33.18	**73**	25.71	**9**	39.34	**190**
A sex-worker organisation (e.g. Ugly Mugs, SWOP Behind Bars, NZPC)	12.22	**11**	22.46	**31**	6.36	**14**	2.86	**1**	11.80	**57**
A manager or someone who you worked for	41.11	**37**	1.45	**2**	6.36	**14**	11.43	**4**	11.80	**57**
A sexual violence support charity (e.g., Rape Crisis)	3.33	**3**	3.62	**5**	2.27	**5**	2.86	**1**	2.90	**14**
A hospital, clinic, health service (e.g. doctor, Sexual Assault Referral Centre—SARC)	6.67	**6**	12.32	**17**	5.00	**11**	2.86	**1**	7.25	**35**
Police	0.00	**0**	2.92	**4**	0.91	**2**	0.00	**0**	1.24	**6**
Total		**90**		**164**		**180**		**22**		**456**

number may be relatively high in the UK due to the prominence of the third-party reporting scheme, National Ugly Mugs, who offer a range of support services for sex workers, particularly after crimes and incidents. Our recruitment methods for the survey in the UK via sex work support projects could also account for this higher number. In the USA, there may be less specialist support services given the emphasis on trafficking and the rescue industry, leaving little support for harm reduction and sexual violence projects per se. In other findings, only 7% of the whole sample told a hospital, doctor, or clinic—although this low response may be because injuries sustained, if any, did not always need a medical response.

Combining these survey findings with qualitative interview data is, however, important as it could be argued that even while the numbers seeking support are low, those who *do* seek support may still have positive experiences in doing so. For instance, after having been stealthed, Chanelle from Aotearoa New Zealand noted how she was "very grateful for the health services and that they would just go and get that sorted out" (Chanelle, ANZ, various). That being said, the very low engagement of sex workers in support services is a significant worry and suggests much work needs to be done regarding reaching out to this group, improving accessibility of services for sex workers, and providing a non-judgemental service for those who experience harms in sex work.

While the survey did not suggest that sex workers in Aotearoa New Zealand report to the police any more than other jurisdictions (explored further in Chapter 6), the qualitative data is much more reassuring in relation to sex workers here knowing their rights, knowing when consent has been breached and knowing what can be done in those situations. There is a better understanding around stealthing and non-payment issues among sex workers in Aotearoa New Zealand, and around recognising how this aligns with formal law, but there remains hesitancy around engaging in the criminal justice process. These sex workers understand how difficult it can be to actually achieve justice without very specific witnesses or evidence. This can be very discouraging for those sex workers who do consider reporting, as they know that it is very difficult to attain the justice they deserve. This can contribute to barriers to reporting, as the process can be traumatic and time-consuming, with extensive delays, and getting an outcome can feel unlikely.

Workplace Actions: Third Parties and Cultural Expectations

Up until this part of the chapter, we have largely discussed and focused on individual sex-worker actions in adopting tactics to mitigate or deal with violations as and when they occur and also actions taken in their aftermath. However, we also note from the analysis that there is a collective response to breaches and harms—supported by security features implemented by workplaces—and this is particularly so among the legalised settings in the Nevada brothels and the decriminalised settings of Aotearoa New Zealand. We already know from decades of literature that spaces possessing better working conditions also have less violence and are safer environments in which to work (Brents & Hausbeck, 2005; Platt et al., 2018). One of the strong messages around rights-based work culture came from Aotearoa New Zealand sex workers, where Christine (ANZ, various) described a non-payment incident from 20 years ago while working on the streets. While it was happening, she had made sure to drop a ripped condom wrapper with the condom in it onto the floor of the car and grabbed his registration on the way out of the car. She immediately reported the incident to the police, who were nearby, providing them with a description and the evidence; additionally, and fortunately, there were people on the corner watching, who also told the police. She had enough facts, and he was eventually convicted and served seven years in prison. Such a result is in major contrast to those working in a criminalised setting when workers try and access criminal justice to report violations. Cody (USA, independent), for example, said of a stealthing incident, "I tried to report it to police and they laughed at me and told me 'What did you expect?'".

The ways in which brothels are organised often adds levels of security that are not possible in other sex markets, particularly the street (Abel, 2010; Brewis & Linstead, 2000; Hubbard and Sanders, 2003; Sanders and Campbell, 2007). There is a range of physical security features, such as panic alarms, CCTV cameras, and others being present (workers, receptionists, managers, and security personnel), that make the context of brothels one that is more organised to deal with problematic situations. This close-to-hand nature of security services in a legalised brothel setting, then, is a clear way that workplace enforcement can happen, as described by one of the Nevada brothel workers:

> The tip of my toe barely taps the alarm, thank goodness. So it triggered it; the cashier comes over the intercom and asks if I'm okay. I tell them 'No'. That's all I just say is 'No', and the guy's still not stopping. He's still trying to take my clothes off. I managed to not let him get inside of me, but he's definitely trying. Security is there in 10 seconds. They bust down the door, they don't even knock. (Abigail, USA, Nevada legal brothel)

While, here, the crime had not been dealt with by law enforcement, but rather, had simply been stopped, preventing further harm, for Abigail there was a sense of justice in having had the client removed forcibly from the premises and barred from entering again. This was important for her, not only in having ensured her own safety at the moment but because she was as concerned with possible future dangerous encounters that her brothel co-workers could have otherwise experienced. With these workplace actions, although not 'formal' with regard to enacting the law, the rest of the workers in that brothel would then be protected from that person doing the same thing to them; however, there were no guarantees that the client could not go to another brothel in the area. Without formal reporting to the police, the emphasis is on enforcing organisational rules and not on the state law, to apprehend and prevent a perpetrator from acting again.

How perpetrators' actions could endanger others was commonly considered by sex workers and contributed towards their decisions about what action to take after a violation had occurred. For some, there was an explicit sense of responsibility towards the safety of others. Explaining why they reported an assault and robbery to the police, one of the few trans-female sex workers we interviewed explained: "I couldn't [...] have lived with myself [...] to let anybody else go through that" (Hunu, ANZ, street-based). In contrast to the experiences of legal alienation discussed earlier, some experiences demonstrated faith in criminal interventions in having the power to be able to make a difference—the opposite of the 'legal powerlessness' sometimes experienced (Hertogh, 2011). The ability to use one's voice, to some, felt like an important obligation to others: "…everyone's got their voice, and then if I withdraw my voice, I could hurt another victim, you know" (Alice, ANZ, various). Christine (ANZ, various) explains what she thinks her approach would be if a sexual assault occurred at work:

> [Interviewer:] If, um, you knew somebody who was assaulted at work, what advice would you give them? Would you encourage them to go to the police?
> [Christine, ANZ, various:] Yeah, I'd tell them, 'You've got to do something about it. You've got to go to the police. If you don't go to the police, it's going to happen over and over and over and over 'til they destroy you, and if you, um, take it to the police and tell them, they will do something about it. Just be open and honest with them'. But there's a lot of those just still won't do it.

Police were sometimes called to brothels in Nevada after an incident and most of the brothel sex workers we interviewed indicated that they felt that the police would take them seriously if they reported something—again, demonstrating a level of confidence with formal legal processes. However, none of these workers had progressed with criminal proceedings, meaning the formal resolution to breaches started and ended at the level of workplace intervention. This could be that feelings of justice had been satisfied outside of traditional criminal justice. It could be, however, that the reality of formal legal mobilisation was not what was expected nor wanted. Abigail expanded on why she never reported after a client was removed from the brothel and management had called the police:

> I didn't personally get to talk to them [the police], they must have dealt with the madams and the head of security directly after I'd already relayed my story to them. But the fact that they showed up right away was very nice. So, from what I heard from everyone, they did follow all the protocol, they asked if I wanted to file a report. So, they were there for me if I needed them to be. … On the surface, they've been very polite with me, when I do go get my licence every year. But it's almost as if they're an employee having a bad day, so they're nice but seemingly irritated, and I found that odd the first time. … I could file a police report,

> but I hear so many cases of friends and family who do that and nothing happens from there. They'll even fight back a little bit saying, 'Well, it was your boyfriend so it wasn't sexual assault'. 'You know the person'. So, it feels like it's always kind of a struggle to be safe, and then take care of yourself after something does happen, even after the #MeToo movement. There was so much pushback from that too: 'Well, now women can just lie whenever they want'. That's not the point. Why would we do that? Just the entitlement almost, of people, to our bodies is very hard to navigate when we're constantly told that it's our fault and our responsibility, rather than being given resources to protect ourselves. So, I feel really lucky to work here [in the brothel] where it's very safe. (Abigail, USA, Nevada legal brothel)

There is much to unpack in this story from Abigail, about the likelihood of engagement, or not, with law enforcement, the probabilities of the police disbelieving the assault claim in the USA sex-work setting, and the broader cultural context of responsibilisation of women's behaviour to avoid sexual violence. Abigail notes a persistent misogynistic acceptance of sexual violence as ordinary and even acceptable as a normal reaction from police in the USA. What underpins the story is that ultimately Abigail felt the legal brothel system in Nevada gave her the assistance and protection she needed—including how they empowered and enabled her to make a formal report—and that this was more effective than recompense via the police. The informal norms and rules within the workplace of the regulated brothel provided protections and a response that she sought and was not likely to get from the USA police.

This demonstrates further how, regardless of sex workers' understanding of the protections that should be afforded to them under formal law, support and resolution are more readily available in the workplace environment of the legal brothels.

Conclusion

However sex workers experience sexual violations within their work, they adopt a range of pathways—to greater or lesser extents of formality—for them to respond to the breach in a way that is most suitable for them at that time. These responses exist along a continuum, from minimal or no action to informal resolutions to approaches based on the organisational culture and workplace norms. As we see in Chapter 6, very rarely is the criminal justice service approached as a course of action after a violation. Behind each response is a reason for engaging with that option—be that out of necessity due to the circumstances of the violation (for instance, where no action may be considered possible in a criminalised setting or where there is a risk of harm), or on the basis of the understanding the worker has of what options are available to them. This is then further influenced by the experiences of others, both those within close social structures (particularly the workplace) and those in wider society. The concept of second-order legal consciousness (Young, 2014) can be applied to this cohort of participants, whereby an individual sex worker's beliefs and attitudes towards violations and the actions that can be taken as a result of breaches are heavily influenced by their interpretation of the beliefs and attitudes of those around them.

The process of learning about appropriate and inappropriate behaviours (within and outside the context of sex work) can lead sex workers to be able to consider their options, and then ultimately choose to take formal or informal action against the perpetrator. Having a better understanding of formal laws can lead sex workers to legal mobilisation (e.g. Lehoucq & Taylor, 2019). It appears vital how sex workers learn about both formal and informal norms in the local context of the sex industry, which contributes to sex workers' attitudes and perceptions of the formal law and their actions after sexual violence and breaches of agreements. This determines whether sex workers would use informal enforcement mechanisms or whether they feel able to report more formally.

Legal consciousness research to date is largely constructed at the level of individuals, as victims and their interaction with support agencies and/or legal professionals. Our understanding of the data in this project flags how a focus on only the individual victim misses out so much of the broader understanding of how communities have knowledge of and utilise the law, if they do at all. Our data go beyond examining legal knowledge and consciousness at an individual sex-worker level by exploring the structural elements of how mobilisation by sex workers is constrained or promoted at meso and macro levels, by organisations, legal hegemonies, and cultural formations in different countries in our study.

The social and legal context in which the sexual violation occurred is also, of course, a significant factor in how such behaviour could feasibly be responded to. There are still strong cultural narratives and legal norms, particularly in criminalised settings, regarding sex workers not being able to be raped or being capable of non-consent because of the work they do. Such external social attitudes encourage clients to push boundaries, disregard consent, and violate sex workers' sexual autonomy. It is also the same type of narrative against sex workers that makes them highly vulnerable to occupational homicide and targets by serial killers and perpetrators of hate crime (see Cunningham et al., 2018).

Additionally, this 'tolerance' to legally and morally egregious behaviour, as noted by Felstiner and colleagues (1980), can be a cause and an outcome of not being able to identify where harm has been caused. In contexts where there is legality and regulation around selling sex, such as brothels in Nevada or in the decriminalised setting in Aotearoa New Zealand, there was, among our study participants, a stronger sense of rights and knowing when a harm had occurred around condom removal/stealthing and non-payment. Ultimately, understanding formal laws was more evident, as well as trust in the formal process in Aotearoa New Zealand, where talk about rights and understanding the law was passed on through brothel workplace culture and between the individuals working together. Yet, there was still a reluctance to engage law enforcement, and a low engagement in generic support services (such as Rape Crisis centres) more broadly. This suggests that, even with knowledge around legal interventions, and the opportunity to engage in criminal processes, the type of 'justice' sought by many sex workers falls into a more informal category of resolution, with strong intentions of wanting to keep others and themselves safe.

References

Abel, G. (2010). *Decriminalisation: A harm minimisation and human rights approach to regulating sex work* (PhD thesis, University of Otago). Christchurch.

Bernstein, E. (2001). The meaning of the purchase: Desire, demand and the commerce of sex. *Ethnography, 2*(3), 389–420.

Blackstone, A., Uggen, C., & McLaughlin, H. (2009). Legal consciousness and responses to sexual harassment. *Law & Society Review, 43*(3), 631–668. https://doi.org/10.1111/j.1540-5893.2009.00384.x

Brents, B. G., & Hausbeck, K. (2005). Violence and legalized brothel prostitution in Nevada: Examining safety, risk, and prostitution policy. *Journal of Interpersonal Violence, 20*(3), 270–295. https://doi.org/10.1177/088626050 4270333

Brewis, J., & Linstead, S. (2000). 'The worst thing is the screwing'(1): Consumption and the management of identity in sex work. *Gender, Work & Organization, 7*(2), 84–97.

Cunningham, S., Sanders, T., Platt, L., Grenfell, P., & Macioti, P. G. (2018). Sex work and occupational homicide: Analysis of a UK murder database. *Homicide Studies, 22*(3), 321–338.

Day, S. E. (2007). *On the game: Women and sex work*. Pluto Press. Decriminalise Sex Work. (2024). *What is SESTA/FOSTA?* Retrieved June 20, 2024, from: https://decriminalizesex.work/advocacy/sesta-fosta/what-is-sesta-fosta/#What-Is-SESTA-FOSTA

Felstiner, W. L. F., Abel, R. L., & Sarat, A. (1980). The emergence and transformation of disputes: Naming, blaming, claiming... *Law & Society Review, 15*(3/4), 631–654. https://doi.org/10.2307/3053505

Hertogh, M. (2011). Loyalists, cynics and outsiders: Who are the critics of the justice system in the UK and the Netherlands? *International Journal of Law in Context, 7*(1), 31–46. https://doi.org/10.1017/s174455231000039x

Hertogh, M. (2018). *Nobody's law: Legal consciousness and legal alienation in everyday life*. Palgrave Pivot.

Hubbard, P., & Sanders, T. (2003). Making space for sex work: Female street prostitution and the production of urban space. *International Journal of Urban and regional research, 27*(1), 75–89.

Jones, A. (2015). Sex work in a digital era. *Sociology Compass, 9*(7), 558–570.

Lehoucq, E., & Taylor, W. K. (2019). Conceptualizing legal mobilization: How should we understand the deployment of legal strategies? *Law & Social Inquiry, 45*(1), 166–193. https://doi.org/10.1017/lsi.2019.59

Platt, L., Grenfell, P., Meiksin, R., Elmes, J., Sherman, S. G., Sanders, T., Mwangi, P., & Crago, A. L. (2018). Associations between sex work laws and sex workers' health: A systematic review and meta-analysis of quantitative and qualitative studies. *PLOS Medicine, 15*(12), e1002680.

Pyett, P., & Warr, D. (1999). Women at risk in sex work: Strategies for survival. *Journal of Sociology, 35*(2), 183–197.

Sanders, T. (2004a). *Sex work. A risky business.* Cullompton Devon.

Sanders, T. (2004b). A continuum of risk? The management of health, physical and emotional risks by female sex workers. *Sociology of Health & Illness, 26*(5), 557–574.

Sanders, T., & Campbell, R. (2007). Designing out vulnerability, building in respect: Violence, safety and sex work policy. *The British Journal of Sociology, 58*(1), 1–19.

Young, K. M. (2014). Everyone knows the game: Legal consciousness in the Hawaiian cockfight. *Law & Society Review, 48*(3), 499–530. https://doi.org/10.1111/lasr.12094

6

Formal Reporting: The Barriers and Enablers of Legal Mobilisation

Teela Sanders, Harriet Smailes, Barbara G. Brents, Jane Scoular, and Gillian Abel

Introduction

The global #MeToo digital campaign has brought significant attention to the criminal justice system's continued failures to deal with sexual harassment, rape, and sexual assault (Mendes et al., 2018). Many victims still do not report sexual violence to the police, rarely are perpetrators punished, and those who do report have negative interactions with the

T. Sanders (✉) · H. Smailes
University of Leicester, Leicester, UK
e-mail: teela.sanders@leicester.ac.uk

B. G. Brents
University of Nevada, Las Vegas, Nevada, USA

J. Scoular
Strathclyde Law School, University of Strathclyde, Glasgow, UK

G. Abel
University of Otago, Dunedin, New Zealand

T. Sanders et al. (eds.), *Voicing Consent*, Palgrave Advances in Sex Work Studies,
https://doi.org/10.1007/978-3-031-77715-8_6

system. Zvi (2022) conducted a perceptions-based study of 220 police officers in Israel (in the context of client criminalisation) and concluded that victim credibility in rape against sex workers was low, with higher rates of victim-blaming and a tendency to treat the consequences of rape as if they were less severe. It is in this context that—rather than being able to reach out for support or justice—sex workers are left to deal with their own experiences of crime, sexual violence, and other incidents that are harmful and often illegal. Stigma and exclusion have long silenced sex workers, and, in many places, their work itself is criminalised. As a result, they are even less likely to formally report sexual violence or other crimes compared to non-sex workers, a finding consistently supported by decades of research (Amnesty International, 2016; Kinnell, 2008; Krüsi et al., 2014; Penfold et al., 2004; Spencer et al., 2018). It is this problematic context that has led us to ask questions to find out more about the dynamics of sex workers' experiences.

Do different legal landscapes affect sex workers' interactions with criminal justice systems? We know that when aspects of their work are criminalised, they are less likely to use the criminal justice system to deal with violence. Are they likely to access the criminal justice system to manage other disputes such as non-payment or 'stealthing'? Are there differences in legal systems that may lead to different outcomes? This chapter examines the impact of different legal landscapes on sex workers' engagement with the criminal justice system.

Drawing on surveys and interviews (see Chapter 9 for a discussion of our methods), we explore the experiences shaped by legal frameworks, ranging from Aotearoa New Zealand's decriminalisation to complete criminalisation in the USA. We detail sex workers' experiences with the reporting, investigation, and prosecution of sexual offences and other forms of unwanted contact. The chapter investigates how confidence in the police varies among sex workers, both within and across these jurisdictions. We present the accounts and experiences of those who have and have not navigated the criminal justice system—outlining the reasons why the majority will not report, and, conversely, the experiences of the police and courts for those who did. Included are the reasons why many sex workers choose to seek alternative, more informal routes to resolution. By contrasting Aotearoa New Zealand's decriminalised approach with the semi-legal structure in the UK, and the mixed legal environment in the USA, we explain how legislation influences sex workers' interactions with law enforcement. We use this novel lens to provide a comprehensive understanding of how legislation shapes interactions between sex workers and law enforcement.

What We Know About Sex Workers and the Criminal Justice System

We know that, even more so than non-sex workers, sex workers of any socio-demographic status would rarely consider seeking assistance from the police, or attempt to seek justice through the courts in dealing with any crime. In a systematic review of research, Struyf (2023) finds that sex workers do not report victimisation for four main reasons: (i) fear of being punished; (ii) fear of being mistreated; (iii) fear of exposure, and; (iv) fear that perpetrators will not be punished. Sex workers fear being re-traumatised and those who have had bad previous experience in non-sex-work cases also fear arrest or a criminal record. In the USA, in a collection of essays titled *We Too* (West & Horn, 2021), current and former sex workers point out that despite public concern about violence and exploitation in the sex industry, they are left out of these mainstream 'Me Too' debates. Instead, their experiences of harassment and violence are funnelled into the USA trafficking rescue industry (Weitzer, 2020). This highlights the policymakers' and the general population's perceptions of sex workers' experiences, which they view as an issue belonging to the criminalised debate, rather than a mainstream public rights debate. This separation could be seen as furthering the stigma attached to sex-working populations.

We also know that sexual violence victims are more willing to report any potential future crimes when they perceive adherence to elements of procedural justice (for instance, empathy with survivors) in their interactions with the criminal justice system (Lorenz & Jacobsen, 2021). The varying legal status of sex workers in different countries could, thus, make a difference. Yet, we have little comparative data on how these experiences differ in different legal contexts. What we did know leading up to our project was that sex workers rarely engage with the police (Bowen et al., 2021) and that police attitudes can often be stereotypical, stigmatising, and problematic. Stardust and colleagues (2021) examined trust and experiences with police across Australia's diverse legal contexts and found that police consistently see sex workers as 'irresponsible citizens' and blamed them for their experiences of crime. The authors conclude that "... 'Whore stigma' is entrenched in the criminal legal system and requires a systemic response that necessitates but goes beyond the decriminalisation of sex work" (Stardust et al., 2021, p. 142).

Even for non-sex-working populations, we know little about how different legal contexts matter. Evidence so far indicates some strong similarities across many countries. In the UK, trust in the police is at an all-time low, and trust around safety for women is questionable, particularly for many women who are in marginalised groups and live in London (see Marquis & Langlois, 2023). A recent poll of all crime victims in England and Wales found that only 17% believed the criminal justice system was fair and 8% thought they would receive justice by reporting a crime (Victims' Commissioner UK, 2023). From this knowledge it is clear we need more nuanced ways of understanding sex workers' low (or, in the case of the USA, next-to-no) engagement with the criminal justice system.

Attitudes Towards the Criminal Justice System

Our survey assessed attitudes towards the criminal justice system by asking whether respondents agreed or disagreed with three key statements:

1. The police take rape against sex workers seriously.
2. I have confidence in getting justice if a case is taken to court.
3. Overall, I have confidence in the criminal justice system.

Table 6.1 reports across all sites for those who disclosed an incident and also shared their attitudes to the criminal justice system. The data is reported across four categories, which reflects the different legislative frameworks like so: Aotearoa New Zealand (ANZ); Nevada (NV) brothels; the rest of the USA (where sex work is criminalised); and the UK (including Northern Ireland data due to small numbers; see Chapter 9 for more detail). From this data, we can say the following:

- Participants in the USA (including those in criminalised and legalised brothel settings) had the poorest attitudes towards police, courts, and the criminal justice system generally.
- Participants in the ANZ decriminalised system were more likely to believe the police will take rape seriously.

Table 6.1 Respondent percentage of agreement with criminal justice system attitudinal statements

Percentage and number of respondents who have experienced incidents and who agree ('agree' or 'strongly agree') with attitudinal statements concerning the criminal justice system										
	ANZ		NV Brothel		UK		USA		All Sites	
	%	n	%	n	%	n	%	n	%	n
The police take rape against sex workers seriously	34.57	28	3.33	1	25.81	32	10.50	21	18.85	82
I have confidence in getting justice if a case is taken to court	17.28	14	4.17	1	17.86	20	6.99	13	11.91	48
Overall, I have confidence in the criminal justice system	12.05	10	0.00	0	13.27	15	6.32	12	9.00	37

- The UK participants generally had low opinions of the police, courts, and criminal justice system.

There was a notable difference in perceptions of police attitudes across the different legal contexts. Across all sites and among respondents who reported violence, only 19% of sex workers (n = 82) agreed that 'The police take rape against sex workers seriously'. Across all sites, 66% of survey respondents who experienced violence/unwanted contact strongly disagreed that police take rape against sex workers seriously. In ANZ, 35% of sex workers agreed or strongly agreed that police take rape against sex workers seriously, compared to 11% in the USA criminalised market. In ANZ, 44% of sex workers strongly disagreed that the police take rape against sex workers seriously, compared to 78% USA who strongly disagreed. This suggests that even while numbers who are supportive of police attitudes are low in ANZ, the decriminalised setting may increase the number of sex workers who believe the police will support sex workers.

Within countries, there are some subtle differences. In the USA, 63% of sex workers in Nevada's legal brothels strongly disagreed that the police take rape against sex workers seriously, compared to 79% of respondents working in illegal sex work elsewhere in the USA. ANZ had the greatest proportion of respondents who agreed that the police take rape against sex workers seriously (35%). By contrast, only 10% of all USA sex workers agreed. The 'confidence in getting justice' question responses were very low for the USA, with only 7% from illegal settings in the USA agreeing and 4% (one respondent) from the Nevada brothels. Irrespective of setting, sex workers in the USA were dubious of the court system assisting them when they were a victim of sexual violence or unwanted contact in their sex work. The lack of engagement with the criminal justice system in the USA can be explained by the intense criminalisation of sex work in the vast majority of states. Data from respondents from the semi-legal structure in England and Wales lay largely in between the USA and ANZ results: distrust was still significant, with 70% strongly disagreeing that they have confidence in the criminal justice system. When we compare these attitudes across jurisdictions, there is an indication that, in a decriminalised setting, there is more belief that the police will take account of unwanted contact seriously. In those where the sex worker is heavily criminalised, there is little faith. The Nevada brothel workers, despite working in a regulated system, ultimately are situated in a culture of anti-sex work, in a country that generally criminalises the sex industry. Decriminalisation, therefore, does not eliminate distrust of the courts or law enforcement. Sex workers' lack of trust in seeking formal redress is most likely impacted by the general populations' perception towards sex workers and the dominant legal position in that context, alongside sex workers' perceptions of the criminal justice system in its response to sexual violence more broadly. In other words, these factors combined contribute to sex workers' understanding and perception of engaging with the police and going through criminal justice proceedings, which ultimately affects their intentions around legal mobilisation.

Who Reported to the Police?

From our comparative survey, we wanted to know, from those who had experienced forms of unwanted contact, how many respondents reported any incidents to the police. We asked respondents to tell us whether or not they had reported to the police the last incident that had happened to them (from a list of non-/underpayment; condom removal; physical assault; penetration; person not stopping when asked to; being threatened or harassed into having sex). Of the 425 participants who responded, only 35 reported any incident to the police. While the numbers are incredibly small, which means not much can be inferred, this was broken down by site as follows:

- Four from Aotearoa New Zealand (4% of ANZ respondents who experienced unwanted contact);
- 17 from the UK (13% of UK respondents who experienced unwanted contact); and
- 14 from the USA (USA criminalised market = 5.8%, 2 from the Nevada brothels = 6.45%).

Given the barriers that previous research has found that prevent access to criminal justice for sex workers (see 'What We Know About Sex Workers and the Criminal Justice System', above), it was no surprise that so few in our sample reported unwanted contact or sexual violence to law enforcement. However, there are differences between countries that are worth discussing. We think a likely explanation for the lowest reporting to police being from the decriminalised setting is because the sex workers use a wider range of other interventions—from their brothel manager, to reporting to (and getting support from) the New Zealand Collective of Prostitutes, and even Human Rights Tribunals where they can report breaches of contract by clients (see Wilkinson, 2023 and Chapter 2 of the current volume). Other legal mechanisms are explored in the ANZ system, below (see 'Decriminalised Settings' within this chapter). It also stands, as argued in Chapter 5, that despite a decriminalised setting where better relationships between marginalised groups and the police might be expected, behaviour does not always follow legal change/reform. To further understand the trends from the survey, then, the qualitative data (mainly from interviews but some from free-text responses in the survey) will now be discussed.

The sex-worker interviewee sample for this project is made up of 41 interviews across the sites as follows: England, Wales, Scotland, and Northern Ireland (UK) = 15; USA (both Nevada brothels and the criminalised setting) = 14; Aotearoa New Zealand (ANZ) = 11 (see Chapter 9 for a detailed account of the study design and socio-demographics of participants).

Among those interviewed in ANZ who had reported their assaults to the police, there is a common theme connecting the women in terms of their reasons for reporting. The main reason most of the workers reported their assaulters was so that the perpetrator could not go on to assault more sex workers. It is a commonly shared thought, and evident reality, that if he (because it is usually a 'he') would do this to one woman/sex worker, then he probably has done it before, and he will likely do it again. It is an important and also inspiring reason for reporting as it shows their sense of solidarity and desire to protect fellow workers from harm—for example:

> I've considered what would happen if I took any of these many people to court, um, and I think for me the change was that with one of these ones I can't discuss, the event that occurred to me, occurred to someone else as well. And I saw that if I do not report what's happened to me as a sex worker from a customer and try and get justice, then it's going to keep happening to these other people. … So that's what made me change, and press for justice, because I wanted to protect my peers. And I am glad that I did it. It's just, I just, it's why I have regrets about not reporting other things sooner, is because I know those people are probably still reoffending and causing more harm. (Talia, ANZ, brothel)
>
> I feel a responsibility as a human to, if that were to ever happen to me again or if something, sexual violence were to happen to me again, to protect other people from having that happen to them. And part of it was why I went through with the court process as well, is that no-one really wants to go to court, for any reason, on either side, but sometimes it's like a personal obligation, yeah. (Jane, ANZ, brothel)

Reporting incidents to the police shows that some sex workers would want to engage in formal ways to seek justice and they knew the mechanisms to initiate this—however, they generally perceived that they could not trust the criminal justice system. In some cases, when sex workers chose to engage in the criminal justice system, they gained a better understanding of how the system worked and their understanding of formal law changed or broadened. Talia, for instance, demonstrated knowledge she had learned throughout the legal process:

> ... for someone back-handing you, you can get them convicted. For someone touching you after you told them, 'I don't want you to touch me anymore', that's also a crime. So yeah, I've learnt a lot about consent and, um, stuff I didn't know before doing all this justice experience. (Talia, ANZ, brothel)

We knew there would be few people in the survey who had experience in the criminal justice system because of low reporting rates and high attrition, yet we were still keen to capture sex workers' experiences of taking formal pathways to seek justice from those who did take this step of reporting. In the survey, we asked '*What happened after you*

Table 6.2 The number of participants by outcome after having reported to the police

What happened after you reported to the police?	ANZ	UK	USA	Total number
There was nothing done about it	1	10	10	21
Police arrested or charged the person who did it	2	4	2	8
The person was convicted	2	3	0	5
I received compensation	2	3	0	5
Other	1	4	2	7
Total number	8	24	14	46

reported to the police?'. Table 6.2 provides the responses (respondents could choose more than one answer). We note that there was only one person from Aotearoa New Zealand who replied that nothing was done after a report, whereas this was ten times higher with both the UK and USA respondents. As expected, convictions are low and compensation is even lower.[1]

Experiences with Police

Criminalised Settings

We know that, in general, the rate of sex workers reporting to the police is extremely low. Sex workers' comments in interviews reflected what the survey data said: "I think I would have to think I was going to be dead within the next five minutes to dial 911. They're not going to help" (Bella, USA, independent).

Sex workers realised that they are certainly likely to be treated the same as non-sex workers in one sense, in not being believed, but in addition they felt that they face more discrimination from the police, because of their line of work. One survey respondent wrote:

[1] We want to flag that in the UK, conviction rates for violence against sex workers are higher than those for non-sex workers, according to case-file analysis by Lea et al. (2016).

> There's no reason to trust the police; they don't do anything about sexual assault for non-sex workers and certainly not for sex workers. I don't need a target on my back. (Survey respondent, USA)

But, in addition, the fact that sex workers are criminalised can mean that they feel they risk being arrested themselves when they report crimes. The USA sex workers working in criminalised spaces were clear in their beliefs:

> [Few sex workers would report because] they don't want to risk going to prison themselves (Nancy, USA, independent)
> On a number of occasions, I've had law enforcement choose not to believe me, choose not to assist me, or choose that I'm actually the person they should pursue with charges. (Bella, USA, independent)
> The police will never help a sex worker, only hurt her further. I will never, even if in serious trouble, reach out to my enemies who are ready to ticket me and stain my name and who do not care in the slightest. (Survey respondent, USA)

There may be instances, however, whereby reporting may feel more like a necessity or an expected course of action. Jessica recalled that because sex work is criminalised in the USA, sex workers do not usually report anything until they have to—for example, when they are in the emergency room or hospital:

> Because it's not legalised, and we're doing it illegally, you don't have anybody to call, report. It's not even like they're going to care. Usually we don't report things, unless like ... I've had a friend that had been strangled, or things like that, then they reported it, because they've ended up in the hospital. Usually the only time a woman will report it, is if they end up in the hospital, and then they're getting questioned. Other than that, they're more likely not to. (Jessica, USA, various)

Dewey and St. Germain (2014), from a large three-year study of street-based sex workers in Denver Colorado, note that the reluctance from sex workers to report is because both sex work and drug use are criminalised, which determines the approach of police officers. In this jurisdiction, sex workers perceived that the laws criminalised them and that, therefore, it could ultimately hurt them if they did report formally, which also affected their willingness of seeking redress formally. This means, then, that while sex workers' understanding of client-breach behaviours may actually be entirely aligned with a formal legal understanding, their experience of the law with regard to their sex work more generally presents as a significant barrier to reporting. Moreover, the barrier in reporting is not, in itself, that the state law criminalises sex work, but, rather, because of the police's interpretation and perception of these laws, which seems to support a stigmatised understanding of the nature of sex work, even beyond the scope of the law.

A trans woman in the USA who we interviewed suggested the innate level of assumptions around gender identity and sex work can lead police officers to make judgements and not see the crime that is being presented to them:

> It's hard enough for a trans woman to get a police officer to take you seriously, because when I was raped the first time I wasn't doing anything, I wasn't even dressed provocatively, I was just raped, and the first [thing] the cop asked me was, was I soliciting. And I'm kind of like, 'What the fuck?!' ... Yeah. I discovered recently that it's not a question that they just ask any woman, it's a question that they tend to ask a lot of trans women, because automatically they think that because we're trans, we're sex workers or we're doing this for the kink. (Kassandra, USA, independent)

Kassandra told the story of the one time she did report a rape: "I wasn't expecting closure in that sense, if I had to be honest with you. But if I didn't report it, somebody else in the area would probably be hurt". Afterwards she was called to the police station and told to pick out her rapist from a line-up of all black men. None of them were the perpetrators, and because she did not select anyone, the only thing that was done was a temporary increase in the police presence in the area:

> I'm not just picking out the random black guy because you think that all black guys look alike or whatever. I'm not doing that... And I haven't heard anything more about that investigation since. Again, I'm probably

> just another one of the 98% statistics then of rape that are never resolved. (Kassandra, USA, independent)

While this is a rare occasion of a sex worker reporting a rape in the USA context and appropriate initial investigations taking place, the dissatisfaction with the investigation is evident.

Semi-Criminalised Settings

In semi-criminalised settings, sex workers expressed similar reluctance to go to the police because of the fear of disbelief and belittlement. However, there were subtle differences in perception, resulting in a slightly higher proportion (13% of the sample) in the UK having engaged with the police. The two interviewees who had reported to the police had experienced very high levels of violence and the conditions in which they were attacked left them especially vulnerable: the women were alone when they were attacked and in a context where the perpetrator had complete control of the surroundings. These two cases were taken to court and convictions were secured.

Rather than a fear of arrest, sex workers in semi-criminalised settings that we interviewed reported a perception that police believed crime was an 'occupational hazard' in the sex industry. Two interviewees from England, for example, recounted police attitudes encountered when working in a street environment:

> Every working girl I know never wanted to report it, never wanted to report it because they either get away with it or they're not arrested anyway… In a way, we should get more support because there's reasons why we do what we're doing. No-one wakes up in the morning and says, 'I'm going to be a prostitute'. We've all got a story, unfortunately; we've all got reasons why we do it, whether it be addiction or whatever. But yeah, it's like they just see it, I feel anyway, that police just see it as an occupational hazard. (Anna, UK, street-based)
>
> I've had it all over the years, 'Well, you do that job', and there's the look. Yeah, there's so much judgement. They need talking to, as well, because

> there's so much judgement in their faces and it's like, 'Come on!'. (Emily, UK, various)

There was a recurrent theme that emerged in the UK context: sex workers experienced being treated less favourably than non-sex workers because they were selling sexual services:

> The first thing the copper asked me were, 'Did they know you were a working girl?' What difference does that make? Why have you asked that? Whether they had known or not, what difference does that make? And they said, 'Oh, there's no reason why we've asked you'. Well, there clearly is because you wouldn't have asked! So, and that made me feel like, and this is the question you're coming out with, what girl is going to feel like they can go and report? They're not going to feel like they can report it. (Tess, UK, street-based)

This experience that Tess had with the police—suggesting that violence committed against sex workers could be contextualised, and was perhaps even permissible, because of their work—clearly demonstrates why many sex workers do not report. If there is even a perception that their case will follow a different trajectory compared to a non-sex-worker victim's case, the criminal justice process becomes, at best, a mystery, if not explicitly discriminatory.

There was little regard for treating non-payment as any kind of harm from police in the UK, and in fact, it was rare for sex workers across all jurisdictions to pursue a criminal-reporting route for this type of breach. Recounting interactions with a police officer regarding non-payment by a client, Anna explains this lack of understanding:

> But again, I've had other incidents, like I said, where it's 'Occupational hazard', 'Are you sure this really happened? Did he just not pay you?', 'There's a difference between not being paid and being raped'… (Anna, UK, street-based)

For some sex workers, they had internalised police responses to these breaches and were of the same view—that it was a hazard of the work. For others, they perceived it as something more violating and their responses reflected this. Halley, an independent sex worker in the UK, described an incident where the client had not paid and she had tried to tell people with no success. She clearly saw this as an act of violence:

> One time on the job, I was outsmarted, yes. At the end, the client didn't pay me and he absconded with my money and I wasn't able to contact him. ... Would I consider that an act of violence? Yes, I would. ... I was trying to let the people know what was going on but nobody was hearing me or no-one was trying to speak up for me, or trying to accuse the person: 'Why would you do that?' (Halley, UK, independent)

We interviewed some street-based sex workers in the UK who had experience working in the only officially managed street area in Leeds, Yorkshire, which was open during 2014–2020.[2] Even while they felt safer in this managed zone (also a feeling reported by other sex workers outside of this study; see Brown & Sanders, 2017), they still felt police often did not take their claims seriously:

> I used to get fined if I was out outside the times of the zone. But that's pointless because you just have to go out earlier the next day and do more jobs to pay the fine. And I told the police that, but they just laughed. There are two police who used to come around the area who harassed us worse than the punters. Then the men wouldn't come up to you if the police were hanging around, but it was safer on the whole. I don't know why they stopped it because it's worse now without the managed area. (Tess, UK, street-based)

Tess discussed not taking forward her (earlier mentioned) claim of sexual violence to the police as she was concerned that the accused could harass her online and cause reputational damage, which could devastate her income: "He could easily go online and say, 'this escort lies about rape'. And then I've got no clients if they do that. So I didn't end

[2] For more information about the first managed approach in the UK, see here: https://democracy.leeds.gov.uk/documents/s208220/Managed%20Approach%20Independent%20Review%20Report%20Appendix%2008072O.pdf And here: https://prostitutescollective.net/tag/leeds/

up doing the statement" (Tess, UK, street-based). The lack of protection Tess felt a police report would afford her clearly informed her decision-making here.

As has been described in other literature (e.g. Minichiello & Scott, 2014), sex workers reported experiencing incidences of police performing additional, gendered discrimination. There were only six male or trans sex workers interviewed across the project/sites; this smaller group, who responded to the survey also, flagged some essential points around policing and male sex work:

> I strongly feel that male escort/sex workers are taken less seriously and are given far fewer resources to deal than females. There are no men's shelters for abuse victims in this country. There is a clear bias in how cases are taken, reported, and dealt with, which disproportionately affects men. (Survey respondent, UK)

Additional discrimination was felt by Queen whereby she felt additional vulnerability engaging with the police, being a sex-working mother.

> I'm speaking from personal experience. You report a crime to the police, rightly. So, they'll immediately contact Social Services because that's a vulnerable child. Social Services go, 'You're doing what?' and remove your child. So that is weaponised against us; you will have your children removed from you if you report a crime. Whereas the experience in New Zealand, because people in sex work are acceptable human beings, social workers don't immediately go, 'We're going to remove your child because you're bad'. They'll go, 'Oh okay, so you're doing sex work, fine'... (Queen, UK, various)

For Queen, even without full criminalisation of sex work in the UK, there is still an experience felt by some that the legislation is perhaps still focused on ending prostitution, not protecting workers. In fact, Queen felt as though "The crime of being a whore is worse than crimes against whores" and that "That's very much the feeling of if we report a crime against us". This shows that legislation can have unintended consequences, which might affect sex workers' perception of the law and their trust in formal reporting mechanisms.

Understanding the specific vulnerabilities that may be experienced by sex workers is something that has been noted as being an important element of policing crimes against them (Brown et al., 2024). A recent review of UK specialist police sex worker liaison officers (SWLOs) found that a focus on vulnerabilities over enforcement, and using discretion with regard to whether individuals were considered as victims or offenders, was incredibly important and considered as best practice (Brown et al. 2024). These principles are particularly pertinent in semi- or fully criminalised jurisdictions, where the unknowns around whether sex workers will be afforded victim or offender status is noted as a significant barrier for them in reporting to the police. These uncertainties experienced by sex workers around the police's interpretation of the law contributed to their perceptions that formal reporting is not available for them or it is not in their interest. The unpredictability of laws being enforced, with regard to the feeling that they are responded to differently to those in the sex industry when reporting crimes, was often a well-understood context to which sex workers referred when making decisions around reporting.

Legal and Managed Settings

When asked about interactions with or attitudes about the police, Nevada brothel workers mostly felt that because they were working in licensed brothels and were, therefore, working legally, they would be treated well by the police, and many said that the police would be respectful:

> ... they [the police] seem to have respect when situations have happened. I haven't experienced a situation like that, to that level, where the police had to come and everything. Incidences of the alarms going off, being a legit situation, are pretty rare. I do feel like in Nevada, where it is legal in the brothels, that we are looked at in a better light. (Jessica, USA, various—experience working independently and in brothels)

> In the brothels, because it is legal, so you can file a police report and not get arrested, it's still stigmatised and judged, so some people still might not feel comfortable. But I think it's easier, because you won't get arrested for being a sex worker. (Chrissie, USA, various—experience in brothels)

However, none of the sex workers from the legal brothels that we interviewed had ultimately reported anything to the police:

> Everybody should be able to report it to the police if something violent happens to them, and find the perpetrator and all that. But I just know that I personally wouldn't, and that's a shame. And I'm sure most sex workers feel that same way. (Chrissie, USA, various—experience in brothels)

As discussed in Chapter 5, the impact of practical adjustments that could be made in decriminalised settings—for instance, having security in legal brothels—allowed for alternative routes for safety and justice, not involving the police. Security systems and safety processes in brothels (as has been testified for many decades; see Brents & Hausbeck, 2005) provide protection and a quick, direct form of intervention for the incidents that occur in the licensed brothels. Of course, some brothels are more supportive than others and can help sex workers in reporting incidents to the police, as well as implementing their own response measures. Importantly, this affords sex-worker victims with some additional choices, not available in other jurisdictions or work settings. For Chrissie, with experience of working independently and in brothels, her view was clear that "Let's say if I had actually be raped in the brothel, I would have gone to the police". However, she followed to consider the same scenario in a different setting:

> If I was working independently or illegally, and if something happened to me, I'm pretty sure I wouldn't go, I'm almost positive I wouldn't go to the police. I do know that, because I would be too afraid of getting arrested and judged and not believed. … I just know that I personally wouldn't and that's a shame. (Chrissie, USA, various)

Decriminalised Settings

The attitude of the brothel workers in the Aotearoa New Zealand decriminalised setting was the reverse of that expressed above by the workers in the Nevada brothels. There was a stronger sense of justice and doing the 'right thing' in involving the police if harm was done, which was embedded in the workplace norms of the brothel—if not through members of staff, through other workers:

> There was one other girl on shift, and then I just said—I can't remember what I said, but I just said, like, 'Something has happened. Like, something has happened'. And then she, um, she went up and she talked to him. And at that time, my head was sort of spinning. I couldn't really think. ... I was like, 'Should I call the police?' and the other girl in the room, she was like, 'Yeah, you should', like, 'You should definitely call the police'. But the way the receptionist was talking to me, it felt like I shouldn't. She was like, 'I don't know. It's, like, up to you', and stuff, and in that situation, I couldn't really think for myself. So, they had asked me, 'What do you want?' like, 'What do you want done?', and I just said, 'I just want him to leave so I can think'. [Her partner came and] he was like, 'We're calling the police'. That's when I realised we should call the police. ... I told the Chinese lady that ran the house and that I'd rung the police and the police might be coming here. She freaked the fuck out, told me she didn't want the police to come and she left the building. So yeah, that caused a big fissure in our relationship and I no longer work from that house, because she didn't want the police there. ... It was absolute bullshit, but it was a real sort of power trip. Like, 'Oh, if you're my friend, you don't bring the police into my house. That's disrespectful', and I'm like, 'No, it's not. The police are here to help us'. (Talia, ANZ, brothel)

In a contrasting account, Jane recalled how brothel staff had been enabling in their response to her experience of a client breach:

> I think our manager said, 'Do you want me to call the police?' Yeah, and I said 'Yes', and so she did it, yeah ... He did try to leave ... he wasn't aggressive about it. Like, he did kind of try to step past, but, um, our

> manager has a bit of air of respect about her; she calmly told him, 'You have to stay here'. (Jane, ANZ, brothel)

The brothel workers in Aotearoa New Zealand appeared, then, to have a different attitude to more regularly reporting incidents to the police compared to Nevada brothel workers, despite sex work being licensed and legal in both contexts. We would suggest that the anti-sex-work narrative, and perhaps the context around the criminal justice system more broadly, in the USA negatively affects the belief that sex workers will be protected in the brothels in Nevada. Supporting this assertion, in a quote presented above in the USA (Nevada) context, Chrissie noted that she perceived that the police would treat sex workers respectfully, because "*it* is legal" (emphasis added), and not because she is legal or sex work is accepted.

While the survey reported some feelings of distrust in the police by Aotearoa New Zealand sex workers, they were among the most trustful from all three countries. The Aotearoa New Zealand sex workers we interviewed reported that they understand that the police can be on their side and that the laws to protect them will be implemented: for some, this was a process of gradual realisation; for others, it has always been their perception:

> The whole time I have been having sex it has been legal to be a sex worker. So I've never understood that fear of going to the police. The whole time I have been employed as a sex worker the police have been there, in my mind's eye, to help. ... Last year was the first time I ever took any assaults to court or anything. I never reported it or anything ever before. So, I'm proud of myself and glad that I do have something to say, you know, 'Oh, it does work. You can get a conviction and get some justice'. (Talia, ANZ, brothel)

Talia went on to describe in detail the breach she reported to the police and the conviction that followed:

> He knew what my rules were around the practice of safe sex, which includes using condoms and dental dams for oral sex on each other in penetrative, vaginal and oral sex. And he decided that he was going to

> ignore my rules and he put his mouth on my vagina without a dental dam. So that's one I have taken to the police and he ended up pleading guilty to indecent assault. Yay. And he got sentenced to six months detention, which is amazing. (Talia, ANZ, brothel)

Talia went on to explain that, in her experience, the police in Aotearoa New Zealand were solely focused on the victimhood of the person and not any other potential misdemeanour that might surround the case:

> I was talking with the detective, and he said, 'Well, we don't care about whether you're committing benefit fraud. We're not going to tell IRD [the benefit authorities]. We've got bigger fish to fry. We're not, we don't care about that stuff. We care about whether you're safe'. So, it really needs to be the thing drilled into all of this is that the police are there to keep us safe. (Talia, ANZ, brothel)

Aotearoa New Zealand's sex workers were able to refer to a section in the Prostitution Reform Act that provides special protections for sex workers and that indicates that, even if there is a contract for sexual services, a sex worker can stop contact at any point. This section of the law has proven among the most important for giving sex workers confidence that they can report crimes to the police. As a result, crimes such as removing a condom (stealthing), non-payment, and any form of non-consent can be taken to the police. Details of the legislation are discussed further in Chapter 2.

All this being said, it is the case that sex workers recognised the need to be aware of rules of evidence:

> I thought because there's a witness involved, we might be able to get justice here. And my thinking around it was 'I don't really care for my own justice, but I'd like to go through the process to see what happens and then set a precedent'. I wanted to set a precedent for the stealthing incident, 'cause I went, 'Well this directly breaches the PRA, you know, Section 9, up to 1, 3 and 4'. You know, it's not okay. I screamed at him. The witness saw me screaming. That would make a really solid case. (Carrie, ANZ, independent)

In this way, Carrie demonstrates how being aware of the details of legislation not only helped her at the time of a breach, but gave her additional confidence to report what had happened. Even then, the actual reason for reporting, as is often the case, was not necessarily having laws in place, but the potential for using these laws to protect someone else in the community:

> I'm proud of myself and glad that I do have something to say, you know: 'Oh, it does work. You can get a conviction and get some justice.' … The event that occurred to me, occurred to someone else as well, and I saw that if I do not report what's happened to me as a sex worker from a customer and try and get justice, then it's going to keep happening to these other people… (Talia, ANZ, brothel)

Others expressed that, irrespective of the response from the police, there was a high emotional price to pay for reporting and going through the criminal justice system. Chanelle, for instance, described her reluctance:

> I'm not sure if, for me personally, it would help just with my mental health and that sort of thing. If my client was to, like, you know, be prosecuted and to go into prison, that would probably be cool. I'd be like, 'Cool, they can't do that to other people'. They actually do deserve to be there, yes. But does that take away the flashbacks? Does that take away the fact that he did do that? (Chanelle, ANZ, various)

Yet despite the more pronounced understanding of rights and access to justice, this did not dilute the experiences of re-trauma in recounting horrific incidents. The re-victimisation of survivors by the criminal justice system in sexual violence cases has been documented, even from the point of view of police (see Spencer et al., 2024).

As considered earlier in this chapter, speaking out and reporting unwanted sexual contact was seen as protection for other sex workers, especially by Aotearoa New Zealand sex workers. They saw that the law was there to protect them and, as has been discussed, felt a personal obligation, both to prevent other sex workers from experiencing what they had experienced and to feel that justice had been served. The perpetrator was positioned as responsible and had to answer for their actions. These sex workers felt a sense of pride in standing up to anyone who overstepped their boundaries:

> It's not just that he disregarded my safety and my boundaries and the rules I set in that room. It's that he disregarded a legal regulation of the industry I work in. So, it would be the same if you didn't wear a hard hat at a construction site or shit like that. (Talia, ANZ, brothel)
>
> I feel a responsibility as a human to, if that were to ever happen to me again or if something, sexual violence were to happen to me again, to protect other people from having that happen. (Jane, ANZ, brothel)
>
> ...because I feel really disgraced that he did what he did and the way it happened; it seemed like he'd done it before… I would feel even worse if I withdrew it and then heard something happened, you know. Not even with the same guy, just to hear something happened to another girl, say at work or something, I would just feel, you know, almost like everyone's got their voice, and then if I withdraw my voice, I could hurt another victim, you know. (Alice, ANZ, various)

Even though no sex workers in any of the jurisdictions had attempted to test whether non-payment could be prosecuted as rape, the context of decriminalisation, again, appeared to support resolution—or at least some form of it in Christine's (ANZ, various) case. Christine recounted a situation where she had been picked up by a client who she argued raped her because he dropped her back on the street without paying her and also, to her dismay, did not put the condom on. As she got out of the car, she "ripped the registration out of the window" and gave it to police officers who happened to be across the road. They intercepted his car on the motorway.

> … and they arrested him there and then, but he was saying that he paid me the money and, and done the deed and dropped me off, and I said, 'No, he didn't pay me the money'…There's a ripped condom packet too, but the condom's still in the packet, and I deliberately dropped it on the floor beside the front seat, and um on the side of the front seat' and they found that too. (Christine, ANZ, various)

The offender was charged and ultimately convicted of rape and sentenced to seven years' imprisonment.

Working in a decriminalised setting allowed for different perceptions of breaches that would otherwise be considered quite common among sex workers. Jane went on to recall that unwanted sexual contact is "not like someone left the heater on all day or, you know, that's not a workplace complaint. That's a human rights issue" (Jane, ANZ, brothel). Of course, those attitudes may still exist in formal and informal settings. Erihapeti (ANZ, independent) reported an assault to the police, and a family member subsequently asked her if that was not something she should expect in her job. She said "that was pretty... like, pulling the knife out on you... Whoa, how out of touch". However, for the most part, the Aotearoa New Zealand sex workers *themselves* never saw any form of unwanted sexual contact as an occupational hazard.

Court Experiences: What Helps?

We were interested in sex workers' experiences after they reported a crime, and, in particular, what happened once they were involved in the criminal justice system. In the survey, we asked whether people agreed or not with the statement: 'I have confidence in getting justice if a case is taken to court'. Across all sites, only 12% of respondents agreed with this statement (see Table 6.1). Respondents with the most confidence in court justice came from the UK (18% agreement), very closely followed by those from Aotearoa New Zealand (17% agreement). Overwhelmingly, survey respondents from the USA—both across legalised settings in Nevada brothels and criminalised states—showed the least confidence in attaining justice through the courts, with 4% and 7% agreement respectively. Again, this suggests that those in criminalised states, or even legalised and managed settings which are broadly surrounded by criminalisation (i.e. Nevada brothels), are most alienated from the criminal justice system and less likely to believe that it is there for them to obtain justice through the courts.

No study participants from the USA (whether survey respondent or interviewee) had court experience—a situation that can be explained by virtue of the fact that, as mentioned earlier, sex work in most states is intensely criminalised.[3] In the quasi-criminalised context of the UK, meanwhile, experiences were more varied. Below, we explore some of the participants' experiences in court.

Experiences in UK Courts

It is well known and well documented that, in the UK court context, victims of sexual violence and assault are often treated inadequately. Indeed, the response here on such issues has not kept up with policy, to the extent that Smith and Skinner (2012) suggest that there remain "fundamental inadequacies" in the UK courts. Our interviewees' experiences of the courtroom reflect some of these failings. Interviewees recounted stories of stigma and of being treated differently and unfairly because of the sex-work context in which they experience harms. Even though the UK had the most survey respondents who spoke more positively about getting justice through criminal proceedings, respondents also identified a number of problems that contributed to their negative experiences. Many of them reported problems regarding the healthcare system, connected to gathering forensic evidence for criminal justice investigations. When Emily was violently raped this was her experience in a hospital:

> There was one occasion, I had to ask for a test, a swab test because I said the situation, and they were like, 'Oh okay, right okay, I'll go and speak to someone, get a doctor to come over'. And they had a look and that but they didn't do any swabs. I went, 'Are you not even going to do a test?' They were like, 'Yeah, but that's the kind of job you do', and I was like, 'You fucking what?' Oh, and I had to really keep it cool because I was ready to hit the roof. Yeah, I was fuming; I was like, 'I want to speak to...' And I made complaints and everything. But no-one should get treated like that; it's disgusting. (Emily, UK, various)

[3] Other than ten regions in the state of Nevada, the rest of the USA criminalises any sexual services, relationships or organising. See, for example, https://decriminalizesex.work/advocacy/prostitution-laws-by-state/

As Emily's experience demonstrates, police investigations can involve medical examinations; and Anna also felt as though healthcare staff were particularly insensitive to her needs after a male client had raped her just hours earlier:

> … 'You want a male to go near me after I've just been… What? No mate! See you later'. I think they should make it that rape victims, that it's a female police surgeon because the last thing you want is a male going near you. And then… the officer was, 'Why are you being difficult? They've got other things to be doing; they don't have to be here'. Hang on a minute, 'I don't want to be here mate, I don't have to be here either, yeah? I'm a victim and you want a man to come near me after I've just gone through whatever I've gone through, it ain't gonna happen is it?' Like come on, let's be real, yeah? (Anna, UK, street-based)[4]

Although these experiences were not with police officers or criminal justice staff directly, they were barriers along the pathway of intervention and support—in these cases, the collation of forensic evidence—that should be afforded to all sexual violence victims/survivors.

Further along the criminal justice timeline, those who had gone through the UK court system explained how standing in the witness box was a brutal experience:

> The trial was horrible because basically the [perpetrator's defence] made it sound like I wasn't raped, I just weren't paid, do you know what I mean? … I know it's the [defence's] job but come on, man … my injuries was horrific. I was raped anally and vaginally. I had stitches anally and so it was obvious that it was a violent rape. It was obvious. I spent three weeks in hospital, like I said. They don't keep you in hospital for nothing, do they? But they still put me in; they rung me through the mill. (Anna, UK, street-based)

---

[4] Guidance provided to Sexual Assault Referral Centres in England and Wales does consider the need to be able to offer victim/survivors a choice of gender of the forensic examiner, where it is possible to do so (see National Service Specification for Sexual Assault Referral Centres, p. 33, https://www.england.nhs.uk/wp-content/uploads/2018/04/PRN00577-national-service-specification-sexual-assault-referral-centres-updated.pdf). However, this may not always be supported by the necessary staffing at the time of the examination.

This differs from the experiences of non-sex-working victim/survivors because of the defence being able to suggest it is part of the job (an 'occupational hazard') and perhaps the only issue is with regard to whether payment occurred or not—and not whether rape occurred or not. However, there were differences in experiences of participants that can be noted. When asked about the evidence-giving process, Tess was relatively positive:

> I found it alright. I mean, the only thing when I was going on my interview, is my [support] worker is not allowed in the room with me when I'm getting my interviews to court. But I could have stopped it at any point and I could have gone out to him, so it were alright. (Tess, UK, street-based)

The English Collective of Prostitutes in the UK continually raises awareness of the problems with sex workers accessing justice in rape cases (Elks, 2019). In Anna's case, her first trial resulted in a hung jury and her second trial resulted in the perpetrator getting a jail sentence. She recounts the prejudice and stigma against sex workers she felt from those members of the jury who did not believe her, even though the jury were shown evidence of visible signs of the injury she had sustained:

> [During the first trial (hung jury)] there was no doubt that something happened because of my injuries. But I honestly believe it was people's perception of working girls that made them say 'Not guilty'... I'm looking at the jury and it's like you can just see, just with body language and that, and I'm thinking, 'You lot need your eyes opening because not everybody lives in that comfortable world'. (Anna, UK, street-based)

There were sex workers who reported on the aspects that made the process better for them, from kind and understanding officers to procedures that made the process easier, such as support workers and various identity protections. Participants described the impact of professionals supporting them through the court process:

> ...I went to court with [my support worker] and [the support worker] did half the work... (Tess, UK, street-based)

> On that occasion, the head officer, she was brilliant. She went out of her way to get in court and I was never doubted whatsoever; she was behind me all the way. (Anna, UK, street-based)

There are, then, some 'take homes' here in terms of better practice, particularly around forensic investigations and where sex workers feel supported in the UK context. Ensuring that support workers, who have a clear focus on the sex worker as the complainant, are present is key, and a practitioner who is not connected to a state criminal justice agency appeared to make a significant difference to the experience.

Experiences in Aotearoa New Zealand Courts

In Aotearoa New Zealand, the interviewees revealed a legal system that protected the victim by mostly keeping their identity out of records and maintaining their anonymity during the trial. One respondent who worked in a brothel explained the different measures that were in place to facilitate her witness statement:

> I could [testify] behind a screen, or actually because of Covid, I could have done it just remotely, as a video thing. I could have done it in a different room while being in the courthouse. There was all sorts of different things, um, sort of offered to me. (Talia, ANZ, brothel)

Since New Zealand Prostitutes Collective (NZPC, a sex-worker-led organisation in ANZ) have begun liaising with police, there is a mechanism that is increasingly being used when sex workers are reporting sexual harm crimes against clients. It protects the legal name of the sex worker up until trial. The sex worker still must provide their legal identity to the police; however, when charges are laid, this is redacted in the documents provided to the defence. They provide their legal details for the administration part of their statement, but when they write their statement, they identify themselves as their workname. This way the offender is still able to know who is accusing them of a crime (see Chapter 2).

Unfortunately, this does not apply to charges of harassment or harmful digital communication, as they do not meet the threshold. However, this is often when sex workers are feeling most fearful of their legal identity being known. Also, it runs into problems when charges are reduced. In a recent case relayed to us by NZPC colleagues, the sex worker withdrew her complaint altogether when her sexual harm complaint was reduced to a Section 9 (of the Prostitution Reform Act) charge and it no longer counted as a Category 3 charge, so her legal identity could no longer be redacted. However, if the offender pleads guilty, the sex worker's name is protected from them completely. This is where the legal provisions work effectively. For example, in 2022, there was a case of complaints of intimate visual recording of 14 sex workers (see Osborne, 2022), and, in the same year, a case of a customer receiving a six-month community sentence for not using a dental dam despite clear instructions from the worker. This was considered an indecent assault charge (see Galuszka, 2022). There are laws in Aotearoa New Zealand that enable the protection of the sex worker, which encourages engagement in the criminal justice system; but the nuances of how these laws are applied may create additional barriers for some, even within decriminalised settings.

Conclusion

This chapter has explored sex workers' perceptions and experiences with the criminal justice process across various legislative contexts. We documented accounts of workers who navigated formal reporting processes, highlighting diverse impacts and outcomes. The differences between decriminalised, semi-criminalised, and criminalised settings were considered and recognised as factors influencing sex workers' legal mobilisation. How individuals understand formal law reflects the legal context in which they work. Additionally, their understanding is shaped by how law enforcement and other actors in the criminal justice system interpret the law and perceive sex workers' legal and social standing.

Previous research shows that both sex workers and sexual violence survivors often have negative experiences with criminal justice proceedings, facing victim-blaming and re-traumatisation. When these two identities overlap (i.e., a sex worker who is also a survivor of sexual violence), the likelihood of seeking formal redress is significantly lower. This chapter specifically explores how different legal contexts affect these perceptions and outcomes for sex workers.

Our survey found varying attitudes towards the criminal justice system and the belief that the police and courts would take their reports seriously. The greatest difference emerged when comparing decriminalised (ANZ) and criminalised (USA) settings. A relatively positive experience with formal law in decriminalised markets, compared to where they could be subject to prosecution in criminalised states, appears to reduce feelings of legal alienation. Their own prior experiences, as well as the experiences of their peers, with the criminal justice process also informed sex workers' perceptions and understanding of formal law and affected their willingness to seek justice formally.

When it came to actually engaging with criminal justice proceedings, only a minority of survey participants reported incidents to the police. Reporting was not more common in decriminalised settings, despite generally more positive attitudes towards these processes. Most of those who did report to the police did so to help protect others. Those who chose not to report cited reasons such as the fear of being criminalised themselves, particularly in the USA.

Additionally, the attitudes of criminal justice professionals and how they responded—often viewing violations against sex workers as merely occupational hazards—affected sex workers' experiences with formal reporting options. Positive experiences were more likely in legal contexts like Aotearoa New Zealand, where the Prostitution Reform Act specifically requires sex-work clients to wear condoms, supporting a more positive response from criminal justice professionals. Conversely, in criminalised contexts, the application of the law against sex workers or a misunderstanding of the law surrounding sex work led to poorer experiences for those who did come forward.

These contextual factors highlight the importance of considering how sex workers' understanding of formal law and their perceived possibilities for legal mobilisation are influenced by the perceptions and attitudes of other actors. These actors include other sex workers, brothel management, the police, various parties connected to the justice system (such as healthcare providers, jury members, and case workers), as well as general society and representatives of social movements like #MeToo. While sex workers often expressed a willingness to report sexual violence, this rarely led to formal reporting, and seeking formal redress through the criminal justice system was even more uncommon.

Sex workers' willingness to report formally was primarily affected by the legislative context around sex work in their areas and their broader perceptions of the criminal justice process. Their legal mobilisation was also influenced by informal routes for resolution, which were more common in decriminalised settings. Therefore, for those involved in criminal justice processes to better engage with sex workers, they must understand and dismantle the barriers related to the criminalisation of sex workers.

References

Amnesty International. (2016). *Sex workers at risk: A research summary on human rights abuses against sex workers*. Retrieved July 14, 2024, from: https://www.amnesty.org/en/documents/pol40/4061/2016/en/

Bowen, R., Hodsdon, R., Swindells, K., & Blake, C. (2021). Why report? Sex workers who use NUM opt out of sharing victimisation with Police. *Sexual Research and Social Policy, 18*, 885–896. https://doi.org/10.1007/s13178-021-00627-1

Brents, B. G., & Hausbeck, K. (2005). Violence and legalized brothel prostitution in Nevada: Examining safety, risk, and prostitution policy. *Journal of Interpersonal Violence, 20*(3), 270–295. https://doi.org/10.1177/0886260504270333

Brown, K., & Sanders, T. (2017). Pragmatic, progressive, problematic: Addressing vulnerability through a local street sex work partnership initiative. *Social Policy and Society, 16*(3), 429–441.

Brown, K., Grace, S., & Redman, S. (2024). Policing vulnerability: The care and control of sex workers through designated police officers. *British Journal of Criminology*, Open access.https://doi.org/10.1093/bjc/azae026

Dewey, S., & St. Germain, T. (2014). "It depends on the cop:" Street-based sex workers' perspectives on police patrol officers. *Sexuality Research and Social Policy, 11*, 256–270.

Elks, S. (2019). Sex workers denied justice over rapes says UK prostitutes' collective. *Thomson Reuters Foundation*. Retrieved February 8, 2024, from: https://news.trust.org/item/20191105120530-v6kp7/

Galuszka, J. (2022, June 3). Sex worker indecently assaulted by man who failed to practice safe sex. *Stuff*. Retrieved July 18, 2024, from: https://www.stuff.co.nz/national/crime/300605102/sex-worker-indecently-assaulted-by-man-who-failed-to-practice-safe-sex

Kinnell, H. (2008). *Violence and sex work in Britain* (1st ed.). Willan. https://doi.org/10.4324/9781843926887

Krüsi, A. (2014). *The social and structural production of violence, safety and sexual risk reduction among street-based sex workers* (PhD thesis, University of British Columbia).

Lea, S. J., Callaghan, L., Grafton, I., Falcone, M. A., & Shaw, S. (2016). Attrition and rape case characteristics: A profile and comparison of female sex workers and non-sex workers. *Journal of Interpersonal Violence, 31*(12), 2175–2195.

Lorenz, K., & Jacobsen, C. (2021). Sexual violence survivors' experiences with the police and willingness to report future victimization. *Women & Criminal Justice,* pp. 1–23. https://doi.org/10.1080/08974454.2021.1985045

Marquis, C., & Langlois, A. (2023, January 20). Met Police: 'Women don't feel safe approached by a policeman...because we're not safe,' say campaigners. *London World*. Retrieved February 8, 2024, from: https://www.londonworld.com/news/crime/met-police-we-dont-feel-safebecause-were-not-safe-says-campaign-group-3994311

Mendes, K., Ringrose, J., & Keller, J. (2018). # MeToo and the promise and pitfalls of challenging rape culture through digital feminist activism. *European Journal of Women's Studies, 25*(2), 236–246.

Minichiello, V., & Scott, J. (Eds.). (2014). *Male sex work and society*. Columbia University Press.

Osborne, H. (2022, December 22). Man sentenced for secretly filming his consensual encounters with 14 sex workers. *New Zealand Herald*. Retrieved July 18, 2024, from: https://www.nzherald.co.nz/nz/man-sentenced-for-secretly-filming-his-consensual-encounters-with-14-sex-workers/3XTJLEZSIFCNFIPE2WHVOFVQD4/

Penfold, C., Hunter, G., Campbell, R., & Barham, L. (2004). Tackling client violence in female street prostitution: Inter-agency working between outreach agencies and the police. *Policing & Society, 14*(4), 365–379.

Smith, O., & Skinner, T. (2012). Observing court responses to victims of rape and sexual assault. *Feminist Criminology, 7*(4), 298–326.

Spencer, D., Dodge, A., Ricciardelli, R., & Ballucci, D. (2018). "I think it's re-victimizing victims almost every time": Police perceptions of criminal justice responses to sexual violence. *Critical Criminology, 26*(2), 189–209.

Stardust, Z., Treloar, C., Cama, E., & Kim, J. (2021). "I wouldn't call the cops if I was being bashed to death": Sex work, whore stigma and the criminal legal system. *International Journal for Crime, Justice and Social Democracy, 10*(3), 142–157.

Struyf, P. (2023). To report or not to report? A systematic review of sex workers' willingness to report violence and victimization to police. *Trauma, Violence, & Abuse, 24*(5), 3065–3077.

Victims' Commissioner UK. (2023). *Victims' experience: Annual survey 2022.* Retrieved July 14, 2024, from: https://cloud-platform-e218f50a4812967ba1215eaecede923f.s3.amazonaws.com/uploads/sites/6/2023/11/Victim-Survey-2022.pdf

Weitzer, R. (2005). Flawed theory and method in studies of prostitution. *Violence against Women, 11*(7), 934–949. https://doi.org/10.1177/1077801205276986

West, N., & Horn, T. (Eds.) (2021). *We too: Essays on sex work and survival: Essays on sex work and survival*. Feminist Press at CUNY.

Wilkinson, J. (2023, May 30). Only one claim decided by Human Rights Review Tribunal so far this year. *New Zealand Herald*. Retrieved December 30, 2023, from: https://www.nzherald.co.nz/nz/only-one-decision-issued-by-human-rights-review-tribunal-so-far-this-year/BVAWQBCRZRBXJFR7UTJO5USFDE/

Young, K. M. (2014). Everyone knows the game: Legal consciousness in the Hawaiian cockfight. *Law & Society Review, 48*(3), 499–530. https://doi.org/10.1111/lasr.12094

Zvi, L. (2022). Police perceptions of sex-worker rape victims and their offenders: A vignette study. *Journal of Interpersonal Violence, 37*(15–16), NP14189–NP14214.

7

Bridging Gaps: Peer Recommendations for Better Services

Susie Balderston, Alessandra Lanti, Samuel Thomson, Jessica Hyer Griffin, Cherida Fraser, Caoimhe Ní Dhónaill, and Teela Sanders

Introduction

Looking across all sites in our research, it has become apparent that many of our participants have been denied—however unintentionally—what they needed, from a myriad of services, in the aftermath

S. Balderston · S. Thomson · J. H. Griffin
University of Strathclyde, Glasgow, UK

A. Lanti
University of Nevada, Las Vegas, Nevada, USA

C. Fraser
NZPC: Aotearoa New Zealand Sex Workers' Collective, Wellington, New Zealand

C. N. Dhónaill
Queen's University Belfast, Belfast, UK

T. Sanders (✉)
University of Leicester, Leicester, UK
e-mail: teela.sanders@leicester.ac.uk

T. Sanders et al. (eds.), *Voicing Consent*, Palgrave Advances in Sex Work Studies,
https://doi.org/10.1007/978-3-031-77715-8_7

of their experience of rape, sexual assault, and/or unwanted contact. Some were told that 'that's just the way the system is', while others were more openly discriminated against because they were a sex worker. Against this backdrop, this chapter will pull together nine key recommendations for implementing and delivering sex-worker-knowledgeable support services, which we have identified in association with the sex workers from this study.

As well as discussing challenges they faced, through the surveys and interviews that have informed this book, participants (from Aotearoa New Zealand (ANZ), Nevada in the USA, and the UK) were also asked to tell us what they would change or improve—including their hopes for violence prevention, service improvements, and legal changes. These recommendations were then coded, collated, and arranged into key themes using NVivo software. We used the James Lind Priority Setting Method (Staley et al., 2020) to iteratively discuss and prioritise the recommendations in workshops and to remain aware of our own biases. Although some recommendations may be more relevant to specific organisations—such as health, NGOs, the criminal justice service, or sex-work organisations—it is best practice for all services to learn from one another. The recommendations in this chapter, therefore, are cross-service and have been grouped into the following core themes: developing trauma-informed services; working with and for sex workers; and improving safety through lobbying for decriminalisation and supporting the improvement of working conditions.

The aim of outlining these recommendations is to help counter the invalidation, stigma (Sweeney et al., 2018), and attitudinal barriers that many sex workers and survivors have faced during their journey through services, by valuing and highlighting the importance of their views; sex workers are the experts in identifying what they need. In sharing the recommendations from participants and further disseminating them to relevant services, we hope that readers and allies will use them to improve experiences and outcomes in the future.

Cross-Service Recommendations

Trauma-Informed Services

Trauma-informed working offers a culture in which a professional can meet a person to address their needs in a non-stigmatising fashion (SAMHSA, 2014). A trauma-informed professional must understand that sex work is not inherently traumatising or violent (Sanders, 2016), but that trauma can be recreated inadvertently by stigma (discussed further later in this chapter). Asking what has happened to a person and what they need, not who they are, is the first step to providing adequate support. Operationalising a trauma-informed approach involves recognising and embedding key principles of empowerment, voice and choice; trustworthiness and transparency; peer support; collaboration and mutuality; and safety (SAMHSA, 2014). These principles also map onto the recommendations discussed in this chapter.

Recommendation 1. Allow Survivors Choice Through Processes, Including Accessing Healthcare and Through the Criminal Justice System

All survivors of sexual violence (in some shape or form) have had choice and control taken away from them and need services to assist them in a way that is appropriate to their needs. Sharing decision-making with patients is shown to improve affective-cognitive outcomes—that is, how patients feel, longer term, after their experience of healthcare (Shay & Lafata, 2015). For example, after a rape, Alice was taken to the sexual assault clinic in an ambulance, but, "I felt like, 'Why do I need an ambulance? I can just go in a car, you know' and they go, 'No, no, you have to. It's just, like, the way it is'" (Alice, ANZ, various). A first responder explaining what was going to happen to Alice, and why, could have made a difference to her feelings of control and dignity. Talia, another sex worker also raped in Aotearoa New Zealand, explains why this kind of approach is important: "I wanted to drive myself because, I don't know, I just wanted to have some control still" (Talia, ANZ, brothel).

This choice, where possible, should also extend to the criminal justice system. For instance, survivors should be allowed to choose the gender of the police officer handling their report following a crime. For example, Sheryl was left crying in the police station for over an hour by a front-desk policeman before being referred to a female sexual assault specialist: "… the support that I got, which is probably my main support, was the detective that was working on my case, to be honest. She was lovely. She went up and over and beyond to help me" (Sheryl, ANZ, independent). Talia similarly argued for specialist police: "… the detectives that are in the Adult Sexual Harm thing. They were just so onto it the whole way through, and it's just this lack of education with the new guys in the front of the building [police at the front desk of the police station]" (Talia, ANZ, brothel). Sex workers who experience violence should be able to report to a specialist detective in sexual assault and have a consistent, trained, police liaison contact, and victims should be provided with clear victim-support information about every step of the process.

Recommendation 2. Support Sex Workers to Be Empowered, and Build Trust Through Developing Relationships

Through discussion with participants, we became aware of a case where an 11-year sentence was handed to a man who secretly filmed his encounters with 14 sex workers. A positive news article about the conviction, in the *New Zealand Herald*, quoted one of the sex workers involved, whose statement in court read, "I feel empowered by reporting. … I want him to learn from this that you respect women the same way you respect men …" (Osborne, 2022). Justice for our participants has been a rare occurrence, particularly in the USA, and media reporting of sex work is usually highly problematic in criminalised and partially criminalised settings. Therefore, sex-worker-led organisations feel that positive reporting of those cases where sex workers have achieved justice—including when this has involved the support of sex-worker-led organisations—might help improve trust and confidence for other sex workers in the future.

Trauma-informed services can help to reduce stigma and ensure dignified, safe access for sex workers, through empowerment and trust. This is particularly important for mental health services, where a therapeutic alliance for positive outcomes cannot be achieved in the face of stigma and preconceived views. As one practitioner explained to us:

> Yeah, there's a lot of support required in terms of trust-building for sex workers because it's not always easy to access sex-working-knowledgeable practitioners in our field. So, the kind of support that I provide, in developing a relationship with the people I'm doing therapy with, looks quite different to what I would usually do with folks ... I'm sex-worker friendly and I'm going to be there to support them rather than save them or change them or try and move them into different industries. (Practitioner, ANZ)

Working with and for Sex Workers

To address the trauma-informed principles of peer support, collaboration, and mutuality, services must work with and for sex workers—that is, engage in collaboration in order to be culturally competent and sex-worker-informed.

Recommendation 3. Mainstream Services Should Partner with Sex Workers and Sex-Work-Specialist Organisations

In this study, 39% of survey respondents who had experienced unwanted contact told another sex worker about what had happened to them, while 12% told a sex-worker organisation (see Chapter 5). As the first point of contact, then, such peer support can provide a crucial link to the trusted services that a sex worker needs. Where convictions and good health outcomes were achieved for participants, there was usually a sex-worker-led organisation advocating alongside and navigating barriers with them through difficult systems. Mainstream services can also partner with specialist, user-led organisations, to better support clients who have not traditionally accessed their services. For example, in San Francisco, the

St James Infirmary—the first occupational safety and health clinic for sex workers, run by sex workers, in the USA—provides sex-worker-led medical and social health services for sex workers of all genders and their families.

One of the critical ways that police officers and their services can become more trusted by sex workers is to work with sex-worker-led organisations. As one therapist explained, "… listening to sex workers and sex worker organisations is going to empower those systems to provide a much, much better service and one that's more reflective of the rights of sex workers" (Practitioner, ANZ). However, sex-worker-led organisations are rarely adequately funded (see Grenfell et al., 2016), and so funding is an area in which public bodies, commissioners, and communities can powerfully ally with sex workers and specialist organisations.

Recommendation 4. Services Can and Should Engage Sex Workers in Delivering Education Programmes

Many of our sex-worker respondents showed expert knowledge of the different elements of consent, which could be of great value to non-sex-working populations for staying safe in relationships and perhaps in reducing sexual violence. Sex workers like these participants could take a leading role in educational campaigns and training, to improve public understanding of these issues, which, in turn, could help to prevent sexual violence, harassment, and unwanted contact in the future. As Linda and Emily explain:

> It's all about awareness, isn't it, really? You know, like people never used to wear a seatbelt until it was aware. People never knew not to smoke on buses until it was aware. It's about making things aware to people and then maybe things will change. (Linda, UK, street-based)
>
> They just need people like us ... [to] get in the police station and talk to these officers. … they need those specially trained just for sexual assaults and working women, dedicated to them … give them a whole list of things to do and what not to say as well, because when they talk they don't realise how offensive they are. (Emily, UK, various)

Educational training in Aotearoa New Zealand is relatively common and made possible given that sex work is decriminalised. However, there is a limited ability for this in the UK and practically none in the USA outside of the Nevada brothels.

Recommendation 5. Services Should Understand the Specific Requirements of Sex Workers, and How These Differ from Other Survivors

It is the responsibility of every practitioner who is in a position of power and privilege in working with survivors and sex workers, particularly after rape or sexual assault, to be knowledgeable and culturally competent in providing an equal service to marginalised communities and in acting with empathy for the person in front of them. Each person's unique experience matters and sex workers typically face more barriers than do other patients (Lazarus et al., 2012). The value of health allies working with sex-worker-led organisations to ensure access to services cannot be underestimated. As we were able to interview practitioners who were very experienced in working with the sex-work community, it became clear that being 'sex-worker friendly' was only the start, and that much more could be done by practitioners to enhance their position of understanding. One practitioner explained:

> ... [being] sex-worker knowledgeable goes beyond that and is fully allied with the sex worker industry and has understanding around what's actually happening for them, in depth. So, I would say, in my time working there, I've moved from being sex-worker friendly to sex—worker knowledgeable. (Practitioner, ANZ)

Sex-worker-led organisations, crucially, do not give up on sex workers in difficult situations and they have a non-judgemental approach. With many other services rationing appointments, due to tight parameters over who their service users should be, and limiting the length of time that someone can access their services, having the right attitude is crucial. Several sex-worker-led organisations may provide support for sex workers to transition to legalised sex work (for example, in brothels) and offer educational and career training opportunities for sex workers who want to pursue other careers, but taking up these opportunities is not a prerequisite for engaging with their services. Ensuring consistency across services in terms of how sex workers are responded to, in line with being 'sex-worker knowledgeable', may require training of professionals:

> And I think, you know, police departments get all this training and all these other different topics. There should be some training about sex work and about how to deal with vulnerable populations. And I think there should be some kind of … some kind of competency training for how to deal with these situations. (Chrissie, USA, various)

Improving Safety: Decriminalisation and Improved Working Conditions

To address the trauma-informed principle of safety, services and practitioners should support a change in legislation for the decriminalisation of sex work, and, in turn, support the process of improving and standardising of working conditions for sex workers that comes with this legislative change.

> Just because you think what I do is wrong, doesn't make my safety and life worth less. And that's really what it comes down to: just because you don't agree with it, doesn't mean I shouldn't have a safe place to work, the same as anybody else. (Abbey, USA, independent)

Recommendation 6. Sex-Worker Organisations Should Continue to Educate and Help Lobby for Changes and Improvements in Law to Move to Full Decriminalisation

Sex-worker organisations have a powerful voice through which to lobby for changes and improvements in laws and working conditions. These should include allowing sex workers to work together (in the UK and USA) for greater safety, as recommended by sex workers in all of the sites (see Chapter 3). This is already legal in Aotearoa New Zealand and

Nevada brothels. One Nevada brothel worker also explained how the regulated environment helped her feel respected as a sex worker:

> I feel like a lot more people have respect for it, and it's not as looked down upon. ... You're working with staff that are house-keepers and chefs, and security and cashiers — which I consider normal jobs — and they're working all with us. And they treat us all with the same respect. We're treated just as everybody else. (Jessica, USA, various)

Bella (originally from the USA but who had worked in ANZ, independent) explained that "working under decrim, I felt safe for the first time in my life. A game changer, because now I can tell on you and you can't threaten me". Not only was this seen as a way of improving feelings of safety, but also a way to empower sex workers: "to decriminalise sex work would then put more power in the women's hands" (Abigail, USA, Nevada legal brothel).

Recommendation 7. Services and Organisations Should Support the Consistent Application of Regulation

This research has demonstrated, to a large extent, that the decriminalisation of sex work in ANZ and, in more limited ways, the legalisation of sex work in Nevada helps sex workers in their negotiation for health and safety. However, consistency of regulation could improve this situation even further. One important recommendation for regulated establishments in ANZ and Nevada is for sex-worker-led organisations to work closely with, or even form part of, inspection regulatory teams—for example, WorkSpace New Zealand. Several sex-worker participants told us that standards in different establishments varied considerably and that this has a direct relationship to safety:

> So, basically, if a woman was getting assaulted in her room during a party, what we were always told to do was, the whole house is going to rush in there and gang up on this one guy. And a lot of brothels are like that, because the owners are cheap. They don't want to hire extra staff to be security guards ... I think if clients don't see those security guards walking

> around, they're going to think 'Maybe I can get away with a little bit more', right … (Roxanne, USA, Nevada legal brothel)

Improving safety, again, goes hand-in-hand with sex-worker empowerment, through providing information on their rights. Although standards are generally higher in ANZ than are typical elsewhere, there are still improvements to be made in different brothels, as Jane explained: "The previous place … didn't really take it upon themselves to give the ladies as much information as they could" (Jane, ANZ, brothel). Importantly, improving safety and rights knowledge does not have to be costly: "We do have the [Prostitution] Reform Act printed out where we work, so we can just, like, see it and have a good read, which is awesome" (Chanelle, ANZ, various).

There are also many practical steps that can be taken by organisations. For instance, establishments should have alarms regularly tested, and ensure new sex workers understand how to use the security system: "We do have panic buttons in every room that we can activate discreetly in case we need [to]" (Dace, USA, Nevada legal brothel). In addition, organisations can support sex workers in sharing information with one another. In the UK, National Ugly Mugs provides a regularly updated blacklist that sex workers and their organisations can use free of charge. This is invaluable, particularly in criminalised and partially criminalised settings, as one sex worker explained: "But I think the only safety issue we have is being able to communicate with each other and being able to share information with each other on platforms … We'll use Ugly Mugs to record" (Queen, UK, various). In ANZ and Nevada, there are several 'bad date' lists, and many brothels keep their own lists, but these are not always shared, allowing perpetrators to move around establishments.

Recommendation 8. Ensure Better Welfare and Health Support for Sex Workers

Several of our respondents advocated for greater welfare and health support for sex workers. Services working with sex workers to remove barriers to equity were found to be particularly effective in improving health outcomes, in a systematic review of healthcare interventions for sex workers (Johnson et al., 2023). Trauma-informed services can help to reduce stigma and ensure dignified, safe access for sex workers, across physical, sexual, and mental health services, where a therapeutic alliance for positive outcomes cannot be otherwise achieved in the face of stigma and preconceived views. One independent sex worker in the USA reflected:

> ... if you can give out free condoms at schools, why can't you do it at a sex club? You could provide resources like that very easily. You could provide more testing; you could provide free testing ... Even just set up a sex workers' fund for day care. (Abbey, USA, independent)

Basic health and safety provisions can assist sex workers in ways that are expected in other workplaces:

> So, it's not just that he disregarded my safety and my boundaries and the rules I set in that room. It's that he disregarded a legal regulation of the industry I work in. So, it would be the same [as] if you didn't wear a hard hat at a construction site ... (Talia, ANZ, brothel)

To provide an example of good practice, NZPC, Aotearoa New Zealand Sex Workers' Collective, a sex-worker-led organisation, receives core funding from the Ministry of Health, and they are contracted to provide advocacy, as well as health promotion in sexual and reproductive health. This is an evidence-based model; peer outreach has, elsewhere, been shown to lead to sex workers being more likely to access clinics at an earlier point in a crisis (Krishnamurthy et al., 2016).

Recommendation 9. Challenge and Dismantle the Stigma Against Sex Work and Sex Workers

> End the stigma around it, because that's just like rape culture and everything else — you've got to end the stigma around it in order to fix anything. (Roxanne, USA, Nevada legal brothel)

Many of these recommendations may seem surprisingly minor to people who are not sex workers, victim-survivors of violence, or both. At the heart of these recommendations, though, is the need to address the stigma of sex workers in mainstream services and communities. The stigma against sex workers—particularly as described by participants in criminalised and partially criminalised sites—can be entrenched, even in the most necessary of crisis services, and has produced perverse and damaging results. The externally facing stances of organisations can be incredibly important with regard to how accessible they appear to sex workers. As one third-sector advocate told us, if an organisation has a position suggesting that sex work equates with sexual violence, "that's definitely a huge barrier in terms of accessing, like, sexual violence support, I think" (Practitioner, UK).

Stigma entrenched in policy is also (even when unintentional) a barrier to services for sex workers. In tackling institutional barriers, co-producing with and involving sex workers in training, conducting audits, and working as expert partners is a powerful approach based in relationship, which can have invaluable benefits for mainstream organisations. Equality Impact Assessments are a statutory requirement in the UK, designed to remove barriers to publicly funded services; but best practice can go further by including sex workers as a minority group in these activities. Training and co-production with and by sex workers can help to remove stigma and barriers to equity (Bowen & Bungay, 2016).

Through this project, we have been heartened and impressed by the visible impact of best practices on the attitudes, safety, and justice for sex workers in Aotearoa New Zealand. This approach has been hard-won and has been demonstrated as working after 20 years of decriminalisation, although we recognise there is still more to do, even there. ANZ has shown that if there are improvements in services for sex workers, who experience persistent stigma and discrimination (a particularly crucial point in criminalised jurisdictions), positive changes for other minoritised groups and most service users will likely be made.

References

Bowen, R., & Bungay, V. (2016). Taint: An examination of the lived experiences of stigma and its lingering effects for eight sex industry experts. *Culture, Health & Sexuality, 18*(2), 184–197.

Grenfell, P., Eastham, J., Perry, G., & Platt, L. (2016). Decriminalising sex work in the UK. *British Medical Journal, 354*. https://doi.org/10.1136/bmj.i4459

Johnson, L., Potter, L. C., Beeching, H., Bradbury, M., Matos, B., Sumner, G., Wills, L., Worthing, K., Aldridge, R. W., Feder, G., & Hayward, A. C. (2023). Interventions to improve health and the determinants of health among sex workers in high-income countries: A systematic review. *The Lancet Public Health, 8*(2), e141–e154.

Krishnamurthy, P., Hui, S. K., Shivkumar, N., Gowda, C., & Pushpalatha, R. (2016). Assessing the impact of peer educator outreach on the likelihood and acceleration of clinic utilization among sex workers. *PLoS ONE, 11*(7), e0159656. https://doi.org/10.1371/journal.pone.0159656

Lazarus, L., Deering, K. N., Nabess, R., Gibson, K., Tyndall, M. W., & Shannon, K. (2012). Occupational stigma as a primary barrier to health care for street-based sex workers in Canada. *Culture, Health & Sexuality, 14*(2), 139–150.

Osborne, H. (2022, December 22). Man sentenced for secretly filming his consensual encounters with 14 sex workers, *New Zealand Herald*. Retrieved July 18, 2024, from https://www.nzherald.co.nz/nz/man-sentenced-for-secretly-filming-his-consensual-encounters-with-14-sex-workers/3XTJLEZSIFCNFIPE2WHVOFVQD4/

Sanders, T. (2016). Inevitably violent? Dynamics of space, governance, and stigma in understanding violence against sex workers. *Studies in Law, Politics and Society, 71* (Special issue: Problematizing prostitution: critical research and scholarship), 93–114. https://doi.org/10.1108/S1059-433720160000071005

Shay, L. A., & Lafata, J. E. (2015). Where is the evidence? A systematic review of shared decision making and patient outcomes. *Medical Decision Making, 35*(1), 114–131.

Staley, K., Crowe, S., Crocker, J. C., Madden, M., & Greenhalgh, T. (2020). What happens after James Lind alliance priority setting partnerships? A qualitative study of contexts, processes and impacts. *Research Involvement and Engagement, 6*, Article no. 41. https://doi.org/10.1186/s40900-020-00210-9

Substance Abuse and Mental Health Services Administration (SAMHSA). (2014). Concept of trauma and guidance for a trauma-informed approach. Substance Abuse and Mental Health Services Administration *Briefing*, 14–4884. Retrieved December 13, 2023, from: https://ncsacw.acf.hhs.gov/userfiles/files/SAMHSA_Trauma.pdf

Sweeney, A., Filson, B., Kennedy, A., Collinson, L., & Gillard, S. (2018). A paradigm shift: Relationships in trauma informed mental health services. *Bjpsych Advances, 24*(5), 319–333.

8

Legal Consciousness and Sex Work: Towards More Inclusive Policy

Jane Scoular, Fanni Gyurko, Barbara G. Brents, Teela Sanders, and Gillian Abel

Introduction

In previous chapters, we have shown that different legal contexts have a profound influence on sex workers' experiences with unwanted sexual contact. We have explored how these legal frameworks influence the perceptions and responses of victims, offering a victim-led perspective.

J. Scoular
Strathclyde Law School, University of Strathclyde, Glasgow, UK

F. Gyurko
University of Oxford, Oxford, UK

B. G. Brents
University of Nevada, Las Vegas, Nevada, USA

T. Sanders (✉)
University of Leicester, Leicester, UK
e-mail: teela.sanders@leicester.ac.uk

G. Abel
University of Otago, Dunedin, New Zealand

T. Sanders et al. (eds.), *Voicing Consent*, Palgrave Advances in Sex Work Studies,
https://doi.org/10.1007/978-3-031-77715-8_8

Moreover, by using the concept of legal consciousness, we have shown how different legal environments impact sex workers' experiences and actions, providing a comprehensive picture that we hope will lead to greater understanding and more effective policies.

The legal context for sex work, whether criminalised, partially criminalised, legalised, or decriminalised, significantly influences how sex workers negotiate consent, define unwanted contact, assert their rights, and seek justice. In decriminalised settings like Aotearoa New Zealand (ANZ), sex workers report feeling more empowered to handle violations, whereas in criminalised settings, fear of legal repercussions often prevents them from seeking help outside their informal networks.

But to fully understand experiences of unwanted contact, we must distinguish the law around sex work from that around sexual violence, for the two interact. On the one hand, sexual violence laws often fail sex workers in the same ways they fail non-sex workers. Few general victims of violence report to the police and most do not trust the legal system. While our study has focused only on sex workers, reforms to the criminal legal system that help victims of sexual violence generally will undoubtedly benefit sex-worker victims as well. On the other hand, our findings show that sex workers can be both better prepared and less able to deal with unwanted contact than non-sex workers. Their experience in negotiating sexual contracts better equips them to manage boundaries and express conditions of consent. At the same time, material conditions may impact their ability to enforce these conditions, and the stigma and legal status of their work, as determined by sex-work laws, can hinder their ability to respond and to seek justice. Thus, sex-work laws are important in addition to sexual violence laws.

Further, sex workers' perceptions and responses are shaped by more than just formal statutory law (Hertogh, 2004). Sex workers have diverse experiences even within the same legal jurisdiction. Unwanted incidents range from minor boundary pushing to violence. 'Stealthing' and payment problems are much more frequent than incidents defined by formal law as constituting sexual violence or those that would trigger a formal legal response. The sector—whether the victim works independently or in a brothel—matters. Even across brothels, informal workplace policies and cultures differ significantly.

These informal rules, norms, and community support play a more significant role in how sex workers manage and respond to unwanted sexual contact than does formal sexual violence law. To be sure, the law around sex work provides a strong basis for support (or the lack thereof); but many sex workers rely on peer networks and informal community and workplace norms and practices to navigate their safety and consent. For those able to work legally in brothels, workplace support staff, the informal norms embedded in workplace policies and culture, and simply being around peers are all factors that significantly enhance their personal safety. This reliance is even more important in settings where trust in formal legal systems is low, demonstrating the importance of support mechanisms outside of formal criminal law.

Additionally, our research has highlighted that consent in sex work is dynamic. Sex workers engage in ongoing negotiations and establish clear boundaries. But sometimes these boundaries need to change during a sexual service, and sex workers need the power to do this as they see fit. This complexity is often misunderstood or oversimplified by legal systems. The research underscores that consent is not a one-time or inflexible agreement but a continuous process that sex workers manage through their negotiations with clients. This dynamic understanding of consent is crucial for both preventing and addressing any unwanted contact, especially sexual violence in sex work.

The previous chapters have used both qualitative and quantitative data to provide an in-depth and nuanced exploration of our three main goals:

1. To understand how sex workers experience sexual violence by exploring a nuanced, victim-led definition of consent and harm;
2. To examine the dynamics between different legal contexts (criminalised, legalised, and decriminalised systems) and victims' responses to sexual violence and unwanted sexual contact, focusing on how laws, awareness of legal rights, and law enforcement actions help or hinder in managing these experiences; and

3. To explore the extent to which the legal context affects sex workers' actions, perceptions, understandings, and experiences of sexual violence and unwanted contact.

The book's structure mirrors the process that sex workers follow in setting boundaries and negotiating agreements (Chapter 3), defining and interpreting unwanted incidents (Chapter 4), responding to breaches of those boundaries (Chapter 5), and interacting with the formal criminal legal system (Chapter 6). This approach provides a comprehensive understanding of sex workers' experiences with sexual violence in different legal contexts regulating sex work, the factors influencing sex workers' perceptions of formal sexual violence law, and the actions sex workers take when violations occur.

In this conclusion, we focus on the impact of law on both sex work and sexual violence, in terms of sex workers' experiences and their legal consciousness. Section 8.1 discusses the gap between legal definitions and sex workers' lived realities. Section 8.2 addresses three key themes that sex workers identified as crucial for improving working conditions and mitigating sexual violence: empowerment; peer communication; and learning opportunities. We then provide a brief overview of this study's contributions to research on legal consciousness and then compare our findings on the impact of formal law on sex work with sex workers' experiences of violence. Finally, we discuss the policy implications for balancing regulations on sex and labour within sex-work policy.

Law and Experiences of Sexual Violence

The Gap Between Legal Definitions and Lived Realities

Our research finds that there is a big difference between formal legal definitions of sexual violence and the real-life experiences of sex workers. Formal laws on sexual violence often define the issue narrowly, excluding critical concerns for sex workers, like non-payment and 'stealthing'. These limited legal scopes fail to capture the full range of violations that sex workers face, leading to a disconnect between their experiences and what is legally recognised.

Our data shows that sex workers perceive 'non-payment' as a significant form of sexual violation, both in terms of frequency and in terms of harm. Agreed payment and the clients' use of protection (i.e. a condom) are essential elements of the sexual contract. Sex workers see any breaches of these conditions as violations. Our survey data indicates that 75.6% (365 out of 483) of sex workers who had experienced an incident reported some sort of payment problem. In addition, there are a variety of other breaches sex workers must constantly manage, ranging from minor to violent. These registered on our survey as incidents involving unwanted penetration or a person not stopping when having been asked/told to.

While most clients are respectful of conditions of consent, cultural beliefs about male sexual privilege, combined with racism, classism, xenophobia, cisnormativity, and other systems of inequality, frame how they think of differences between themselves and sex workers, how they will respect boundaries of consent, whether they accept changing conditions of consent or whether they will register a breach as non-consent. Our data shows that sex workers consider it a violation when clients: (1) engage in acts explicitly prohibited prior to the booking; (2) engage in acts not formally discussed; or (3) fail to warn or request consent for certain acts during services.

This broad understanding of sexual violation affects how sex workers mobilise formal legal codes for enforcement and redress. The frequency of formal reporting is very low. In criminalised or semi-criminalised settings, sex workers fear that police will label these events as 'occupational hazards', something expected in their line of work. Any past problematic interactions like this with law enforcement influences their understanding of sexual violence and their willingness to seek formal redress in the future.

There is a clear tension between what sex workers experience as unwanted contact, what the law considers sexual violence, and what sex workers can formally report as such. Law enforcement tends to align more with formal sexual violence laws, which often do not recognise non-payment and 'stealthing'. In contrast, sex workers' understanding of a sexual violation includes these issues, and they are ranked by some as seriously as physical violence. Stealthing is likely also a serious issue for non-sex workers too. This disparity highlights the need for a more inclusive and flexible legal framework that addresses the full spectrum of violations that sex workers (and others more generally) may face.

Legal Alienation and Barriers to Seeking Formal Redress

We know that legal alienation accounts for many of the barriers to seeking formal redress for unwanted contact. Research finds that marginalised groups have: (1) a disbelief in the effectiveness of the law; (2) a fear of negative consequences; (3) a perception of inefficiency in the formal legal system; (4) the constraint of living in a jurisdiction where there is an absence of formal laws to govern the particular situation they face; and/or (5) a lack of knowledge about the law (Ewick & Silbey, 1998; Hertogh, 2018).

Our survey results show that sex workers have little trust in the justice system and the police across all jurisdictions. However, there was a correlation between sex workers' attitudes towards the justice system and the legal context of sex work. Sex workers in the criminalised USA demonstrated the poorest levels of trust in the police and the justice system, followed by semi-criminalised UK sex workers' low opinions of formal law enforcement. In contrast, decriminalised sex workers in Aotearoa New Zealand felt that they were more likely to be believed and taken seriously when formally reporting incidents. This aligns with our findings that, in decriminalised settings, sex workers are more knowledgeable about their rights, leading to higher trust in the justice system. Nonetheless, even in these settings, sex workers rarely reported incidents or sought formal redress.

Our research reveals a shared perception among sex workers that formal law could be used against them when reporting incidents, although this varied by legal context. In criminalised settings, sex workers' legal status itself acts as a significant barrier to reporting. This barrier is exacerbated by the police's stigmatised perception of sex workers. In the USA, sex workers felt that police viewed them as deviant and criminal, further discouraging formal reporting. Formal reporting typically occurred only if sex workers were hospitalised.

Even in decriminalised settings, challenges persisted. One sex worker in Aotearoa New Zealand mentioned she did not report stealthing because the use of condoms in sexual contracts is compulsory by law (Prostitution Reform Act, s.9), and she feared the police might think she was breaking the law. Additionally, Aotearoa New Zealand sex workers reported that minor sexual violence happened so frequently that they perceived reporting it to the police as impractical. They regarded such incidents as the 'reality of the job'. This perception indicates that sex workers feel the law does not serve its intended purpose because, in practice, they cannot effectively mobilise it.

Informal vs. Formal: The Role of Workplace Rules, Informal Norms, and Peer Networks

Our research finds that sex workers rely more on informal norms, conventions, and rules than on formal statutory law to prevent and manage unwanted contact. The interview data reveals that, across all jurisdictions, these informal practices guide sex workers in negotiating and enforcing sexual contracts.

Sex workers, regardless of their setting, implement various practices to ensure their personal safety. These include screening clients, outlining services, setting timing and duration ahead of services beginning, and establishing boundaries, either through advertising or verbal agreements. They stipulate terms for the use of condoms or dental dams and develop specific methods for collecting payment. Additionally, they share their location with others for safety. Techniques for managing pushy clients include using certain body movements, articulating specific warnings, and adjusting their tone of voice. These proactive measures help sex workers maintain control and safety in their work environments.

In brothels or managed settings, workplace rules and informal norms play a crucial role, especially in handling violations that are not covered at all by formal laws on sexual violence, such as payment and condom use.

Brothels often handle advertising and payment through various workplace procedures. Health statutes mandate condom use in Nevada's legal brothels and in Aotearoa New Zealand. Brothel workers often mentioned health codes and condom use as part of negotiating boundaries with clients. However, some sex workers in Aotearoa New Zealand reported less support from management regarding condom use. UK brothels do not have the backing of formal law.

In dealing with boundary pushing, sex workers must constantly negotiate and may amend their conditions of consent during the service they provide, for a variety of reasons. Managed settings offer a structured and adaptable framework for sex workers to negotiate boundaries effectively. Workers in brothels benefit from having other workers nearby, for both safety and advice on preventing violations. These settings provide training, management advice, and informal sharing of tricks and tips among workers. The workplace culture determines a broad range of acceptable and unacceptable acts. Security staff and other workers help enforce rules and norms. Sex workers in Nevada and Aotearoa New Zealand mentioned various resources, including panic alarms, CCTV cameras, and support staff (such as managers, security personnel, and receptionists).

In criminalised contexts, these informal mechanisms outside of formal law were essential in protecting sex workers. In Aotearoa New Zealand's decriminalised setting, meanwhile, formal laws were more helpful. Sex workers that we interviewed often referenced formal laws, recounting having quoted sections of the Prostitution Reform Act 2003 (PRA) and case law rulings when managing clients. (Some brothels support Sections 16 and 17 of the PRA, which allow workers to refuse a client and choose their services, or even to change their mind partway through a booking.)

Despite having formal legal recourse, sex workers in both criminalised and decriminalised settings rarely took formal action when experiencing a breach of contract. They reported that informal actions provided a greater sense of security, safety, and justice, preferring informal redress over formal reporting, the latter being something that they did not expect or desire. While brothel environments offered protection through internal mechanisms and support from management, security staff, and peers, they did not facilitate formal reporting to authorities, leaving a gap in legal recourse.

In Nevada's legal brothels, sex workers believed the police would take them seriously if called, indicating some confidence in the formal legal process. However, even in this seemingly protected environment, they rarely pursued formal reporting. Instead, they often blamed themselves, feeling they should have been clearer in their negotiations or sounded the alarm sooner. Interviews revealed that Nevada brothels would assist sex workers in making formal reports to the police, but most interviewed sex workers did not follow through with this, reporting to us their belief that involving the police would result in no action. This reinforced their reliance on informal norms and rules within the brothel for protection.

Safety measures and support for reporting were inconsistent across brothels. In Aotearoa New Zealand's decriminalised setting, workers often referenced formal laws in client negotiations, quoting sections of the PRA. However, some reported less support from management on condom use and were discouraged from involving the police. Our peer recommendations in Chapter 7 suggest that services and organisations should support the consistent application of formal and informal workplace rules to provide better protection and justice for sex workers.

The structured environment of brothels benefits workers in both criminalised and decriminalised settings by offering dual layers of protection through workplace rules and informal norms. However, this structure stops short of bridging the gap to formal legal systems for enforcing sexual violence laws.

Independent sex workers face a unique set of challenges. Without the support of a brothel's structured rules, they must implement the practices of boundary setting outlined above, typically learned through experience, on their own. Only a few independent sex workers can also rely on a network of peers to navigate their work safely.

This underscores the resilience and resourcefulness required to work independently, but also highlights the absence of formal support structures and the heavy burden on individuals. While independent workers in decriminalised contexts can rely on formal laws if needed, those in criminalised settings must depend solely on informal mechanisms, which sometimes conflict with the formal laws governing sex work.

The Need for Flexibility in Consent and Boundary Setting

We found that sex workers exercised considerable flexibility in defining consent as they negotiated with clients. Our research reveals that sex workers' verbal agreements with clients are binding but also adaptable as a service progresses. Sex workers continuously assess whether clients are breaching consent and determine how to respond. Responses can include warning the client or negotiating higher payments for additional services, and are influenced by various factors, such as financial needs or the relationship with the client, particularly if the client is a regular. For some sex workers, boundaries are rigid, while for others, they are fluid and adaptable.

Versatility is also crucial when sex workers decide how to act upon breaches of agreement. Across all jurisdictions, sex workers reported considering the same factors, such as job security, regular income, and relationships with clients, before taking formal or informal actions. Personal priorities and power dynamics in the situation drive the chosen actions. Some sex workers might consider physically removing either the client or themselves from the situation as being the best option to mitigate breaches of contract.

This dynamic understanding of consent complicates the situation when it comes to how formal law can protect sex workers. We found that, for sex workers, consent is viewed as ongoing, allowing them to withdraw or renegotiate services as needed. This variability highlights that a one-size-fits-all approach to consent, that is necessary in formal criminal law, does not work for everyone. Courts in some jurisdictions are, however, beginning to recognise that consent is contextual, ongoing, and conditional. Nevertheless, the court process remains risky and most victims do not engage with formal systems.

Addressing Challenges in Legal Reform

Our research findings reveal that the flexible ways in which sex workers set and maintain the boundaries of the sexual contract do not easily translate into the seeking of formal redress. Is reform of formal criminal justice law, then, the best solution? We often look to formal law for answers. However, just as advocating for stricter penalties alone has not effectively addressed sexual violence, our study shows that reforms aimed at improving sex worker safety must ensure they do not inadvertently worsen conditions for sex workers.

The primary objective for sex workers is to stay safe while earning money. Our peer recommendations in Chapter 7 emphasise the need for flexibility. Sex workers need choices in the processes affecting their lives, such as accessing healthcare and deciding whether to engage with the criminal justice system. Our research indicates that providing these choices gives sex workers control and dignity, which are essential for their well-being.

Empowerment, Peer Communication, and Opportunities to Learn

Our research finds three important factors that sex workers mentioned for preventing and dealing with unwanted sexual contact: empowerment; communication with peers; and the opportunity to learn. These mechanisms support each other. For example, in criminalised settings where sex workers could not engage, communicate, or network with their peers, they had to learn by trial and error about setting boundaries. This lack of peer support diminished their power to negotiate and enforce boundaries. They had fewer opportunities to understand or access formal legal processes and were less likely to trust criminal legal and other support services.

Empowerment

Empowerment was a recurring theme throughout the chapters and across the different stages of dealing with sexual violence. Our peer researchers also frequently highlighted this theme in their recommendations (Chapter 7). This section discusses the importance of empowerment for sex workers and what it means to be empowered.

Being empowered involves having the power to set and enforce one's boundaries of consent and sexual contracts in all sexual exchanges. In negotiating a sexual contract, empowerment means that sex workers can establish their own consent boundaries in a way that benefits them, maintain those boundaries, and seek redress if those boundaries are breached.

Maintaining and potentially extending the boundaries of consent requires constant assessment of actions during a service. Sex workers that we interviewed explicitly stated that they could handle their own safety when they have greater power. One ANZ sex worker said that she felt more powerful than her client because she determined what the client could or could not do. This underscores that central arguments about consent are fundamentally about having power during the service—clients should respect the sex worker's agency and personhood, and ask for consent and, moreover, adhere to it throughout the service. Sex workers had the power to say no to those clients who asked for discounted rates, or for extra or uncomfortable services, and they could end negotiations at any time. This ability required both experience and relative power.

Being empowered also means having the support of formal law, which was most prevalent in decriminalised settings. In ANZ, the use of condoms is compulsory when providing a sexual service (under PRA, s.9). When a client refused to use a condom, sex workers could assert that it was against the law. Official statutes reinforced their ability to negotiate and maintain boundaries.

For workers in criminalised and semi-criminalised settings who cannot rely on the support of formal law, developing a set of skills and knowledge on how to set and maintain boundaries is crucial. Many sex workers, especially in criminalised contexts, experienced their most violent incidents when they first started working, as offenders took advantage of their inexperience in protecting themselves. In these settings, where experiencing violence is part of learning the 'rules of the game', it is particularly important to learn how to become more empowered in setting boundaries and enforcing them informally.

Our data clearly demonstrates that being or becoming empowered is a process. As sex workers gain more experience, they often change their reactions to violations as they become more aware of the power dynamics at play and how to navigate them. This evolving awareness and adaptation contribute to their empowerment. By learning from others and honing their skills, sex workers can better protect themselves and assert their boundaries, leading to a greater sense of control and safety in their work environments.

Peer Communication

Our research finds that sex workers' ability to interact with their peers is a key factor in safely managing sexual contracts, setting boundaries, enforcing those boundaries, and reporting any violations. Sex workers we spoke to wanted interaction with peers to learn skills, to receive help and to seek justice for others. However, legal barriers often hindered these collective efforts, especially in semi-criminalised and criminalised contexts where such interactions could be construed as trafficking. This limited communication made sex workers less able to learn, and meant they felt powerless and vulnerable. (Our peer recommendations (Chapter 7), likewise, emphasise the need for allowing sex workers to work together.)

The data also shows that a collective sense can be manifested in various ways. Workplace norms, on what services individual sex workers would provide, were crucial in constructing a workplace culture where workers felt empowered to maintain boundaries. Different brothels had distinct collective cultures that influenced client expectations and workers' willingness to do more.

Sex workers were more willing to take formal action when they had close relationships with their peers and co-workers. Our survey data supports this finding. When asked whom they told after their last incident, 39% of sex workers told another sex worker, finding most support through their colleagues and the peer community. By comparison, 24%

of respondents told no one and only 3% reported to sexual violence support charities.

This collective sense of responsibility was crucial in encouraging sex workers to report sexual violence, especially in Aotearoa New Zealand, where recent court cases made clear that formal law may benefit them. Many felt reporting incidents could prevent future harm to others. Indeed, in Aotearoa New Zealand, some saw speaking out as a duty to the community. Building trust and relationships empowered sex workers to seek justice and improve their mental health.

Opportunities to Learn

This theme includes learning about both formal law and informal norms through experience and peer interaction. The ability to interact with peers provides opportunities to learn, leading to empowerment. In this section, we explore *what* sex workers learn, *how* they learn, and *who* they are learning from.

Chapter 3 shows that sex workers learn informal norms for negotiating and maintaining boundaries from peers. Despite some reliance on formal laws in decriminalised settings, managed settings can provide opportunities for training and from both management and co-workers. Practices like 'big sister' mentorships help new workers learn negotiation skills. Learning and teaching the 'rules of the game' aids in preventing, deterring, and protecting against unwanted contact.

Sex workers also learn through experience. In criminalised settings, there are limited opportunities to interact with others and so sex workers must learn by trial and error because of the inability to communicate legally with other sex workers. Decriminalised and managed settings offer more chances to learn from peers. Informal interactions and shared experiences in these settings help sex workers learn how to educate clients on boundaries and consent.

Experienced sex workers play a crucial role in passing information to less experienced workers about which informal actions to take when experiencing sexual violence. Our peer recommendations (Chapter 7) emphasise the need for sex workers to engage in public education programmes and specialist services, as they are experts in elements of consent. Continued education on legal rights is also crucial for their empowerment and safety.

Sex workers gain insights into formal law and their rights in the justice system through interactions with law enforcement and various criminal legal institutions, including caseworkers, healthcare providers, juries, and lawyers. Unfortunately, these experiences often lead to a sense of legal alienation. Sex workers across all jurisdictions reported that police often responded to their complaints with disbelief, belittlement, judgement, or unfavourable treatment because of their profession. These interactions led sex workers to believe that reporting to the police would not offer them protection, shaping their attitudes towards seeking justice through the criminal system. Despite the low reporting and high attrition rates, however, Chapter 6 shows that even limited experiences with the criminal justice system can positively shape sex workers' understanding of formal law, including issues of consent and other legal areas.

Contributions to the Study of Legal Consciousness

This book makes important contributions to the study of legal consciousness by exploring the unique context of sex work. Sex workers managing unwanted sexual contact navigate laws regarding sex work and laws on sexual violence. By examining both formal law and informal practices, the research provides a comprehensive view of how marginalised groups, specifically sex workers, interact with the law at all levels. This approach illuminates the complexities of legal engagement and offers valuable insights into the realities faced by sex workers.

A key theoretical contribution highlights how sex workers perceive breaches of contractual agreements, such as non-payment or removing a condom without consent, as serious violations. This perspective both expands traditional legal definitions of sexual violence and calls for more nuanced and flexible legal frameworks that align with sex workers' lived experiences. By emphasising these differences, the book underscores the need for legal reforms, to both sex-work and sexual violence law, that recognise the dynamic nature of consent and the importance of informal norms and community support in empowering sex workers.

Additionally, the research demonstrates the impact of different legal contexts—criminalised, semi-criminalised, legalised, and decriminalised—on sex workers' legal consciousness. This comparative analysis shows how important legal environments are in shaping legal consciousness and highlights the importance of creating inclusive and effective legal frameworks that account for the realities of sex work.

Comparing Formal Legal Frameworks on Sex Work

The research clearly demonstrates that the legal context in which sex work is situated profoundly shapes the experiences, safety, and empowerment of sex workers. In decriminalised settings like Aotearoa New Zealand, sex workers benefit from a legal framework that provides recognition and certain protections, fostering an environment where they, potentially, can assert their rights more confidently. The aforementioned Prostitution Reform Act offers legal backing that empowers sex workers to handle breaches of consent and encourages them to seek formal redress. However, it is important to note that legal alienation persists. Even in decriminalised settings, sex workers are hesitant to involve law enforcement due to a fear of resultant negative experiences or perceived inefficiencies in the system. This legal alienation is not that different from what non-sex-worker victims of sexual violence experience.

In criminalised settings, sex workers face significant barriers that hinder their ability to protect themselves and seek justice. The fear of arrest and legal repercussions often prevents them from reporting violations or seeking help from authorities. This environment of heightened legal alienation forces sex workers to rely heavily on informal networks and personal strategies to manage their safety and consent. The absence of formal legal protections increases their vulnerability, making it more challenging to establish and enforce boundaries with clients. Consequently, sex workers in these settings have little ability to seek supportive formal legal recourse.

The distinction between how sex workers perceive violations and the public's understanding of sexual assault further explains their responses in these differing legal contexts. In decriminalised environments, sex workers view breaches of agreement, such as non-payment or removing a condom without consent, as serious violations. This understanding helps them navigate their professional interactions with a clearer sense of agency and control. However, this does not always translate into action, as many sex workers still prefer informal resolution methods and may avoid formal reporting due to mistrust or dissatisfaction with legal processes.

Conversely, in criminalised settings, the pervasive stigma and lack of legal support contribute to a more fragmented and precarious experience of consent and violation, where sex workers often feel isolated and powerless. Here, sex workers are less likely to perceive the legal system as an ally and more likely to prioritise immediate safety and practical resolutions over formal legal action.

These findings underscore the critical need for flexible and supportive legal frameworks that recognise the unique realities of sex work. We require an environment where sex workers are empowered to negotiate their conditions of consent and seek justice when violations occur. A holistic approach not only enhances the safety and well-being of sex workers but also fosters a more equitable legal system that respects and protects the rights of all individuals involved in sex work.

Balancing Sex and Work in Policy

How, then, do we address sexual violence—indeed, all unwanted sexual contact—in sex work? The transactional nature of sex work presents a conundrum in addressing sexual violence. There are two main tensions: how effectively the criminal legal system can handle sexual violations, and how well the law can manage the contractual nature of the sex business. Is it SEX work or sex WORK when it comes to dealing with unwanted sexual contact?

Our findings show that there is no single easy answer to these questions. Any solution must both empower sex workers to negotiate the terms of consent effectively and provide meaningful, effective mechanisms to deal with violations. These mechanisms must protect human rights and sex workers' abilities to earn a living. The same improvements to the criminal legal system (including alternatives to that system) that help victims of sexual violence generally will undoubtedly benefit sex-worker victims as well.

Alongside that, we need to navigate the line between protecting sex workers' rights to negotiate flexible conditions of sexual consent and their rights to negotiate and enforce transactional contracts in their work. Legislatures must reconcile the criminal statutes of sex work while also addressing workplace laws that impact these negotiations and enforcement. Additionally, we need to acknowledge how law interacts with and influences the informal mechanisms that protect and empower workers. This requires a nuanced approach that balances legal protection with the realities of sex workers' experiences.

Finally, social norms, institutions, and structural power dynamics—such as race, class, gender, sexuality, citizenship, and ability—shape sex workers' ability to prevent, think about, define, and manage unwanted sexual contact, just as they do in the general population. The forces of classism, racism, ableism, heterosexism, ageism, xenophobia, cisnormativity, and sizeism, the systems of white supremacy, patriarchy, and immigration policies, and the legacies of colonialism all stigmatise and marginalise sex workers. These systems shape how sex workers understand and interact with the law, as well as influence those who create the laws. Recognising these intersections is crucial for developing laws and policies that truly protect and empower sex workers.

References

Ewick, P., & Silbey, S. S. (1998). *The common place of law: Stories from everyday life*. University of Chicago Press.

Hertogh, M. (2004). A 'European' conception of legal consciousness: Rediscovering Eugen Ehrlich. *Journal of Law and Society, 31*(4), 457–481. https://doi.org/10.1111/j.1467-6478.2004.00299.x

Hertogh, M. (2018). *Nobody's law: Legal consciousness and legal alienation in everyday life*. Palgrave Pivot.

9

The Sex Work and Sexual Violence Study: Research Methods

Teela Sanders, Susie Balderston, Chris Wakefield, Jane Scoular, Barbara G. Brents, and Gillian Abel

Introduction

This chapter summarises the values and methodology for the mixed methods, international research from which the data used in this book were drawn.

The Sex Work and Sexual Violence project is described extensively in the project protocol (Scoular et al., 2023). Protocols (cf. Pemberton

T. Sanders (✉)
University of Leicester, Leicester, UK
e-mail: teela.sanders@leicester.ac.uk

S. Balderston · J. Scoular
Strathclyde Law School, University of Strathclyde, Glasgow, UK
e-mail: jane.scoular@strath.ac.uk

C. Wakefield
Whitman College, Walla Walla, Washington, USA

B. G. Brents
University of Nevada, Las Vegas, Nevada, USA
e-mail: barb.brents@unlv.edu

T. Sanders et al. (eds.), *Voicing Consent*, Palgrave Advances in Sex Work Studies,
https://doi.org/10.1007/978-3-031-77715-8_9

et al., 2021) are increasingly adopted in the social sciences, particularly because they help to ensure consistent standards and quality across multiple research sites, as well as transparency in large studies. The protocol describes the eligibility of the participants, the length of the study, anticipated ethical concerns, and details around data storage and methods of analysis in the study. The research was funded by the Economic and Social Research Council (ESRC) (ES/V002465/1).

Mixed Methods Research

The study began in July 2021 and data collection took place over a 12-month period, from March 2022 to March 2023. The mixed research methods in this study included:

- thematic literature reviews, to produce a contemporary knowledge base on the themes of the project and to inform research design;
- an academic advisory board, project steering group, and advisory groups of key academic, sex worker, and NGO advisers in the UK, USA, and Aotearoa New Zealand (ANZ), to provide oversight and assistance at key stages, including in the recruitment of participants, and to guide the research in ensuring ethical, transparent engagement and delivery;
- an expert peer research group with lived experience of sex work and/or sexual violence, who were involved in designing the survey and interview schedules, prioritising recommendations, writing up, and disseminating findings;
- an action learning set, which helped ensure equal and participatory action learning with the team throughout the project;

G. Abel
University of Otago, Dunedin, New Zealand
e-mail: gillian.abel@otago.ac.nz

- qualitative interviews in each research site with sex workers, practitioners, and criminal justice system professionals;
- an international survey, with multivariate statistical analysis and descriptive findings;
- statistical multivariate cluster analysis and descriptive statistics (the latter from responses in which sex-worker respondents disclosed that unwanted sexual contact had happened to them); and
- analysis workshops with the co-investigators, and triangulation of the survey and interview results.

Project Values

Ethics and values were of the highest importance to everyone involved in the project, particularly given the study's sensitive nature, with its focus on sexual violence and barriers to justice for sex workers. Underpinning this research, then, were core values adopted by the research team, including involving experts at every stage and a commitment to trauma-informed design and delivery.

Ethical Research

Ethical approval was granted for this study by the following ethics committees:

- University of Strathclyde Approval;
- University of Leicester Approval;
- Queen's University Belfast: School of Law, Research Ethics Committee;
- University of Otago Approval;
- University of Nevada, Las Vegas; and
- The Commissioner of New Zealand Police: Approval signed by the Director of Evidence Based Policing.

(Ethical research approval was also sought from the Crown Prosecution Service in England and Wales, with the intention of including crown prosecutors in the participant sample; regrettably, however, this approval was not acquired. Crown prosecutors in England and Wales were, therefore, not recruited or interviewed for this project.)

This ethical approval ensured that the project delivered the highest standards of data security and participant safeguards, even where legislation in the research sites did not strictly require this. For example, the personal sensitive data requirements of the European Parliament (2016) General Data Protection Regulation (GDPR), which is in place in the European Union but not the USA or Aotearoa New Zealand, were adopted in respect of all participant data in the project. The research data were anonymised and stored securely, with open-access findings only being deposited in ways that could not allow any participants to be personally identified.

"No Research About Us, Without Us"

The participation slogan "Nothing about us, without us" has been employed by marginalised communities to promote 'voice' and democratic involvement in the face of injustice for many decades (cf. Stone, 1997; Yarbrough, 2019). It is as relevant to academia and sensitive research today and it has been to community involvement promoted by sex workers as survivors of violence, abuse, and criminal injustice for decades. Involving people with lived experience also means that the questions, findings, and impact of research can be more relevant and targeted to where they are needed most. The expert peer researcher group was involved in developing research survey and interview questions, collecting and analysing data, and writing up, prioritising, and disseminating the findings and recommendations (Lushey, 2017).

This participatory approach recognises that people from any community being researched have agency and can participate in research as equal researchers (Higgins et al., 2007). In addition, the research assistant role in the Aotearoa New Zealand site was delivered by NZPC: Aotearoa New Zealand Sex Workers' Collective. This equipped the project with resources to deliver capacity-building and to work in partnership with a sex-worker-led organisation.

The National Institute of Health Research's (NIHR, 2023) best-practice payment guidelines for working with peer researchers were adopted. An additional grant of £10,000 was awarded by the University of Strathclyde Faculty of Humanities and Social Sciences, to continue involvement of the peer researchers through prioritising recommendations, writing up, and disseminating findings in an accessible report.

Trauma-Informed Research Design

The project used trauma-informed practice (SAMHSA, 2014) to ensure safety for participants and safe spaces for researchers to share knowledge, in the context of engaging in emotional research work and sharing power within a research hierarchy (PARTNERS2 Writing Collective, 2020). The project was also designed with prevention in mind, that is, to ensure we did not re-traumatise people and to help us raise awareness about the impact of trauma after sexual violence and injustice in services. Although there is ongoing debate about the efficacy of trigger warnings, mostly when used with general student populations (cf. Boysen, 2017), they were designed into the advertisements used to attract study participants and the initial information about the survey and interview. Respondents could skip any questions they did not want to answer after they had consented to take part in either the survey or interviews.

The interview schedules and survey were designed so that distressing details of sexual violence and barriers to justice were asked in the safest way possible, with only very necessary questions being included and potentially triggering ones occurring approximately midway through (in line with the approach advocated by Campbell et al. (2019). This enabled the participant to begin the interview or survey by answering simple questions first, so building up a sense of trust and a feeling of confidence about any disclosure they might then decide to make in response to more sensitive questions. Importantly, questions being organised in this way also allowed the participant to end the session on a constructive note—when they were invited to share their recommendations for improving services in the future—and so avoid leaving them feeling triggered or distressed. Some interviewees chose to see the interview questions in advance and others were accompanied to the interview by an advocate (who separately consented to take part if they joined in with the discussion). Contact details for the research team and appropriate support services in each research site were provided on the project website, with links in the survey. A 16-hour triage system, with a contact log and a process for signposting to helpful resources and services (Campbell et al., 2010) was in place in each site, with resources hosted on the project website. (No participants reached out to gain assistance in any of the sites, despite this safety planning being in place.)

The trauma-informed approach was also important for team members given the subject matter of the research. Reflection de-briefing sessions were offered to all researchers in the team, and delivered after interviews where required, to assist in preventing the impacts of vicarious trauma, as well as to prevent and deal with any triggers reactivated through the research process.

Mixed Methods Research Design

Participatory Action Learning and Action Research (PALAR)

The project adopted a participatory action learning and action research model, as developed and demonstrated by Zuber-Skerritt (2018). Research team participation was structured through ten action learning set (ALS) sessions during the project. The expert peer researchers, research assistants in each site, the project research fellow, co-investigators, and the principal investigator all participated in the action learning set. The first session started with ground rules being co-produced by the team, so that we could ensure safe spaces for discussion. We talked about how we would equalise power dynamics, choice, and control at each stage of the project.

The whole research team, including peer researchers, trained together using action learning set methods. The ALS sessions consisted of the following themes and activities:

- discussing the themes of the research (legal norms of consent, sexual violence, sex-work regulation, reporting, and justice);
- analysing the risks to researcher and participant when interviewing about sex work and sexual violence, as well as learning techniques to mitigate and manage those risks;
- understanding trauma-informed ways of working to protect the researcher and participant from experiencing distress;
- building research interviewing skills (accessibility, active listening, and communication skills, prompting, disclosure, identifying barriers to participation);
- exploring the ethical hurdles in researching vulnerable groups;
- learning about intersectionality and diversity with marginalised communities;
- developing recommendations from interview and survey data;
- supporting the writing process;
- presenting our results to academic and community audiences; and
- organising dissemination of findings and feedback of impacts to participants and projects.

All participants were invited to reflect at the end of every session and task. A record of the action learning sets, with key information, discussion points, and resources shared, is summarised on a private, dedicated project space on the noticeboard site Padlet.

Overseeing the project was a formal project steering group made up of the core team, supported by an advisory board in each site (consisting of practitioners, sex workers, activists, and academics). In addition, an academic advisory board (consisting of eminent experts in sex work and sexual violence research) met periodically, to inform critical stages during the research, as well as to provide written advice and consultation on draft interview schedules and surveys.

Interview Recruitment and Sample

The data for this book was drawn from interviews and surveys with sex workers. Assisting with recruitment for sex workers as well as the other parties in the larger study were stakeholder groups with the following range of characteristics:

1) sexual violence survivors and people with lived experience of sex work;
2) sex-worker-led NGOs in each jurisdiction and brothel managers in Nevada;
3) sex workers in a wide range of sectors and the broader sex-work community;
4) criminal justice professionals, including police officers and prosecutors;
5) practitioners from outreach charities, third-sector NGOs, user-led sex-worker organisations, health services for sex workers, and sexual violence advocates; and
6) academic advisors specialising in law, criminology, and social research methodology.

Each site aimed to gather interviews with victim-survivors of sexual violence in sex work. In addition to the interviews used for this book, the larger project also gathered data from practitioners from NGOs, health providers, police, and prosecutors. The interview sample sizes aimed to reach thematic saturation at ten practitioners (including criminal justice professionals, NGO sex-work-project advocates, outreach workers, and health service—including sexual violence—practitioners) and ten sex workers at each of the four sites (see Guest et al., 2020 for a discussion of saturation calculations).

The interviews were semi-structured conversations, designed to explore themes from the study research questions, including unwanted contact experiences in sex work, criminal justice system experiences (including reporting, police investigation, and court experiences/outcomes), signposting, support services, and, crucially, recommendations for future improvements for sex workers after sexual violence.

Peer researchers were trained to conduct interviews with sex workers. A sample interview schedule is published with the protocol for the study (Scoular et al., 2023).

The trauma-informed principles as set out by Campbell et al. (2019) were followed at every stage of the project. Most interviews were recorded via Zoom, but some interviews with sex workers were conducted in person in brothels and outreach projects. Interviews were transcribed and coded thematically in Nvivo by three researchers, using a bespoke thematic codebook designed by Balderston, building on the aims/research questions of the study and informed by themes from the literature reviews.

In total, 110 semi-structured interviews with sex workers, criminal justice professionals, and practitioners from NGOs, charities, and health-care providers were conducted, transcribed, and analysed (see Tables 9.1, 9.2, 9.3, 9.4 and 9.5).

Cross-National Survey Design, Recruitment, and Sample

Following the interviews discussed above, an international survey of sex-worker and ex-sex-worker respondents in England, Scotland, Wales, Northern Ireland, Aotearoa New Zealand, the USA, and Nevada legal brothels was developed to gather empirical data about sex workers' experiences of unwanted sexual contact and sexual violence, as well as their experiences of health, advocacy, and the criminal justice system. We designed the survey with sex workers and sex-worker support organisations and included consultation on the drafts with sexual violence survey experts, academics, and professionals from criminal justice and support organisations. The consulting statistician (Marriott) commented on two survey drafts. The online survey was designed to be accessible, took 15 minutes to complete, and was translated into seven languages.

In addition to the sources used to recruit project interviewees described above, social media (Twitter/X, Instagram, and the project website) was utilised to advertise the survey, and chat group messages were distributed. Moreover, sex-work platforms distributed the survey

Table 9.1 Interview frequencies by category and site

Project research site	Criminal justice professionals (including police/ prosecutors)	Practitioners: Sex-worker advocacy, sexual violence NGOs, and health services	Sex-worker interviews	Total interviews
England, Scotland, and Wales	19	13	10	**42**
Northern Ireland	5	2	5	**12**
Aotearoa New Zealand	12	7	11	**30**
United States of America (including Nevada legal brothels)	6	6	14	**26**
Total interviews	**42**	**28**	**40**	**110**

Note One interview in Aotearoa New Zealand involved two participants (although one was the supporter for the main interviewee so their data has not been included); one interview in England, Scotland, and Wales involved two practitioners (one from a charity and one from a health service); and one Northern Ireland interview was conducted with three police officers. This means that a total of 113 interviewees were involved in the 110 interviews outlined above

on their sites in the USA and UK. Some print versions of the survey were distributed to outreach organisations; and the researchers completed some interviews in person through sex-worker NGOs, to ensure on-street sex workers and those without smartphone or computer literacy could participate.

Respondents were eligible to take the survey if they were aged 18 or over, were a current or former sex worker, had sold or exchanged sex for money or something of value (such as somewhere to live or to pay debts), in England, Wales, Scotland, Northern Ireland, the USA (including Nevada's legal brothels), or Aotearoa New Zealand and wanted to share experiences with unwanted sexual contact.

Table 9.2 Sex-worker interview participant demographics/identity (self-described)

Demographics/Identity	Interview participants from:		
	USA	ANZ	UK
Gender			
Female	10	10	11
Male	0	0	2
Non-binary	1	0	0
Trans woman	2	1	1
Trans man	0	0	1
Age			
20–29	5	8	5
30–39	6	2	3
40–49	1	0	4
50–59	1	1	1
Ethnicity (or Nationality as self-defined)			
White (American, Aotearoa New Zealand European, British)	3	3	7
Black/African (American, British)	0	0	3
Māori	0	3	0
Indigenous American	1	0	0
Irish	0	0	1
Romanian	0	0	1
Spanish	0	0	1
Canadian	0	0	1
Pakeha	0	1	0
Mexican	1	0	0
Dual heritage/Mixed ethnicity	8	3	1
Unknown	0	1	0
Sexual orientation*			
Heterosexual	2	0	6
Lesbian/Gay	0	0	0
Bisexual	4	0	3
Pansexual/Queer/Fluid	4	0	0
Sector			
On-street	0	2	2
Brothel (legal)	4	2	0
Escorting	5	3	7
Massage/Sauna/Stripping/Dancing	1	1	0
Online	1	0	2
Various	3	3	2

*This question was not asked in Aotearoa New Zealand interviews

Table 9.3 Sex-worker interview participants (UK) (self-described)

United Kingdom		
Pseudonym	Gender	Sector
Abuya	Female	Independent
Anna	Female	Street-based
Diamond	Female	Independent
Emily	Female	Various
Halley	Female	Independent
Harrison	Male	Independent
Linda	Female	Street-based
Mo	Male	Independent
Morowa	Female	Independent
Paul	Trans man	Independent
Queen	Female	Various
Sabrina	Female	Independent
Sophia	Female	Independent
Stephanie	Trans female	Street-based
Tess	Female	Street-based

Table 9.4 Sex-worker interview participants (ANZ) (self-described)

Aotearoa New Zealand		
Pseudonym	Gender	Sector
Alice	Female	Various
Athena	Female	Street-based
Carrie	Woman	Independent
Chanelle	Woman	Various
Christine	Female	Various
Erihapeti	Female	Independent
Hunu	Trans female	Street-based
Jane	Female	Brothel
Kat	Female	Various
Sheryl	Female	Independent
Talia	Female	Brothel

Participation was entirely voluntary, and all answers were anonymous, with survey responses kept secure and confidential so that nothing in the survey could be used to identify respondents. Participants were provided with details of ethical approval, independent ethics committee contacts in each site, data protection and privacy notices, and participant information sheets. Sources of support, information, and advice on each site

Table 9.5 Sex-worker interview participants (USA) (self-described)

United States of America (including Nevada's legal brothels)		
Pseudonym	Gender	Sector
Abbey	Female	Independent
Abigail	Female	Nevada legal brothel
Bella	Female	Independent
Chrissie	Female	Various
Cielo	Female	Nevada legal brothel
Cody	Woman	Independent
Dace	Female	Nevada legal brothel
Elisa	Female	Dancing
Jessica	Female	Various
Kassandra	Female	Independent
Nancy	Female Fluid	Independent
River	Female	Various
Roxanne	Female	Nevada legal brothel
Sebastian	Non-binary	Various

were signposted throughout the survey, and participants were provided with direct contact emails for the research team. Trigger warnings for sensitive subjects and explicit questions about unwanted sexual contact were prominent, and respondents were advised that they could ignore any questions they did not want to answer. Respondents had to give consent to participate and acknowledge they were aged 18 years or over to access the survey questions.

The survey consisted of questions that included multiple-choice, four-point Likert-scale questions with 'strongly' and 'slightly' agree and disagree options, accompanied by free-text boxes. These questions focused on the following aspects:

- demographics (sex or gender, sexual orientation, ethnicity, citizenship status);
- sex-work sector (on-street, escorting, brothel, massage parlour or strip club, online, other) and length of sex-work career;
- attitudes to how non-payment should be treated (legal consciousness or how sex workers view their rights and knowledge of the law);
- experiences concerning unwanted sexual contact, without permission, while sex-working. The section included how frequently unwanted

experiences had occurred (daily, weekly, monthly, or only once) and the last time something had happened. The questions were taken from the sexual victimisation module of the Crime Survey of England and Wales (including questions on rape, sexual assault, coercion, threats, physical violence, and non-consent) and were adapted to include sex-work-specific issues (clients not paying, paying less than agreed, and condom removal or 'stealthing'). Respondents were asked for the gender and the status of the person or people who did this (e.g. client) and about any injuries, harms, and effects from what happened. They were asked who they told and if it was reported to the police, and, if so, what happened to the perpetrator through the criminal justice system and whether compensation was awarded if a conviction was gained. If the respondent did not tell anyone or report it to the police, they were asked why that was;

- respondents' thoughts and feelings on how the police and criminal justice system deal with sexual violence against sex workers were sought, by asking them if they strongly or slightly agreed or disagreed with six statements—including "The police take rape against sex workers seriously"—and the extent to which they have overall confidence in the criminal justice system;
- questions about what would make respondents feel safer with a client (for example, if there are other sex workers and/or cameras or alarms in the building, whether they or a manager screen or background-check a client in advance, and the ability to report to blacklists) and how they negotiate and consent to sexual activities; and
- in the USA survey only, some questions regarding control over sex-work processes, age, income, and disability.

Survey Response Analysis

The survey was closed when over 1,000 responses were received. In March 2023, the survey data were cleaned and 693 unique survey responses were accepted. Responses that were duplicate, spurious compared to other data received or that contained less than 40% of answers to the questions were excluded from analysis. The sample included sex workers who had and had not reported incidences of harm.

Unless otherwise noted, descriptive survey results are presented with a subset of respondents who had reported at least one of several forms of harm related to sex work (n = 483). The survey asked about harms in two ways. First, respondents were asked to describe, for several types of harm, how often each had happened over the past 12 months. Respondents were then asked a series of questions about the "last time it happened", including what harmful behaviours they experienced, what kind of sex work they were providing, what the consequences of the harm/s were, and so on. For the purposes of this sample, we only included respondents who provided details for the last time it occurred. Respondents who reported harm in the past 12 months but skipped questions related to the most recent form of harm were not included in the subset we report on here.

We chose to measure harm by the last time it happened so that a full accounting of events could be considered across chapters without extensive instances of missing responses affecting reporting. A second justification for the decision comes from the diversity of working conditions that respondents reported. As other studies have shown (Sanders et al., 2020), sex workers tend to work in multiple environments, shifting from strip clubs to independent escorting to webcamming. The same is found to be the case in this sample, with about a quarter of respondents indicating that the type of sex work they were doing at the time of the most recent harmful incident was not the same as the one they selected as their most common method of selling sexual services. Were we to examine the yearly experiences of harm described by sex workers, we would not be able to know in which types of sex work which forms of harm occur. By limiting harm measures to the last time a harmful incident had happened, we can examine singular events resulting in harm that have a clear type of sex work associated with it.

Harm was measured as either a reported payment issue or a form of non-consensual behaviour, and both of them in the context of in-person sex work specifically. Payment issues included not being paid, being paid less than agreed, or being paid in fake money for sexual services. The options provided for non-consensual behaviour were: threats; assault;

agreeing to have sex but the client not stopping when being asked to; pursuing an exchange when the sex worker was unable to consent due to substance use; non-consensual penetration of the vagina or anus with a penis; non-consensual penetration with a finger or object; and removal of a condom during sex (referred to as 'stealthing'). Respondents were able to write in responses alongside these options, which were manually coded into this framework to account for experiences that did not fit our predefined expectations of harm. We excluded respondents who reported a harm occurring while webcamming (whether relating to payment or non-consensual behaviours), as these cases may function differently than do harms directed at in-person sex workers.

The survey sample has some notable limitations (see Tables 9.6, 9.7, 9.8). Beyond the standard concern that the intentional recruitment model cannot generate representative findings, the sampling procedure yielded limited diversity across each field. Across all sites, fewer cisgender males and transgender women participated than had been hoped for. Street sex work was rare among our respondents in every nation. The USA had lower response rates than was expected at the Nevada brothels, limiting conclusions regarding this special case. Aotearoa New Zealand had low response rates among online sex workers and here we were unable to secure responses from street-level workers. In the UK, very few respondents worked in massage parlours or strip clubs. While it is likely that some amount of difference is due to the differing conditions under which sex work is organised in each nation, it is just as likely that the sampling strategy played a role in these discrepancies. Because of these limitations, the survey data is best used for comparison between groups as opposed to an overall reflection of sex work in each nation. Readers are advised not to take values for a given nation or working condition as demonstrating prevalence rates or population estimates. Given how little is known about the prevalence of sex work, participation in specific types of sex work, or demographics of sex workers, the degree to which these data are skewed towards demographics or working conditions of sex workers is unknown. The concerns we express regarding the conditions of the data are conjecture based on other, non-generalisable data sources and qualitative knowledge of the conditions in each nation.

We originally intended to analyse Northern Ireland separately from England, Scotland, and Wales. England and Wales are partially criminalised—selling sex is not illegal, but managing a brothel, and soliciting and living off the proceeds of prostitution are unlawful. Scotland follows the partially criminalised model from England and Wales. Northern Ireland's Policing and Crime Act of 2009, also criminalises soliciting. Clients face a maximum penalty of 12 months in prison. Unfortunately, there were so few survey responses and interviews that we combined Northern Ireland with the rest of the UK.

Survey Participant Demographics

Table 9.6 Sex-worker survey respondents who disclosed unwanted contact (UK)

United Kingdom		
	UK responses with unwanted contact	% of UK responses with unwanted contact, in this sample
Responses from sex workers who disclosed unwanted contact (England, Scotland, Wales, Northern Ireland*)	**138**	**100%**
What sex or gender are you?		
Female	95	68.84
Male	18	13.04
Non-binary, fluid, queer, or other	10	7.25
Trans man	7	5.07
Trans woman	8	5.80
Total	*138*	*100%*
How do you describe your sexual orientation?		
Heterosexual/'Straight'	55	40.44
Lesbian or Gay	12	8.82
Bisexual	55	40.44
Asexual	5	3.68
Other	9	6.62
Total	*136*	*100%*

(continued)

(continued)

United Kingdom		
	UK responses with unwanted contact	% of UK responses with unwanted contact, in this sample
Where do you, or did you, mostly sell sex?		
Indoors/rented rooms, with other sex workers (brothel)	9	6.57
I normally sell sex from the street—on-street sex work	12	8.76
Escorting in-calls in my own home, hotel room, or apartment	55	40.15
Massage parlour/Strip club (licensed)	6	4.38
Escorting out-calls in client's home, hotel room, or other venue	31	22.63
Online—not in person (for example, webcamming)	20	14.60
Other	4	2.92
Total	*137*	*100%*
What is your ethnic origin?		
White or White British	84	62.22
Any other White background	22	16.30
Black, Black British, Caribbean, or African	5	3.70
Asian or Asian British	3	2.22
Mixed or multiple ethnic groups	13	9.63
Latin, Central American, or Southern American	8	5.93
Total	*135*	*100%*

**Note* 11 respondents from Northern Ireland are included in the UK sample who disclosed violence. The number of respondents from Northern Ireland is too small to report as a separate cohort here

A note on the race and ethnicity data we have collected: as seen from the demographic tables above, it was impossible to use the same categories for each site as there were different race and ethnicity categories relevant to a given site's geography. It can also be seen that there are some very small numbers of certain racial identities (for example, in the

Table 9.7 Sex-worker survey respondents who disclosed unwanted contact (ANZ)

Aotearoa New Zealand		
	Total responses with unwanted contact	% of ANZ responses with unwanted contact in this sample
Responses from sex workers in brothels	**33**	**36.67**
Responses from sex workers not in brothels	**57**	**63.33**
What sex or gender are you?		
Female	79	88.76
Male	1	1.12
Non-binary, fluid, queer, or other	8	8.99
Trans man	1	1.12
Trans woman	0	0
Total	*89*	*100%*
How do you describe your sexual orientation?		
Heterosexual/ 'Straight'	23	26.14
Lesbian/Gay	5	5.68
Bisexual	47	53.41
Asexual	1	1.14
Other	12	13.64
Total	*88*	*100%*
Where do you, or did you, mostly sell sex?		
I normally sell sex from the street—on-street sex work	0	0
Indoors/rented rooms, with other sex workers (brothel)	33	36.67
Escorting in-calls in my own home, hotel room, or apartment	25	27.78
Escorting out-calls in client's home, hotel room, or other venue	7	7.78
Online—not in person (for example, webcamming)	2	2.22
Massage parlour/Strip club (licensed)	22	24.44
Other	1	1.11

(continued)

Table 9.7 (continued)

Aotearoa New Zealand		
	Total responses with unwanted contact	% of ANZ responses with unwanted contact in this sample
Total	*90*	*100%*
Which ethnic group do you belong to?		
New Zealand European	46	51.11
Māori (part or full)	18	20.00
Other (such as Dutch, Japanese, Tokelauan)	26	28.89
Total	*90*	*100%*

USA sample only one person identified as Native Hawaiian or Pacific Islander, and in Aotearoa New Zealand, we were advised to use only three categories). This makes any cross-country comparison very tricky, and in some senses meaningless, as 'like for like' is not being compared. We do believe there is more to think about and discuss in relation to race and ethnicity and our overarching framework of legal consciousness, and we hope that further analysis on each site can bring out some interesting dynamics around different racial experiences.

Dissemination and Impact

In addition to this book, the research team will continue to report project findings to advisory, academic, and stakeholder audiences, through conference presentations, briefings, accessible reports (including infographics and a short animation), events with NGOs and participants, meetings, and submissions to policymakers.

Data Archiving

The ESRC require data to be transparently and accurately archived and shared for the use of other researchers in the future, but there are risks with sexual violence research involving minoritised populations

Table 9.8 Sex-worker survey respondents who disclosed unwanted contact (USA)

United States of America		
	Total responses with unwanted contact	% of USA total responses with unwanted contact in this sample
Responses from sex workers in the USA (illegal)	**220**	**86.27**
Responses from sex workers from Nevada legal brothels*	**35**	**13.73**
Total	*255*	*100%*
What sex or gender are you?		
Female	189	74.12
Male	25	9.80
Non-binary, fluid, queer, or other (Ze)	34	13.33
Trans man	3	1.18
Trans woman	4	1.57
Total	*255*	*100%*
How do you describe your sexual orientation?		
Heterosexual/'Straight'	94	37.15
Lesbian or Gay	18	7.11
Bisexual	103	40.71
Asexual	4	1.58
Other	34	13.43
Total	*253*	*100%*
Where do you, or did you, mostly sell sex?		
I normally sell sex from the street—on-street sex work	10	3.92
Nevada legal brothels	20	7.84
Indoors/rented rooms, with other sex workers	6	2.35
Escorting in-calls in my own home, hotel room, or apartment	80	31.37
Escorting out-calls in client's home, hotel room, or other venue	62	24.31
Massage parlour/Strip club (licensed)	19	7.45

(continued)

Table 9.8 (continued)

United States of America		
	Total responses with unwanted contact	% of USA total responses with unwanted contact in this sample
Online—not in person (for example, webcamming)	54	21.18
Other	4	1.57
Total	*255*	*100%*
Are you of Hispanic, Latino, or Spanish origin?		
Hispanic or Latino	24	9.56
Not Hispanic or Latino	227	90.44
Total	*251*	*100%*
What is your race?		
White	181	78.35
Black or African American	31	13.42
American Indian or Alaskan Native	11	4.76
Asian	7	3.03
Native Hawaiian or Pacific Islander	1	0.43
Total	231	100%

* The total number of persons in Nevada brothels is calculated by combining individuals who reported mostly selling sex through Nevada brothels and individuals whose last experience of harm was reported as occurring in a Nevada brothel

that some respondents could be identified retrospectively by individuals with knowledge of the fields we studied (including clients, third-party managers, other sex workers, or law enforcement agents). A particular concern in this study is that so few successful convictions are secured that respondents who disclose details of such convictions can be relatively easy to identify from the court judgements and news reports that are discussed (and collated in one place). Moreover, in settings where some aspect of sex work is criminalised—as in Northern Ireland and the USA (outside legal sites in Nevada)—sex-worker respondents could potentially be identified from their details, if modifications to the archived data to maintain anonymity had not taken place. This project has undertaken extensive consultation with the funder, advisers, statisticians, and data specialists to agree to a modified data-archiving plan, informed by the method demonstrated by Campbell et al. (2015). Consideration was given to how best to anonymize the interview data to enable interviews for secondary analysis. However, the interviews are very context-specific and detail crimes, workplaces, and information of very unique court cases. Upon taking all the elements of information out to ensure anonymity, the interviews would largely lose comprehensibility and relevance in any secondary analysis scenario. Therefore, it was determined that interview transcripts would not be released in any fashion. As we are firmly committed to secondary data analysis, particularly in populations that are both less easy to reach and equally over-researched, we have deposited the survey data.

References

Boysen, G. A. (2017). Evidence-based answers to questions about trigger warnings for clinically-based distress: A review for teachers. *Scholarship of Teaching and Learning in Psychology, 3*(2), 163–177.

Campbell, R., Adams, A. E., Wasco, S. M., Ahrens, C. E., & Sefl, T. (2010). "What has it been like for you to talk with me today?": The impact of participating in interview research on rape survivors. *Violence against Women, 16*(1), 60–83. https://doi.org/10.1177/1077801209353576

Campbell, R., Fehler-Cabral, G., Pierce, S., Sharma, D., Bybee, D., Shaw, J., Horsford, S., & Feeney, H. (2015). The Detroit Sexual Assault Kit (SAK) Action Research Project (ARP), Final Report. https://www.ojp.gov/pdffiles1/nij/grants/248680.pdf

Campbell, R., Goodman-Williams, R., & Javorka, M. (2019). A trauma-informed approach to sexual violence research ethics and open science. *Journal of Interpersonal Violence, 34*(23–24), 4765–4793. https://doi.org/10.1177/0886260519871530

European Parliament. (2016). *Regulation (EU) 2016/679 of the European Parliament and of the Council of 27 April 2016 on the protection of natural persons with regard to the processing of personal data and on the free movement of such data, and repealing Directive 95/46/EC (General Data Protection Regulation)* [2016] OJ L 119/1.

Guest, G., Namey, E., & Chen, M. (2020). A simple method to assess and report thematic saturation in qualitative research. *PLOS ONE, 15*(5), e0232076. Retrieved June 18, 2024, from https://doi.org/10.1371/journal.pone.0232076

Higgins, J., Nairn, K., & Sligo, J. (2007). Peer research with youth. In S. Kindon, R. Pain, & M. Kesby (Eds.), *Participatory action research approaches and methods* (pp. 104–111). Routledge Ltd.

Lushey, C. (2017). Peer research methodology: Challenges and solutions. *SAGE Research Methods Cases*. https://doi.org/10.4135/9781473994614

NIHR (National Institute for Health and Care Research). (2023). *Payment guidance for researchers and professionals v1.4 July 2023*. Retrieved June 18, 2024, from https://www.nihr.ac.uk/documents/payment-guidance-for-researchers-and-professionals/27392

PARTNERS2 Writing Collective. (2020). Exploring patient and public involvement (PPI) and co-production approaches in mental health research: Learning from the PARTNERS2 research programme. *Research Involvement and Engagement, 6*(1). Retrieved July 14, 2024, from https://doi.org/10.1186/s40900-020-00224-3

Pemberton, S., Balderston, S., & Long, J. (2021). *Trauma, social harm and health in criminal justice involved women: The Women's Risk Needs Assessment Validation Research Study Protocol*. University of Birmingham. Retrieved June 18, 2024, from https://www.protocols.io/view/trauma-social-harm-and-health-in-criminal-justice-5qpvoy239g4o/v1/abstract

Sanders, T., Brents, B. G., & Wakefield, C. (2020). *Paying for sex in a digital age: US and UK perspectives*. Taylor Et Francis Group.

Scoular, J., Sanders, T., Balderston, S., Abel, G., Brents, B. G., Ellison, G., & Marriott, N. (2023). Understanding sexual violence in sex working populations—Law, legal consciousness and legal practice in four countries (2021–2023): Study Protocol v2.5. *PLOS ONE, 18*(11), e0283067–e0283067. https://doi.org/10.1371/journal.pone.0283067

Stone, K. G. (1997). *Awakening to disability: Nothing about us without us*. Volcano Press.

Substance Abuse and Mental Health Services Administration (SAMHSA). (2014). Concept of trauma and guidance for a trauma-informed approach. Substance Abuse and Mental Health Services Administration *Briefing*, 14–4884. Retrieved December 13, 2023, from https://ncsacw.acf.hhs.gov/userfiles/files/SAMHSA_Trauma.pdf

Yarbrough, D. (2019). "Nothing about us without us": Reading protests against oppressive knowledge production as guidelines for solidarity research.

Journal of Contemporary Ethnography, 089124161985713. https://doi.org/10.1177/0891241619857134

Zuber-Skerritt, O. (2018). An educational framework for participatory action learning and action research (PALAR). *Educational Action Research, 26*(4), 513–532. https://doi.org/10.1080/09650792.2018.1464939

Appendix 1: Prostitution, Sexual Violence, and Workers Rights Laws Across Sites

See Tables A.1 and A.2.

T. Sanders et al. (eds.), *Voicing Consent*, Palgrave Advances in Sex Work Studies,
https://doi.org/10.1007/978-3-031-77715-8

Table A.1 Prostitution laws compared

	Aotearoa—New Zealand	Nevada brothels	England & Wales	Scotland	Northern Ireland	USA*
General label	Decriminalisation	Legalisation	Partial criminalisation	Partial criminalisation	Client criminalisation	Full criminalisation
Policy level	Federal	County/city	National	National	National	State for prostitution, federal and state for sex trafficking
Enforcement level	National, employment law	Nevada county/city police	44 police force areas	Police Scotland	Police Service of Northern Ireland (PSNI)	Individual states
Relevant law	Crimes Act, PRA	Nevada Revised Statutes, state health codes, county/city prostitution ordinances	Street Offences Act, 1959; Sexual Offences Act, 2003	Prostitution (Public Places) (Scotland) Act 2007; Sexual Offences (Scotland) Act 2009	The Sexual Offences (Northern Ireland) Order 2008	Federal Trafficking Victims Protection Act, FOSTA/ SESTA, wide variety of state prostitution laws
Offering or providing sexual services for payment	Legal	Legal only in licensed brothels, 18 + or 21 + , work card, must use condom, STI testing	Legal except loitering or soliciting in public areas	Legal except 'kerb crawling' and loitering, walking, or soliciting in public areas	Legal, except soliciting	Illegal except in Maine; in some areas prosecutors have non-prosecution policies
Max. penalty	None	Same as illegal, can shut down brothel	Fine up to £1,000, order to attend support meetings	Fine up to £1,000, order to attend support meetings	Fine up to £1,000	NV Up to $1,000 or six months in jail; varies in other areas
Paying for services	Legal unless from someone forced	Legal from licensed brothels, must use condom	Legal except loitering, soliciting in public areas, or from someone forced	Legal except loitering, soliciting in public areas, or from someone forced	Illegal	Illegal

	Aotearoa—New Zealand	Nevada brothels	England & Wales	Scotland	Northern Ireland	USA*
Max. penalty	None	Same as illegal. If no condom used, brothel can lose licence	Fine up to £1,000; from someone forced up to seven years	Fine up to £1,000; from someone forced up to seven years	Prison up to one year and or fine	Varies by state, in some it's a felony. NV up to $2,000 and one year in jail
Brothel keeping	Regulated if more than five workers, overseen by employment law and local councils	Legal with investigation and licence, in a licensed brothel, regulated by police	Illegal	Illegal	Illegal	Illegal
Max. penalty	Must hold a valid operator's certificate; operator who does not hold a certificate is liable to a fine not exceeding $10,000	Without a licence, same as illegal. If violated, local codes, could lose licence	Up to 7 years or up to 6 months or fine	Up to 7 years or up to 6 months or fine.	Up to 7 years or up to 6 months or fine	Varies by state. Can be a felony if sex worker is under 18
Third parties	Legal	Managers in licensed brothels	Illegal with multi-year penalties	Illegal with multi-year penalties	Illegal with multi-year penalties	Illegal
Max. penalty	None	Legal with licence	Up to 7 years or up to 6 months or fine	Up to 7 years or up to 6 months or fine	Up to 7 years or up to 6 months or fine	Varies by state; NV, five years, $10,000

(continued)

Table A.1 (continued)

	Aotearoa—New Zealand	Nevada brothels	England & Wales	Scotland	Northern Ireland	USA*
Advertising	Advertisements for commercial sexual services may not be— (a) broadcast on radio or television; or (b) published in a newspaper or periodical, except in the classified advertisements section of the newspaper or periodical; or (c) screened at a public cinema	(NRS 201.430) Where local ordinances ban prostitution: brothels are prohibited from advertising Where brothels are legal: it is illegal for them to advertise "in any public theatre, on the public streets of any city or town, or on any public highway"	Illegal for brothels Illegal if 'obscene' or placing adverts for prostitution on a public telephone (carding s46 Criminal Justice and Police Act 2001)	Illegal for brothels	Illegal for brothels	Illegal
Trafficking (sex work)	Illegal; Section 98D of the Crimes Act, 1961	Illegal; NRS 200.467 and 200.468	Illegal; Modern Slavery Act, 2015 and Sexual Offences Act, 2003 (sexual offences)	Human Trafficking and Exploitation (Scotland) Act 2015	Illegal; Human Trafficking and Exploitation (Criminal Justice and Support for Victims) Act (Northern Ireland) 2015	NRS 201.300: B felony for adult victims and A felony with potential for life imprisonment when the victim is a child under 18
Max. penalty	20 years imprisonment, a fine of up to $500,000, or both	May be sentenced to five to 20 years imprisonment (or one to 15 years for recruiting) and a possible fine of up to $50,000	In relation to sexual offences: up to seven years and/or fine Otherwise, imprisonment for life	Imprisonment for life or a fine (or both)	Imprisonment for life	Federal trafficking: 10 years to life in prison, $15,000 fine; state penalties vary

*Thanks to Rebecca (Becca) Cleary, J.D., Staff Attorney, Decriminalize Sex Work for help with US data

Table A.2 Sexual violence legal rules in each case-study jurisdiction

	Nevada	Aotearoa —New Zealand	England and Wales	Scotland	Northern Ireland	USA
Legislation	Chapter 200 Nevada Revised Statutes, under 'Crimes Against the Person' (Section 366)	Crimes Act, 1961—directly defined	Sexual Offences Act, 2003; Modern Slavery Act, 2015; Anti-Social Behaviour Crime and Policing Act 2014	Sexual Offences (Scotland) Act 2009	The Sexual Offences (Northern Ireland) Order 2008	On state level—statutory provisions
Definition of consent	Sexual assaultis defined as sexual penetration "against the will of the victim or under conditions in which the perpetrator knows or should know that the victim is mentally or physically incapable of resisting or understanding the nature of the perpetrator's conduct" Case law has established that it is not necessary to prove overt force and physical force (SA *Dinkens v. State* (1976), which ruled that there is no consent where the victim is induced to submit to the sexual act through fear of death or serious bodily injury) (*State v. Denton* (1966); *State v. Thomas* (1973)) Continues to place the victim's actions as central to the analysis of consent/non-consent <u>Conditional consent</u>—not currently recognised rather narrow understanding of 'rape by deception'	Section 128A outlines that consent is not given in circumstances such as where force has been applied, where the victim is asleep or unconscious, where the victim is mistaken about who the other person is, or where the victim is mistaken about the nature and quality of the act Consent defined in case law as "full, voluntary, free and informed". R v Cook (1986)) <u>Conditional consent:</u> recognised in the case of R v Campos (2021): The victim's consent was conditional on the wearing of a condom in the context of sex work Unclear if this will extend to the condition of payment	Consent, under Sect. 74 of the SOA, is defined as agreeing "by choice", with the "freedom and capacity to make that choice" <u>Conditional consent:</u> *Assange 2011*: The High Court held that removal of a condom could vitiate consent if the complainant made clear that consent was conditional on a condom being worn. An 'emerging concept of conditional consent' is recognised in current CPS guidance (Crown Prosecution Service 2021b) Unlikely to apply to non-payment due to R v Linekar (1995): which held non-payment constituted fraud, rather than rape. Law reform suggested, see CLRNN, (2023)	Consent is covered under Part 2 of the SOSA and is defined as "free agreement" <u>Conditional consent:</u> Assumed to follow E&W, see Scottish Law Commission. (2006)	A person consents if s/he agrees by choice, and has the freedom and capacity to make that choice (Sect. 3) <u>Conditional consent:</u> Assumed to follow E&W	Varies by state—statutory provisions For example, California: affirmative consent model; Pennsylvania: only describes non-consent in relation to forcible compulsion and incapacitation <u>Conditional consent</u>—not currently recognised rather narrow understanding of 'rape by deception' Exception: California—victims of stealthing can file civil lawsuits against their assailants for monetary damages (AB 453)

References

Abel, G. (2010). *Decriminalisation: A harm minimisation and human rights approach to regulating sex work* (PhD thesis, University of Otago). Christchurch.

Abel, G. (2011). Different stage, different performance: The protective strategy of role play on emotional health in sex work. *Social Science and Medicine, 72*(7), 1177–1184.

Abel, G. (2014). A decade of decriminalization: Sex work 'down under' but not underground. *Criminology and Criminal Justice, 14*(5), 580–592. https://doi.org/10.1177/1748895814523024

Abel, G., & Fitzgerald, L. (2012). "The street's got its advantages": Movement between sectors of the sex industry in a decriminalised environment. *Health, Risk and Society, 14*(1), 17–23.

Abel, G., & Ludeke, M. (2021a). Brothels as sites of third-party exploitation? Decriminalisation and sex workers' employment rights. *Social Sciences, 10*(3), 1–15.

Abel, G., & Ludeke, M. (2021b). Business like any other? New Zealand's brothel industry post-decriminalisation. *Culture, Health & Sexuality, 24*(9), 1243–1256.

T. Sanders et al. (eds.), *Voicing Consent*, Palgrave Advances in Sex Work Studies, https://doi.org/10.1007/978-3-031-77715-8

Abel, G., Healy, C., Bennachie, C., & Reed, A. (2010). Five: The Prostitution Reform Act. In G. Abel, L. Fitzgerald, C. Healy, & A. Taylor (Eds.), *Taking the crime out of sex work* (pp. 75–84). Policy Press. Retrieved June 20, 2024, from: https://doi.org/10.51952/9781847423351.ch005

Ahrens, C. E. (2006). Being silenced: The impact of negative social reactions on the disclosure of rape. *American Journal of Community Psychology, 38*(3–4), 31–34. https://doi.org/10.1007/s10464-006-9069-9

Aidinlis, S. (2019). Defining the 'legal': Two conceptions of legal consciousness and legal alienation in administrative justice research. *Journal of Social Welfare and Family Law, 41*(4), 495–513.

Alexander, P. (1998). Sex work and health: A question of safety in the workplace. *Journal of the American Medical Women's Association, 53*(2), 77–82. https://pubmed.ncbi.nlm.nih.gov/9595900/

Amnesty International. (2016a). *Sex workers at risk: A research summary on human rights abuses against sex workers*. Retrieved July 14, 2024, from: https://www.amnesty.org/en/documents/pol40/4061/2016/en/

Amnesty International. (2016b). *The human cost of 'crushing' the market: Criminalization of sex work in Norway*. Retrieved July 7, 2024, from: https://www.amnesty.org/download/Documents/EUR3640342016ENGLISH.PDF

Anderson, M. J. (2004). Negotiating sex. *Southern California Law Review, 78*, 101–138.

AQ Thailand. (2022). NZIPT 505589. Retrieved February 24, 2024, from: https://hyimmigration.co.nz/wp-content/uploads/2023/05/rem_20220729_505589.pdf

Armstrong, L. (2017). From law enforcement to protection?: Interactions between sex workers and police in a decriminalised street-based sex industry. *British Journal of Criminology, 57*(3), 570–588.

Armstrong, L. (2019). Stigma, decriminalisation, and violence against street-based sex workers: Changing the narrative. *Sexualities, 22*(7–8), 1288–1308. https://doi.org/10.1177/1363460718780216

Armstrong, L. (2021). "I can lead the life that I want to lead": Social harm, human needs and the decriminalisation of sex Work in Aotearoa/New Zealand. *Sexuality Research and Social Policy, 18*(4), 941–951. https://doi.org/10.1007/s13178-021-00605-7

Aspinall, G. (2019). A British man has been convicted of rape after removing a condom during sex. *Grazia Magazine*. Retrieved June 20, 2024, from: https://graziadaily.co.uk/life/in-the-news/stealthing-conviction-rape/

Assange v Swedish Prosecution Authority. (2011). EWHC 2849 (Admin). Retrieved July 4, 2023, from: https://www.supremecourt.uk/cases/docs/uksc-2011-0264-judgment.pdf

Atchison, C., Benoit, C., Burnett, P., Jansson, M., Kennedy, M. C., Ouellet, N., & Vukmirovich, D. (2015). The influence of time to negotiate on control in sex worker-client interactions. *Research for Sex Work, 14*, 35–36.

Attride-Stirling, J. (2001). Thematic networks: An analytic tool for qualitative research. *Qualitative Research, 1*(3), 385–405. https://doi.org/10.1177/146879410100100307

Bachman, R., & Paternoster, R. (1993). A contemporary look at the effects of rape law reform: How far have we really come? *Journal of Criminal Law and Criminology, 84*(3), 554–574. https://scholarlycommons.law.northwestern.edu/cgi/viewcontent.cgi?article=6785&context=jclc

Baier, M., Svensson, M., & Nafstad, I. (2019). *Understanding sociology of law*. Studentlitteratur AB.

Barbagallo, C., & Cruz, K. (2022). Dancers win at work: Unionization and Nowak v Chandler Bars Group Ltd. *Studies in Political Economy, 102*(3), 354–375. https://doi.org/10.1080/07078552.2021.2000208

Barr, C., Topping, A., & Bowcott, O. (2019). Rape prosecutions in England and Wales at lowest level in a decade. *The Guardian*. Retrieved May 21, 2024, from: https://www.theguardian.com/law/2019/sep/12/prosecutions-in-england-and-wales-at-lowest-level-in-a-decade

Barry, K. (1995). *The prostitution of sexuality*. NYU Press. http://www.jstor.org/stable/j.ctt9qg779

Bennachie, C., Pickering, A., Lee, J., Macioti, P., Mai, N., Fehrenbacher, A., Giametta, C., Hoefinger, H., & Musto, J. (2021). Unfinished decriminalization: The impact of Section 19 of the Prostitution Reform Act 2003 on migrant sex workers' rights and lives in Aotearoa New Zealand. *Social Sciences, 10*, 79. https://hdl.handle.net/2381/25205339.v1

Benoit, C., Jansson, S. M., Smith, M., & Flagg, J. (2018). Prostitution stigma and its effect on the working conditions, personal lives, and health of sex workers. *The Journal of Sex Research, 55*(4–5), 457–471.

Benoit, C., McCarthy, B., & Jansson, M. (2015). Stigma, sex work, and substance use: A comparative analysis. *Sociology of Health & Illness, 37*(3), 437–451. https://doi.org/10.1111/1467-9566.12201

Bernstein, E. (2001). The meaning of the purchase: Desire, demand and the commerce of sex. *Ethnography, 2*(3), 389–420.

Bishop, S., Dawson, B., Hall, E., Murray, I., Northwood, B., O'Sullivan, J., Sheat, C., & van Echten, A. (2018). *Garrow and Turkington's Criminal Law in New Zealand*. Retrieved June 20, 2024, from: https://www.lexisnexis.com/en-nz/products/legalcontent-library/criminal/garrow-and-turkingtons-criminal-law-in-new-zealand?srsltid=AfmBOoolV2h0G__I3mA6n5XV4yOY1iUB8GVj75POcE9d3ho_Q0sYvMD1

Blackstone, A., Uggen, C., & McLaughlin, H. (2009). Legal consciousness and responses to sexual harassment. *Law & Society Review, 43*(3), 631–668. https://doi.org/10.1111/j.1540-5893.2009.00384.x

Blanco, M. (2018). *Sex trend or sexual assault?: The dangers of 'stealthing' and the concept of conditional consent*. Retrieved December 13, 2023, from: https://www.pennstatelawreview.org/wp-content/uploads/2018/12/123-Blanco-FINAL.pdf

Blunt, D., & Wolf, A. (2020). Erased: The impact of FOSTA-SESTA and the removal of Backpage on sex workers. *Anti-Trafficking Review, 14*, 117–121. https://doi.org/10.14197/atr.201220148

Bond, K. (2023). What is stealthing—and what to do if you think it has happened to you. *Cosmopolitan*. Retrieved June 20, 2024, from: https://www.cosmopolitan.com/uk/reports/a45246257/what-is-stealthing/

Bowen, R., & Bungay, V. (2016). Taint: An examination of the lived experiences of stigma and its lingering effects for eight sex industry experts. *Culture, Health & Sexuality, 18*(2), 184–197.

Bowen, R., Hodsdon, R., Swindells, K., & Blake, C. (2021). Why report? Sex workers who use NUM opt out of sharing victimisation with Police. *Sexual Research and Social Policy, 18*, 885–896. https://doi.org/10.1007/s13178-021-00627-1

Boysen, G. A. (2017). Evidence-based answers to questions about trigger warnings for clinically-based distress: A review for teachers. *Scholarship of Teaching and Learning in Psychology, 3*(2), 163–177.

Brents, B. G., & Hausbeck, K. (2005). Violence and legalized brothel prostitution in Nevada: Examining safety, risk, and prostitution policy. *Journal of Interpersonal Violence, 20*(3), 270–295. https://doi.org/10.1177/0886260504270333

Brewis, J., & Linstead, S. (2000). 'The worst thing is the screwing' (1) Consumption and the management of identity in sex work. *Gender, Work & Organization, 7*(2), 84–97.

Brodsky, A. (2017). 'Rape-adjacent': Imagining legal responses to nonconsensual condom removal. *Columbia Journal of Gender and Law, 32*(2), 183–210. https://doi.org/10.7916/d8708d06

Brown, K., & Sanders, T. (2017). Pragmatic, progressive, problematic: Addressing vulnerability through a local street sex work partnership initiative. *Social Policy and Society, 16*(3), 429–441.

Brown, K., Grace, S., & Redman, S. (2024). Policing vulnerability: The care and control of sex workers through designated police officers. *British Journal of Criminology*, Open access.https://doi.org/10.1093/bjc/azae026

Calavita, K., & Jenness, V. (2013). Inside the pyramid of disputes: Naming problems and filing grievances in California prisons. *Social Problems, 60*(1), 50–80.

California Penal Code. (n.d.). Retrieved June 13, 2024, from: https://leginfo.legislature.ca.gov/faces/codesTOCSelected.xhtml?tocCode=PEN&tocTitle=+Penal+Code+-+PEN

Campbell, R., Adams, A. E., Wasco, S. M., Ahrens, C. E., & Sefl, T. (2010). "What has it been like for you to talk with me today?": The impact of participating in interview research on rape survivors. *Violence against Women, 16*(1), 60–83. https://doi.org/10.1177/1077801209353576

Campbell, R., Fehler-Cabral, G., Pierce, S., Sharma, D., Bybee, D., Shaw, J., Horsford, S., & Feeney, H. (2015). The Detroit Sexual Assault Kit (SAK) Action Research Project (ARP), Final Report. https://www.ojp.gov/pdffiles1/nij/grants/248680.pdf

Campbell, R., Goodman-Williams, R., & Javorka, M. (2019). A trauma-informed approach to sexual violence research ethics and open science. *Journal of Interpersonal Violence, 34*(23–24), 4765–4793. https://doi.org/10.1177/0886260519871530

Campos v R. (2022). NZCA 311. Retrieved July 5, 2024, from: https://www.openlaw.nz/case/2022NZCA311

Christopher, R. L., & Christopher, K. H. (2007). Adult impersonation: Rape by fraud as a defense to statutory rape. *Northwestern University Law Review, 101*, 75.

Chua, L. J., & Engel, D. M. (2019). Legal consciousness reconsidered. *Annual Review of Law and Social Science, 15*(1), 335–353. https://doi.org/10.1146/annurev-lawsocsci-101518-042717

Civic Government (Scotland) Act. (1982). Retrieved May 4, 2024, from: https://www.legislation.gov.uk/ukpga/1982/45/contents

Clay-Warner, J., & Burt, C. H. (2005). Rape reporting after reforms. *Violence against Women, 11*(2), 150–176. https://doi.org/10.1177/1077801204271566

Coates, D., & Penrod, S. (1981). Social psychology and the emergence of disputes. *Law & Society Review, 15*(3/4), 655–680. https://doi.org/10.2307/3053506

Comte, J. (2014). Decriminalization of sex work: Feminist discourses in light of research. *Sexuality & Culture, 18*(1), 196–217. https://doi.org/10.1007/s12119-013-9174-5

Connelly, L., & Sanders, T. (2020). Disrupting the boundaries of the academe: Co-creating knowledge and sex work 'academic-activism'. In S. Walklate, K. Fitz-Gibbon, J. Maher, & J. McCulloch (Eds.), *The Emerald handbook of criminology, feminism and social change* (pp. 203–218). Emerald Publishing. https://eprints.whiterose.ac.uk/181379/

Connolly v R. (2009). HC CHCH CRI 2008–409–014401. NZHC 2473. Retrieved July 11, 2024, from: https://www.nzlii.org/nz/cases/NZHC/2009/2473.pdf

Consumer Guarantees Act (CGA). (1993). Retrieved June 20, 2024, from: https://www.legislation.govt.nz/act/public/1993/0091/latest/dlm311053.html

Cowan, D. (2004). Legal consciousness: Some observations. *Modern Law Review, 67*(6), 928–958. https://doi.org/10.1111/j.1468-2230.2004.00518.x

Crimes Act. (1961). Retrieved June 20, 2024, from: https://www.legislation.govt.nz/act/public/1961/0043/latest/DLM327382.html

Criminal Justice and Police Act. (2001). Retrieved June 20, 2024, from: https://www.legislation.gov.uk/ukpga/2001/16/contents

Criminal Law Reform Network Now (CLRNN). (2023). *Reforming the relationship between sexual consent, deception and mistake*. http://www.clrnn.co.uk/media/1031/clrnn3-deception-report.pdf

Crown Prosecution Service (CPS). (2021a). *Rape and sexual offences—Chapter 6: Consent*. Retrieved June 20, 2024, from: https://www.cps.gov.uk/legal-guidance/rape-and-sexual-offences-chapter-6-consent

Crown Prosecution Service (CPS). (2021b). *Rape and sexual offences—Chapter 3: Case building*. Retrieved June 20, 2024, from: https://www.cps.gov.uk/legal-guidance/rape-and-sexual-offences-chapter-3-case-building

Cruz, K. (2020). *Dancers are workers: Nowak v Chandler Bars Group Ltd and the history of dancer organising in London.* Retrieved June 20, 2024, from: https://uklabourlawblog.com/2020/04/30/dancers-are-workers-nowak-v-chandler-bars-group-ltd-and-the-history-of-dancer-organising-in-london-by-katie-cruz/

Cunningham, S., Sanders, T., Platt, L., Grenfell, P., & Macioti, P. G. (2018). Sex work and occupational homicide: Analysis of a UK murder database. *Homicide Studies, 22*(3), 321–338.

Dalziel, L. (2003). *Prostitution Reform Bill—in committee*. Retrieved June 13, 2024, from: https://www.parliament.nz/en/pb/hansard-debates/rhr/document/47HansD_20030514_00001525/prostitution-reform-bill-in-committee

Davis, K. C., Hammett, J. F., Chen, W., Stewart, R., & Kirwan, M. (2024). A scoping review of nonconsensual condom removal ('stealthing') research. *Trauma, Violence, & Abuse, 152483802211468*. https://doi.org/10.1177/15248380221146802

Day, S. (1994). What counts as rape? Physical assault and broken contracts: Contrasting views of rape among London sex workers. In P. Harvey & P. Gow (Eds.), *Sex and Violence: Issues in Representation and Experience* (pp. 172–189). Routledge.

Day, S. E. (2007). *On the game: Women and sex work*. Pluto Press.

Decriminalise Sex Work. (2024). *What is SESTA/FOSTA?* Retrieved June 20, 2024, from: https://decriminalizesex.work/advocacy/sesta-fosta/what-is-sesta-fosta/#What-Is-SESTA-FOSTA

Deering, K. N., Amin, A., Shoveller, J., Nesbitt, A., Garcia-Moreno, C., Duff, P., Argento, E., & Shannon, K. (2014). A systematic review of the correlates of violence against sex workers. *American Journal of Public Health, 104*(5), 42–54.

Dewey, S., & St. Germain, T. (2014). "It depends on the cop:" Street-based sex workers' perspectives on police patrol officers. *Sexuality Research and Social Policy, 11*, 256–270.

Dinkens v State. (1976). 92 Nev. 74, 546 P.2d 228. Retrieved July 5, 2024, from: https://casetext.com/case/dinkens-v-state-11/case-details

Director of Public Prosecutions (DPP) v Yeong (a pseudonym). (2022). (Victoria, Australia). Retrieved July 5, 2024, from: https://jade.io/j/?a=outline&id=944275

Doig, G. A., & Wortley, N. (2013). Conditional consent? An emerging concept in the law of rape. *The Journal of Criminal Law, 77*(4), 286–291. https://doi.org/10.1350/jcla.2013.77.4.848a

Du Bois, W. E. B. (1903). *The souls of black folk*. A.C. McClurg & Co.

Elks, S. (2019). Sex workers denied justice over rapes says UK prostitutes' collective. *Thomson Reuters Foundation*. Retrieved February 8, 2024, from: https://news.trust.org/item/20191105120530-v6kp7/

Ellison, L., & Munro, V. E. (2010). A stranger in the bushes, or an elephant in the room? Critical reflections upon received rape myth wisdom in the context of a mock jury study. *New Criminal Law Review, 13*(4), 781–801.

Ellison, L., & Munro, V. E. (2013). Better the devil you know? 'Real rape' stereotypes and the relevance of a previous relationship in (mock) juror deliberations. *The International Journal of Evidence & Proof, 17*(4), 299–322.

Elvin, J. (2008). The concept of consent under the Sexual Offences Act 2003. *The Journal of Criminal Law, 72*(6), 519–536.

End Violence Against Women. (2023). *Latest data shows the criminal justice system isn't working for women.* Retrieved July 25, 2024, from: https://www.endviolenceagainstwomen.org.uk/latest-data-shows-the-criminal-justice-system-isnt-working-for-women/

Engel, D. (1998). How does law matter in the constitution of legal consciousness? In B. G. Garth & A. Sarat (Eds.), *How does law matter?* (pp. 109–144). Northwestern University Press.

Estrich, S. (1987). *Real rape: How the legal system victimizes women who say no.* Harvard University Press.

Estrich, S. (2018). Is it rape? In P. Searles (Ed.), *Rape and society* (pp. 183–193). Routledge.

European Parliament. (2016). *Regulation (EU) 2016/679 of the European Parliament and of the Council of 27 April 2016 on the protection of natural persons with regard to the processing of personal data and on the free movement of such data, and repealing Directive 95/46/EC (General Data Protection Regulation)* [2016] OJ L 119/1.

Ewick, P., & Silbey, S. S. (1998). *The common place of law: Stories from everyday life.* University of Chicago Press.

Feis-Bryce, A. (2017). Policing sex work in Britain: A patchwork approach. In *Policing the Sex Industry* (pp. 19–37). Routledge.

Felstiner, W. L. F., Abel, R. L., & Sarat, A. (1980). The emergence and transformation of disputes: Naming, blaming, claiming… *Law & Society Review, 15*(3/4), 631–654. https://doi.org/10.2307/3053505

Fernandez, F. L. (2016). *Hands up: A systematized review of policing sex workers in the US* (PhD thesis, Yale University).

Galuszka, J. (2022, June 3). Sex worker indecently assaulted by man who failed to practice safe sex. *Stuff*. Retrieved July 18, 2024, from: https://www.stuff.co.nz/national/crime/300605102/sex-worker-indecently-assaulted-by-man-who-failed-to-practice-safe-sex

Gardner, J., & Shute, S. (2000). The wrongness of rape. In J. Horder (Ed.), *Oxford essays in jurisprudence* (pp. 193–218). Clarendon Press.

Gash, A., & Harding, R. (2018). #MeToo? Legal discourse and everyday responses to sexual violence. *Laws, 7*(2), 21. https://doi.org/10.3390/laws7020021

Gibson, M. (2019). Deceptive sexual relations: A theory of criminal liability. *Oxford Journal of Legal Studies, 40*(1), 82–109. https://doi.org/10.1093/ojls/gqz031

Gibson, M. (2023). Deception, consent and the right to sexual autonomy. In Criminal Law Reform Now Network (Eds.), *Reforming the relationship between sexual consent, deception and mistake* (pp. 48–55). Retrieved June 10, 2024, from: http://www.clrnn.co.uk/media/1031/clrnn3-deception-report.pdf

Gill, C., & Creutzfeldt, N. (2018). The 'ombuds watchers': Collective dissent and legal protest amongst users of public services ombuds. *Social and Legal Studies, 27*(3), 367–388. https://doi.org/10.1177/0964663917721313

Goh, B. (2021). *Full, free and informed: Assessing the scope of conditional consent*. Retrieved June 20, 2024, from: https://www.equaljusticeproject.co.nz/articles/full-free-and-informed-assessing-the-scope-of-conditional-consent2021

Goldenberg, S. M., Duff, P., & Krüsi, A. (2015). Work environments and HIV prevention: A qualitative review and meta-synthesis of sex worker narratives. *BMC Public Health, 15*(1), 1–15.

Gómez-Durán, E. L., & Martin-Fumadó, C. (2024). Nonconsensual condom-use deception: An empirically based conceptualization of stealthing. *Trauma, Violence, & Abuse, 152483802211417*. https://doi.org/10.1177/15248380221141731

Grenfell, P., Eastham, J., Perry, G., & Platt, L. (2016). Decriminalising sex work in the UK. *British Medical Journal, 354*. https://doi.org/10.1136/bmj.i4459

Guest, G., Namey, E., & Chen, M. (2020). A simple method to assess and report thematic saturation in qualitative research. *PLOS ONE, 15*(5): e0232076. Retrieved June 18, 2024, from: https://doi.org/10.1371/journal.pone.0232076

Gwin, C. (2024). It's time to sue for what we want: New legal tools for strippers. In B. Barton, B. Brents, & A. Jones (Eds.), *Sex work today: Erotic labor in the twenty-first century* (pp. 275–284). NYU Press.

Harris, K. (2021). Survivor of attempted sexual assault says migrant sex workers are targeted due to NZ law. *The New Zealand Herald*. Retrieved September 1, 2022, from: https://www.nzherald.co.nz/nz/survivor-of-attempted-sexual-assault-says-migrant-sex-workers-are-targeted-due-to-nz-law/3H434JHI2SEANQCRWH2PDDBUSA/

Hernandez, J. (2021). California is the 1st state to ban 'stealthing', nonconsensual condom removal. *NPR*. Retrieved June 13, 2024, from: https://www.npr.org/2021/10/07/1040160313/california-stealthing-nonconsensual-condom-removal

Herring, J. J. W. (2005). Mistaken sex. *Criminal Law Review*, pp. 511–524. https://ssrn.com/abstract=1287130

Hertogh, M. (2004). A 'European' conception of legal consciousness: Rediscovering Eugen Ehrlich. *Journal of Law and Society, 31*(4), 457–481. https://doi.org/10.1111/j.1467-6478.2004.00299.x

Hertogh, M. (2009). What's in a handshake? Legal equality and legal consciousness in the Netherlands. *Social & Legal Studies, 18*(2), 221–239.

Hertogh, M. (2011). Loyalists, cynics and outsiders: Who are the critics of the justice system in the UK and the Netherlands? *International Journal of Law in Context, 7*(1), 31–46. https://doi.org/10.1017/s174455231000039x

Hertogh, M. (2018). *Nobody's law: Legal consciousness and legal alienation in everyday life*. Palgrave Pivot.

Hertogh, M. (2023). Relational legal consciousness in the punitive welfare state: How Dutch welfare officials shape clients' perceptions of law. *Law & Society Review, 57*(3), 293–316.

Higgins, J., Nairn, K., & Sligo, J. (2007). Peer research with youth. In S. Kindon, R. Pain, & M. Kesby (Eds.), *Participatory action research approaches and methods* (pp. 104–111). Routledge Ltd.

Home Office. (2000). *Setting the boundaries, reforming the law on sex offences*. Retrieved June 22, 2024, from: https://lawbore.net/articles/setting-the-boundaries.pdf

Horney, J., & Spohn, C. (1991). Rape law reform and instrumental change in six urban jurisdictions. *Law & Society Review, 25*(1), 117.

Hubbard, P., & Sanders, T. (2003). Making space for sex work: Female street prostitution and the production of urban space. *International Journal of Urban and Regional Research, 27*(1), 75–89.

Human Trafficking and Exploitation (Criminal Justice and Support for Victims) Act (Northern Ireland). (2015). Retrieved June 22, 2024, from: https://www.legislation.gov.uk/nia/2015/2/enacted

Huysamen, M., & Sanders, T. (2021). Institutional ethics challenges to sex work researchers: Committees, communities, and collaboration. *Sociological Research Online, 26*(4), 942–958. https://doi.org/10.1177/13607804211002847

Indecent Displays (Control) Act. (1981). Retrieved May 4, 2024, from: https://www.legislation.gov.uk/ukpga/1981/42

Jackson, D. (2020). Six mistakes of law about consent. *New Zealand Women's Law Journal*, Volume IV. Retrieved June 20, 2024, from: https://www.womenslawjournal.co.nz/edition-four-2020

Johnson, L., Potter, L. C., Beeching, H., Bradbury, M., Matos, B., Sumner, G., Wills, L., Worthing, K., Aldridge, R. W., Feder, G., & Hayward, A. C. (2023). Interventions to improve health and the determinants of health among sex workers in high-income countries: A systematic review. *The Lancet Public Health, 8*(2), e141–e154.

Jones, A. (2015). Sex work in a digital era. *Sociology Compass, 9*(7), 558–570.

Kahn, A. S., Jackson, J., Kully, C., Badger, K., & Halvorsen, J. (2003). Calling it rape: Differences in experiences of women who do or do not label their sexual assault as rape. *Psychology of Women Quarterly, 27*(3), 233–242. https://doi.org/10.1111/1471-6402.00103

Keighley, R., Sanders, T., Saunders, L., & Agg, H. (2023). Participatory action research: Developing a collaborative approach to modern slavery research with survivors of exploitation. *Methodological Innovations, 16*(3), 393–404. https://doi.org/10.1177/20597991231208441

Kinnell, H. (2008). *Violence and sex work in Britain* (1st ed.). Willan. https://doi.org/10.4324/9781843926887

Klambauer, E. (2019). On the edges of the law: Sex workers' legal consciousness in England. *International Journal of Law in Context, 15*(03), 327–343. https://doi.org/10.1017/s1744552319000041

KR v Mick Costello and others. (2022). 4111660/2021. Retrieved May 20, 2024, from: https://drive.google.com/file/d/1apU0R0bB0_3mry6qciAuLH0pckXdnwyW/view

Krishnamurthy, P., Hui, S. K., Shivkumar, N., Gowda, C., & Pushpalatha, R. (2016). Assessing the impact of peer educator outreach on the likelihood and acceleration of clinic utilization among sex workers. *PLoS ONE, 11*(7), e0159656. https://doi.org/10.1371/journal.pone.0159656

Krüsi, A. (2014). *The social and structural production of violence, safety and sexual risk reduction among street-based sex workers* (PhD thesis, University of British Columbia).

Krüsi, A., Chettiar, J., Ridgway, A., Abbott, J., Strathdee, S., & Shannon, K. (2012). Negotiating safety and sexual risk reduction with clients in unsanctioned safer indoor sex work environments: A qualitative study. *American Journal of Public Health, 102*(6), 1154–1159.

Krüsi, A., Kerr, T., Taylor, C., Rhodes, T., & Shannon, K. (2016). "They won't change it back in their heads that we're trash": The intersection of sex work-related stigma and evolving policing strategies. *Sociology of Health & Illness, 38*(7), 1137–1150.

Krüsi, A., Pacey, K., Bird, L., Taylor, C., Chettiar, J., Allan, S., Bennett, D., Montaner, J.S., Kerr, T., & Shannon, K. (2014). Criminalisation of clients: reproducing vulnerabilities for violence and poor health among street-based sex workers in Canada—a qualitative study. *BMJ Open, 4*(6). https://doi.org/10.1136/bmjopen-2014-005191

KSB v Accident Compensation Corporation. (2012). NZCA 82. Retrieved July 5, 2024, from: https://armstrongthompson.co.nz/wp-content/uploads/2012/03/KSB-v-ACC-Court-of-Appeal.pdf

Laird, K. (2014). Rapist or rogue? Deception, consent and the Sexual Offences Act 2003. *Criminal Law Review, 1,* 492–510.

Landsberg, A., Shannon, K., Krüsi, A., DeBeck, K., Milloy, M., Nosova, E., Kerr, T., & Hayashi, K. (2017). Criminalizing sex work clients and rushed negotiations among sex workers who use drugs in a Canadian setting. *Journal of Urban Health, 94*(4), 563–571.

Latimer, R. L., Vodstrcil, L. A., Fairley, C. K., Cornelisse, V. J., Chow, E. P. F., Read, T. R. H., & Bradshaw, C. S. (2018). Non-consensual condom removal, reported by patients at a sexual health clinic in Melbourne, Australia. *PLoS ONE, 13*(12), e0209779. https://doi.org/10.1371/journal.pone.0209779

Lazarus, L., Deering, K. N., Nabess, R., Gibson, K., Tyndall, M. W., & Shannon, K. (2012). Occupational stigma as a primary barrier to health care for street-based sex workers in Canada. *Culture, Health & Sexuality, 14*(2), 139–150.

Lea, S. J., Callaghan, L., Grafton, I., Falcone, M. A., & Shaw, S. (2016). Attrition and rape case characteristics: A profile and comparison of female sex workers and non-sex workers. *Journal of Interpersonal Violence, 31*(12), 2175–2195.

Lehoucq, E., & Taylor, W. K. (2019). Conceptualizing legal mobilization: How should we understand the deployment of legal strategies? *Law & Social Inquiry, 45*(1), 166–193. https://doi.org/10.1017/lsi.2019.59

Lévesque, S., Rousseau, C., & Dumerchat, M. (2021). Influence of the relational context on reproductive coercion and the associated consequences. *Violence against Women, 27*(6–7), 828–850. https://doi.org/10.1177/1077801220917454

Lewis, J., & Maticka-Tyndale, E. (2000). Licensing sex work: Public policy and women's lives. *Canadian Public Policy, 26*(4), 437–449. https://ideas.repec.org/a/cpp/issued/v26y2000i4p437-449.html

Licea, R. (2022). How to expand rape by deception and protect consent. *University of Massachusetts Law Review, 17*(2), 1.

Lorenz, K., & Jacobsen, C. (2021). Sexual violence survivors' experiences with the police and willingness to report future victimization. *Women & Criminal Justice,* pp. 1–23. https://doi.org/10.1080/08974454.2021.1985045

Lowman, J. (2000). Violence and the outlaw status of (street) prostitution in Canada. *Violence against Women, 6*(9), 987–1011. https://doi.org/10.1177/10778010022182245

Lushey, C. (2017). Peer research methodology: Challenges and solutions. *SAGE Research Methods Cases*. https://doi.org/10.4135/9781473994614

Marquis, C., & Langlois, A. (2023, January 20). Met Police: 'Women don't feel safe approached by a policeman...because we're not safe,' say campaigners. *London World*. Retrieved February 8, 2024, from: https://www.londonworld.com/news/crime/met-police-we-dont-feel-safebecause-were-not-safe-says-campaign-group-3994311

McNair v State. (1992). 20127 Supreme Court of Nevada. Retrieved May 20, 2024, from: https://justis.vlex.com/#vid/895599504

Mendes, K., Ringrose, J., & Keller, J. (2018). # MeToo and the promise and pitfalls of challenging rape culture through digital feminist activism. *European Journal of Women's Studies, 25*(2), 236–246.

Minichiello, V., & Scott, J. (Eds.). (2014). *Male sex work and society*. Columbia University Press.

Mirren, F. (2019). How sex workers who are sexually assaulted are being failed by the justice system. *I News*. Retrieved Febraury 24, 2024, from: https://inews.co.uk/opinion/how-sex-workers-who-are-sexually-assaulted-are-being-failed-by-the-justice-system-328027

Modern Slavery Act. (2015). Retrieved June 20, 2024, from: https://www.legislation.gov.uk/ukpga/2015/30/contents

Murray, K. L., & Beattie, T. (2021). Conditional consent and sexual offences: Revisiting the Sexual Offences Act 2003 after Lawrance. *Criminal Law Review, 7*, 556–574.

National Institute of Justice. (2016). Five things about deterrence. *U.S. Department of Justice Office of Justice Programs*. Retrieved May 24, 2024, from: https://www.ojp.gov/pdffiles1/nij/247350.pdf

National Police Chiefs' Council (NPCC). (2024). *Sex work national police guidance*. Retrieved June 20, 2024, from: https://www.npcc.police.uk/SysSiteAssets/media/downloads/publications/publications-log/national-crime-coordination-committee/2024/npcc-sex-work-guidance-v2---february-2024.pdf

Nevada Revised Statutes. (n.d.). Retrieved June 20, 2024, from: https://www.leg.state.nv.us/nrs/

New Zealand Police. (n.d.). *Understanding sexual assault and consent*. Retrieved June 20, 2024, from: https://www.police.govt.nz/advice-services/sexual-assault-and-consent/understanding-sexual-assault-and-consent

NIHR (National Institute for Health and Care Research). (2023). Payment guidance for researchers and professionals v1.4 July 2023. Retrieved June 18, 2024, from: https://www.nihr.ac.uk/documents/payment-guidance-for-researchers-and-professionals/27392

Noakes, S. (2022, December). 'Stealthing'—an analysis of 'Campos v R' [2022] NZCA 311. *New Zealand Law Journal*, 395–399.

NR v MR. (2014). 2014, NZHC 863. Retrieved May 20, 2024, from: https://defamationupdate.co.nz/wp-content/uploads/case-database/2014/NR-v-MR-2014-NZHC-863.pdf

O'Neill, M. (1996). Researching prostitution and violence: Towards a feminist praxis. In M. Hester, L. Kelly, & J. Radford (Eds.), *Women, violence and male power*. London: Open University Press.

Oberweis, T., Henry, D., Griner, S., & Gorislavsky, E. (2021). Making the call: College students' legal consciousness and hypothetical activation of police for sexual assaults. *Violence against Women, 27*(12–13), 2399–2423. https://doi.org/10.1177/10778012211021121

Obscene Publications Act. (1959). Retrieved June 20, 2024, from: https://www.legislation.gov.uk/ukpga/Eliz2/7-8/66/contents

Osborne, H. (2022, December 22). Man sentenced for secretly filming his consensual encounters with 14 sex workers. *New Zealand Herald*. Retrieved July 18, 2024, from: https://www.nzherald.co.nz/nz/man-sentenced-for-secretly-filming-his-consensual-encounters-with-14-sex-workers/3XTJLEZSIFCNFIPE2WHVOFVQD4/

Östergren, P. (2006). *Sex workers critique of Swedish prostitution policy*. Retrieved 7 July 2024, from: http://www.petraostergren.com/upl/files/115326.pdf

Palmer, T. (2023). Freedom to negotiate. In Criminal Law Reform Now Network (Eds.), *Reforming the relationship between sexual consent, deception and mistake* (pp. 74–83). Retrieved May 20, 2024, from: http://www.clrnn.co.uk/media/1031/clrnn3-deception-report.pdf

PARTNERS2 Writing Collective. (2020). Exploring patient and public involvement (PPI) and co-production approaches in mental health research: Learning from the PARTNERS2 research programme. *Research Involvement and Engagement, 6*(1). Retrieved July 14, 2024, from: https://doi.org/10.1186/s40900-020-00224-3

Patterson, D., Greeson, M., & Campbell, R. (2009). Understanding rape survivors' decisions not to seek help from formal social systems. *Health & Social Work, 34*(2), 127–136. https://doi.org/10.1093/hsw/34.2.127

Pearce v Brooks. (1866). LR 1 Ex 213. Retrieved July 5, 2024, from: https://www.scribd.com/doc/46735334/Pearce-v-Brooks-1866-Lr-1-Ex-213-Exch

Peleg-Koriat, I., & Klar-Chalamish, C. (2022). Sexual offense victims' responses to the question #WhyIDidntReport? Examining restorative justice as an alternative dispute resolution mechanism. *Conflict Resolution Quarterly, 40*(3), 295–312. https://doi.org/10.1002/crq.21369

Pemberton, S., Balderston, S., & Long, J. (2021). *Trauma, social harm and health in criminal justice involved women: The Women's Risk Needs Assessment Validation Research Study Protocol*. University of Birmingham. Retrieved June 18, 2024, from: https://www.protocols.io/view/trauma-social-harm-and-health-in-criminal-justice-5qpvoy239g4o/v1/abstract

Penfold, C., Hunter, G., Campbell, R., & Barham, L. (2004). Tackling client violence in female street prostitution: Inter-agency working between outreach agencies and the police. *Policing & Society, 14*(4), 365–379.

Perkins, R., & Lovejoy, F. (2007). *Call girls: Private sex workers in Australia*. University of Western Australia Press.

Pinchevsky, G. M., & Hayes, B. E. (2022). Understanding college students' perceived help-seeking knowledge and awareness about sexual misconduct policies and procedures. *Journal of Interpersonal Violence, 088626052210819*. https://doi.org/10.1177/08862605221081935

Pinchevsky, G. M., Augustyn, M. B., Kennedy, A. H., & Rennison, C. M. (2024). Perceptions of sexual violence terms used in statutes throughout the United States. *Violence Against Women, 30*(15–16), 3991–4011. https://doi.org/10.1177/10778012231188088

Platt, L., Grenfell, P., Meiksin, R., Elmes, J., Sherman, S. G., Sanders, T., Mwangi, P., & Crago, A. L. (2018). Associations between sex work laws and sex workers' health: A systematic review and meta-analysis of quantitative and qualitative studies. *PLOS Medicine, 15*(12), e1002680.

Policing and Crime Act. (2009). Retrieved June 20, 2024, from: https://www.legislation.gov.uk/ukpga/2009/26/contents

Prostitution (Public Places) (Scotland) Act. (2007). Retrieved June 20, 2024, from: https://www.legislation.gov.uk/asp/2007/11

Prostitution Reform Act. (2003). Retrieved July 7, 2024, from: http://www.legislation.govt.nz/act/public/2003/0028/latest/DLM197815.html

Pyett, P., & Warr, D. (1997). Vulnerability on the streets: Female sex workers and HIV risk. *AIDS Care, 9*(5), 539–547.

Pyett, P., & Warr, D. (1999). Women at risk in sex work: Strategies for survival. *Journal of Sociology, 35*(2), 183–197.

R (Monica) v DPP. (2018). EWHC 3508 (QB). Retrieved February 24, 2024, from: http://www2.bailii.org/ew/cases/EWHC/Admin/2018/3508.html

R (on the application of F) v DPP and A. (2013). EWHC 945 (Admin). Retrieved December 13, 2023, from: https://www.judiciary.uk/wp-content/uploads/JCO/Documents/Judgments/f-v-dpp-judgment.pdf

R v B. (2007). 1 WLR 1567. Retrieved July 5, 2024, from: https://www.casemine.com/judgement/uk/5a8ff6f960d03e7f57ea4f99

R v Campos. (2021). NZDC 7422. Retrieved July 5, 2024, from: https://www.districtcourts.govt.nz/all-judgments/2021-nzdc-7422-r-v-campos/

R v Clarence. (1889). 22 QB 23. Retrieved July 5, 2024, from: https://www.oxbridgenotes.co.uk/law_cases/r-v-clarence

R v Cook. (1986). 2 NZLR 93 (CA). Retrieved July 5, 2024, from: https://plus.lexis.com/api/permalink/32a11bdc-1f56-40ae-b9fb-956c42dd68c4/?context=1001073

R v Cuerrier. (1998). 2 SCR 371. Retrieved July 5, 2024, from: https://www.hivlegalnetwork.ca/site/wp-content/uploads/2014/02/2.Cuerrier1998summary.pdf

R v Dica. (2004). EWCA Crim 1103. Retrieved June 10, 2024, from: https://www.globalhealthrights.org/wp-content/uploads/2014/06/UK-2004-R-v-Dica.pdf

R v Jheeta. (2007). EWCA Crim 1699. Retrieved May 24, 2024, from: https://ipsaloquitur.com/criminal-law/cases/r-v-jheeta-harvinder-singh/

R v Lawrence. (2020). EWCA Crim 971. Retrieved May 14, 2024, from: https://files.justice.org.uk/wp-content/uploads/2020/09/06165908/Y-R-v-Lawrence-002.pdf

R v Linekar. (1995). QB 250. Retrieved May 24, 2024, from: https://ipsaloquitur.com/criminal-law/cases/r-v-linekar-gareth/

R v Livas. (2015). ACTSC 50. Retrieved June 10, 2024, from: https://jade.io/j/?a=outline&id=369436

R v McNally. (2013). EWCA Crim 1051. Retrieved July 5, 2024, from: https://justis.vlex.com/#vid/793830081

R v Olugboja. (1981). 4875/A/79. Retrieved from: https://justis.vlex.com/#vid/792562701

R v Papadimitropoulos. (1957). HCA 74. Retrieved July 5, 2024, from: https://www8.austlii.edu.au/cgi-bin/viewdoc/au/cases/cth/HCA/1957/74.html

Rogers, J. (2013). The effect of 'deception' in the Sexual Offences Act 2003. *Archbold Review, 4*, 7–9.

Sanders, T. (2002). The condom as psychological barrier: Female sex workers and emotional management. *Feminism and Psychology, 12*(4), 561–566.

Sanders, T. (2004a). *Sex work. A risky business*. Cullompton Devon.

Sanders, T. (2004b). A continuum of risk? The management of health, physical and emotional risks by female sex workers. *Sociology of Health & Illness, 26*(5), 557–574.

Sanders, T. (2016). Inevitably violent? Dynamics of space, governance, and stigma in understanding violence against sex workers. *Studies in Law, Politics and Society, 71*(Special issue: Problematizing prostitution: critical research and scholarship), 93–114. https://doi.org/10.1108/S1059-433720160000071005

Sanders, T., Brents, B. G., & Wakefield, C. (2020b). *Paying for sex in a digital age: US and UK perspectives*. Taylor et Francis Group.

Sanders, T., & Campbell, R. (2007). Designing out vulnerability, building in respect: Violence, safety and sex work policy. *The British Journal of Sociology, 58*(1), 1–19.

Sanders, T., Scouler, J., & Campbell, R. (2022). Sex work, hate crime and the criminal law. *The Journal of Criminal Law, 86*(2), 109–125. https://doi.org/10.1177/00220183221086679

Sanders, T., Vajzovic, D., Brooks-Gordon, B., & Mulvihill, N. (2020a). Policing vulnerability in sex work: The harm reduction compass model. *Policing and Society, 31*(9), 1110–1116. https://doi.org/10.1080/10439463.2020.1837825

Schulhofer, S. (2017). Reforming the law of rape recommended citation. *Law & Inequality: A Journal of Theory and Practice, 35*(2), 335–352. https://scholarship.law.umn.edu/cgi/viewcontent.cgi?article=1577&context=lawineq

Scottish Government. (2024). *Prostitution—challenging and deterring men's demand: Strategic approach.* Retrieved June 20, 2024, from: https://www.gov.scot/publications/scotlands-strategic-approach-challenging-deterring-mens-demand-prostitution-supporting-recovery-sustainable-exit-those-involved-prostitution/

Scottish Law Commission. (2006). *Discussion paper on rape and other sexual offences (Discussion 131).* Retrieved June 20, 2024, from: https://www.scotlawcom.gov.uk/files/3012/7892/7070/dp131_rape.pdf

Scoular, J. (2015). *The subject of prostitution: Sex work, law and social theory.* Routledge.

Scoular, J., Sanders, T., Balderston, S., Abel, G., Brents, B. G., Ellison, G., & Marriott, N. (2023). Understanding sexual violence in sex working populations—Law, legal consciousness and legal practice in four countries (2021–2023): Study Protocol v2.5. *PLOS ONE, 18*(11), e0283067–e0283067. https://doi.org/10.1371/journal.pone.0283067

Sexual Offences (Amendment) Act. (1976). Retrieved July 5 2024, from: https://www.legislation.gov.uk/ukpga/1976/82

Sexual Offences (Northern Ireland) Order. (2008). Retrieved June 20, 2024, from: https://www.legislation.gov.uk/nisi/2008/1769/contents

Sexual Offences (Scotland) Act. (2009). Retrieved July 5, 2024, from: https://www.legislation.gov.uk/asp/2009/9/contents

Sexual Offences Act. (1956). Retrieved July 5, 2023, from: https://www.legislation.gov.uk/ukpga/Eliz2/4-5/69/contents

Sexual Offences Act. (2003). Retrieved July 5, 2024, from: https://www.legislation.gov.uk/ukpga/2003/42/contents

Shannon, K., Kerr, T., Allinott, S., Chettar, J., Shoveller, J., & Tyndall, M. (2008). Social and structural violence and power relations in mitigating HIV risk and drug using women in survival sex work. *Social Science and Medicine, 66*(4), 911–921.

Sharpe, A. (2016). Expanding liability for sexual fraud through the concept of 'active deception.' *The Journal of Criminal Law, 80*(1), 28–44. https://doi.org/10.1177/0022018315623674

Sharpe, A. (2018). *Sexual intimacy and gender identity 'fraud': Reframing the legal and ethical debate.* Routledge.

Shay, L. A., & Lafata, J. E. (2015). Where is the evidence? A systematic review of shared decision making and patient outcomes. *Medical Decision Making, 35*(1), 114–131.

Smith, O., & Skinner, T. (2012). Observing court responses to victims of rape and sexual assault. *Feminist Criminology, 7*(4), 298–326.

Spencer, D., Dodge, A., Ricciardelli, R., & Ballucci, D. (2018). "I think it's re-victimizing victims almost every time": Police perceptions of criminal justice responses to sexual violence. *Critical Criminology, 26*(2), 189–209.

Spohn, C. (2020). Sexual assault case processing: The more things change, the more they stay the same. *International Journal for Crime, Justice and Social Democracy, 9*(1), 86–94. https://doi.org/10.5204/ijcjsd.v9i1.1454

Spohn, C., & Horney, J. (1993). Rape law reform and the effect of victim characteristics on case processing. *Journal of Quantitative Criminology, 9*(4), 383–409. https://doi.org/10.1007/BF01064110

Spohn, C., & Horney, J. (1996). The impact of rape law reform on the processing of simple and aggravated rape cases. *The Journal of Criminal Law and Criminology, 86*(3), 861. https://doi.org/10.2307/1143939

Staley, K., Crowe, S., Crocker, J. C., Madden, M., & Greenhalgh, T. (2020). What happens after James Lind Alliance Priority Setting Partnerships? A qualitative study of contexts, processes and impacts. *Research Involvement and Engagement, 6*, Article no. 41. https://doi.org/10.1186/s40900-020-00210-9

Stardust, Z., Treloar, C., Cama, E., & Kim, J. (2021). "I wouldn't call the cops if I was being bashed to death": Sex work, whore stigma and the criminal legal system. *International Journal for Crime, Justice and Social Democracy, 10*(3), 142–157.

State v Denton. (1966). 101 Ariz.455, 420 [92 Nev. 78] P.2d 930. Retrieved June 20, 2024, from: https://law.justia.com/cases/arizona/supreme-court/1966/1654-0.html

State v Thomas. (1973). 9 Wash.App. 160, 510P.2.d 1137. Retrieved December 13, 2023, from: https://www.courtlistener.com/opinion/1117007/state-v-thomas/

Stevens, R. (2022). 'Stealthing' case: Convicted rapist loses appeal against jail term after removing condom during sex. *New Zealand Herald*. Retrieved July 11, 2024, from: https://www.nzherald.co.nz/nz/stealthing-case-convicted-rapist-loses-appeal-against-jail-term-after-removing-condom-during-sex/KYCSBNMHDLWAGOXGMLJTFCVSX4/

Stone, K. G. (1997). *Awakening to disability: Nothing about us without us.* Volcano Press.

Stonehouse, R. (2021). Stealthing: 'I didn't realise it's rape until it happened to me'. *BBC Newsbeat*. Retrieved June 20, 2024, from: https://www.bbc.co.uk/news/newsbeat-57618003

Street Offences Act. (1959). Retrieved July 7, 2024, from: https://www.legislation.gov.uk/ukpga/Eliz2/7-8/57/contents

Struyf, P. (2023). To report or not to report? A systematic review of sex workers' willingness to report violence and victimization to police. *Trauma, Violence, & Abuse, 24*(5), 3065–3077.

Substance Abuse and Mental Health Services Administration (SAMHSA). (2014). Concept of trauma and guidance for a trauma-informed approach. Substance Abuse and Mental Health Services Administration *Briefing*, 14-4884. Retrieved December 13, 2023, from: https://ncsacw.acf.hhs.gov/userfiles/files/SAMHSA_Trauma.pdf

Sweeney, A., Filson, B., Kennedy, A., Collinson, L., & Gillard, S. (2018). A paradigm shift: Relationships in trauma informed mental health services. *Bjpsych Advances, 24*(5), 319–333.

Syrota, G. (1995). Rape: When does fraud vitiate consent? *The University of Western Australia Law Review, 25*(2), 334–345. https://research-repository.uwa.edu.au/en/publications/rape-when-does-fraud-vitiate-consent

Temkin, J., & Ashworth, A. (2004). The sexual offences act 2003: (1)—Rape, sexual assaults and the problems of consent. *Criminal Law Review,* pp. 328–346. https://ora.ox.ac.uk/objects/uuid:8f9f81d6-e99c-47c5-a8c7-71a952b4cc6d

Trafficking Victims Protection Act (TVPA). (2000). Retrieved April 20, 2024, from: https://www.govinfo.gov/content/pkg/BILLS-106hr3244enr/pdf/BILLS-106hr3244enr.pdf

Victims' Commissioner UK. (2023). *Victims' experience: Annual survey 2022.* Retrieved July 14, 2024, from: https://cloud-platform-e218f50a4812967ba1215eaecede923f.s3.amazonaws.com/uploads/sites/6/2023/11/Victim-Survey-2022.pdf

Weait, M. (2007). *Intimacy and responsibility*. Routledge.

Weiss, K. G. (2011). Neutralizing sexual victimization: A typology of victims' non-reporting accounts. *Theoretical Criminology, 15*(4), 445–467. https://doi.org/10.1177/1362480610391527

Weitzer, R. (2005). Flawed theory and method in studies of prostitution. *Violence against Women, 11*(7), 934–949. https://doi.org/10.1177/1077801205276986

Weitzer, R. (2020). The campaign against sex work in the United States: A successful moral crusade. *Sexuality Research and Social Policy, 17*(3), 399–414.

West, N., & Horn, T. (Eds.) (2021). *We too: Essays on sex work and survival: Essays on sex work and survival*. Feminist Press at CUNY.

WHO, UNFPA, UNAIDS, & NSWP. (2012). *Prevention and treatment of HIV and other sexually transmitted infections for sex workers in low- and middle-income countries*. Retrieved May 21, 2024, from: https://www.unfpa.org/sites/default/files/pub-pdf/9789241504744_eng.pdf

Wilkinson, J. (2023, May 30). Only one claim decided by Human Rights Review Tribunal so far this year. *New Zealand Herald*. Retrieved December 30, 2023, from: https://www.nzherald.co.nz/nz/only-one-decision-issued-by-human-rights-review-tribunal-so-far-this-year/BVAWQBCRZRBXJFR7UTJO5USFDE/

Wilson, L. C., & Miller, K. E. (2016). Meta-analysis of the prevalence of unacknowledged rape. *Trauma, Violence, & Abuse, 17*(2), 149–159. https://doi.org/10.1177/1524838015576391

Yarbrough, D. (2019). "Nothing about us without us": Reading protests against oppressive knowledge production as guidelines for solidarity research. *Journal of Contemporary Ethnography, 089124161985713*. https://doi.org/10.1177/0891241619857134

Young, K. M. (2014). Everyone knows the game: Legal consciousness in the Hawaiian cockfight. *Law & Society Review, 48*(3), 499–530. https://doi.org/10.1111/lasr.12094

Zuber-Skerritt, O. (2018). An educational framework for participatory action learning and action research (PALAR). *Educational Action Research, 26*(4), 513–532. https://doi.org/10.1080/09650792.2018.1464939

Zvi, L. (2022). Police perceptions of sex-worker rape victims and their offenders: A vignette study. *Journal of Interpersonal Violence, 37*(15–16), NP14189-NP14214.

Index

T. Sanders et al. (eds.), *Voicing Consent*, Palgrave Advances in Sex Work Studies, https://doi.org/10.1007/978-3-031-77715-8